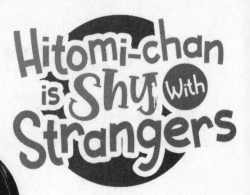

Hitomi-chan is Shy With Strangers

story & art by

Chorisuke Natsumi

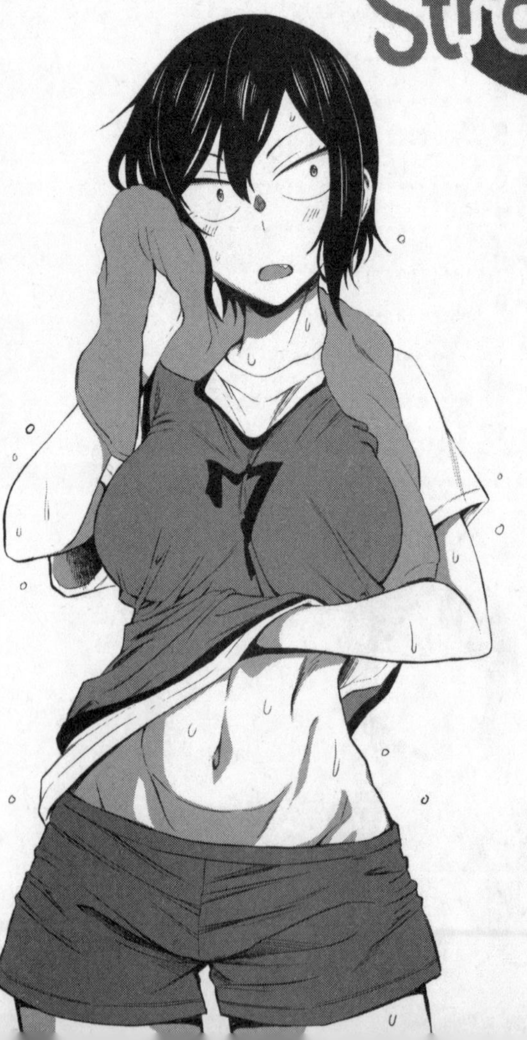

CONTENTS

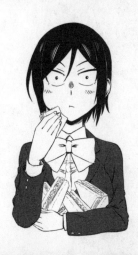

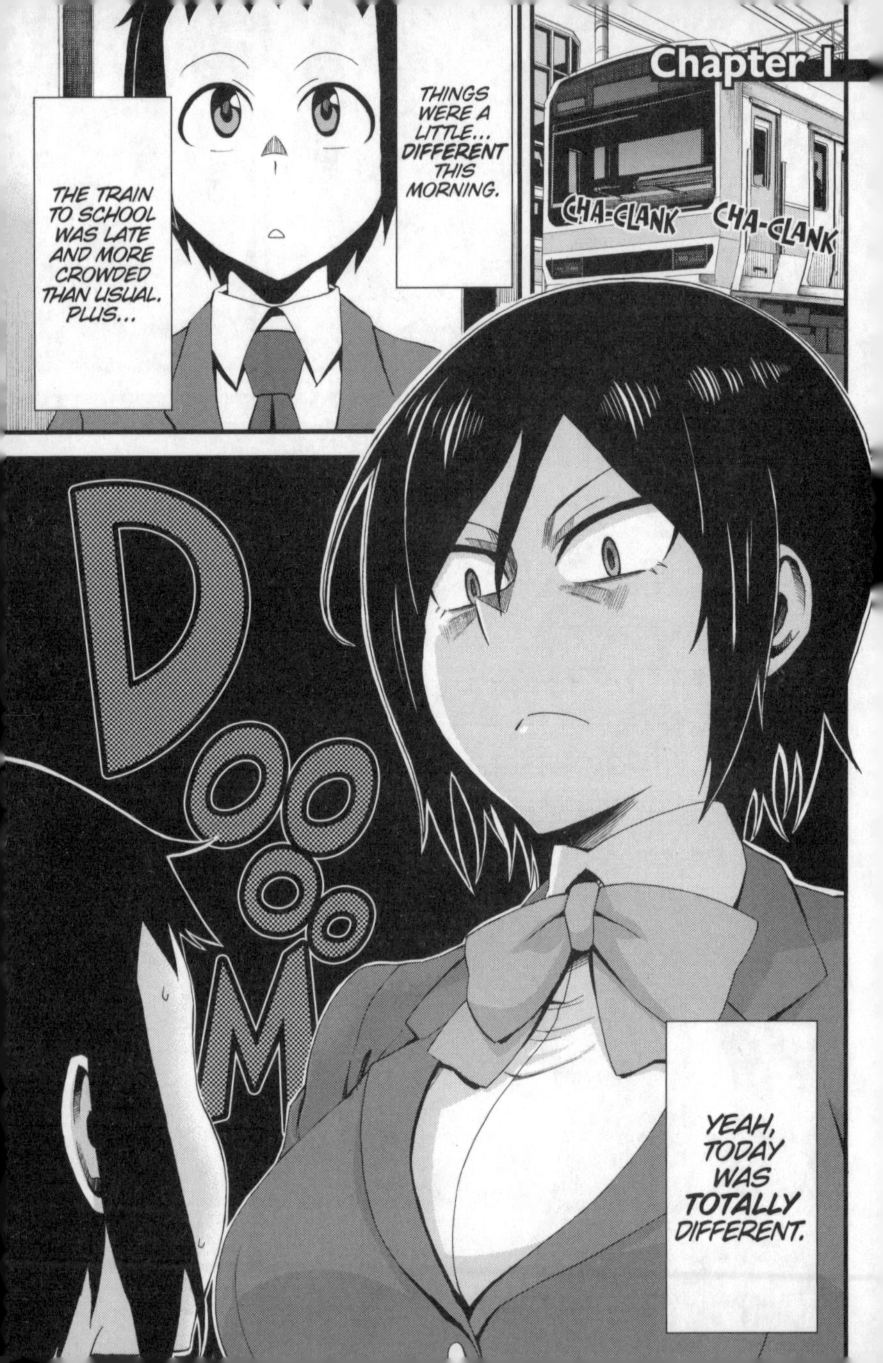
Chapter I
CHA-CLANK
CHA-CLANK
THINGS WERE A LITTLE... DIFFERENT THIS MORNING.
THE TRAIN TO SCHOOL WAS LATE AND MORE CROWDED THAN USUAL. PLUS...
DOOOOM
YEAH, TODAY WAS TOTALLY DIFFERENT.

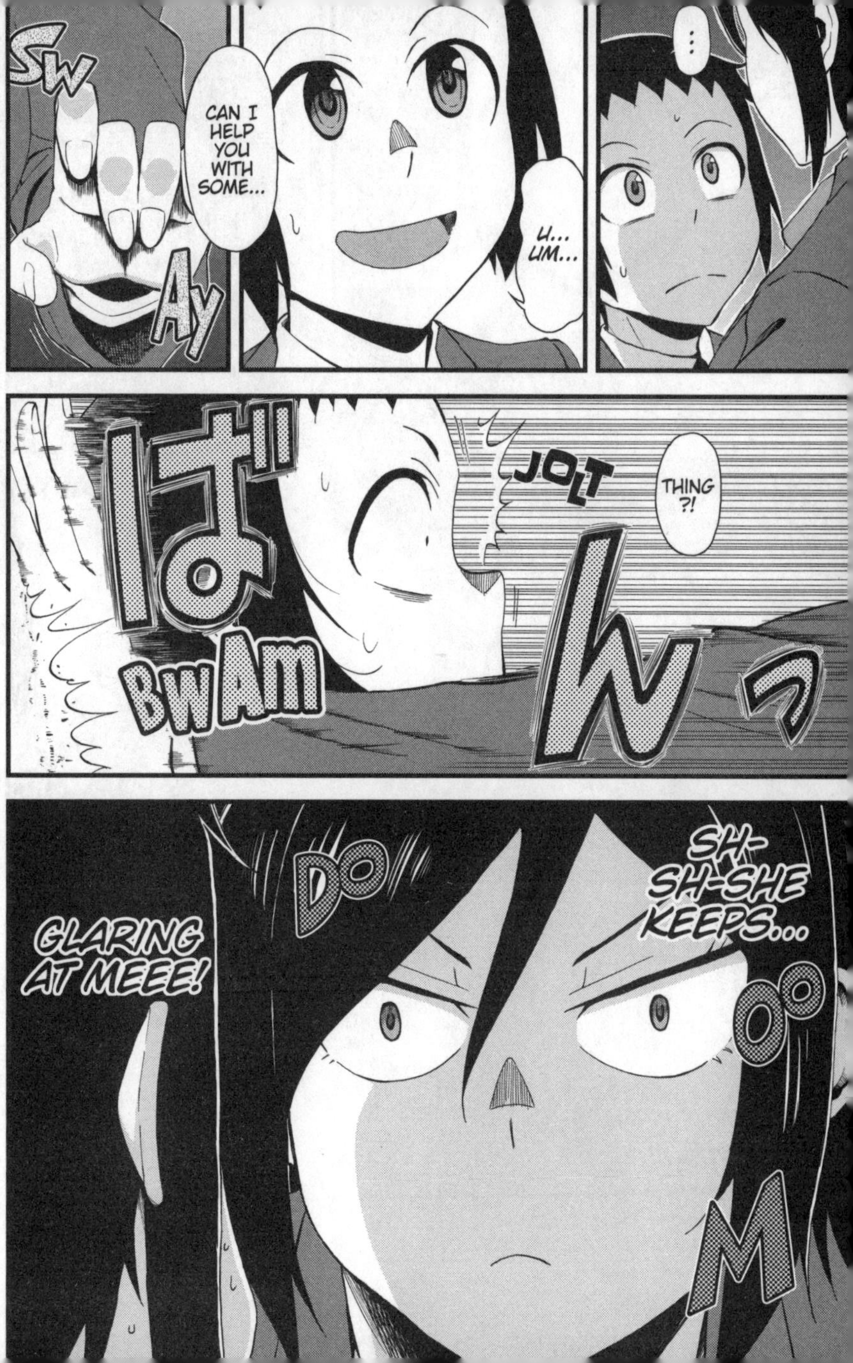
...
U... UM...
CAN I HELP YOU WITH SOME...
SWAY
THING?!
JOLT
ばん っ
BWAM
SH-SH-SHE KEEPS...
DOOOM
GLARING AT MEEE!

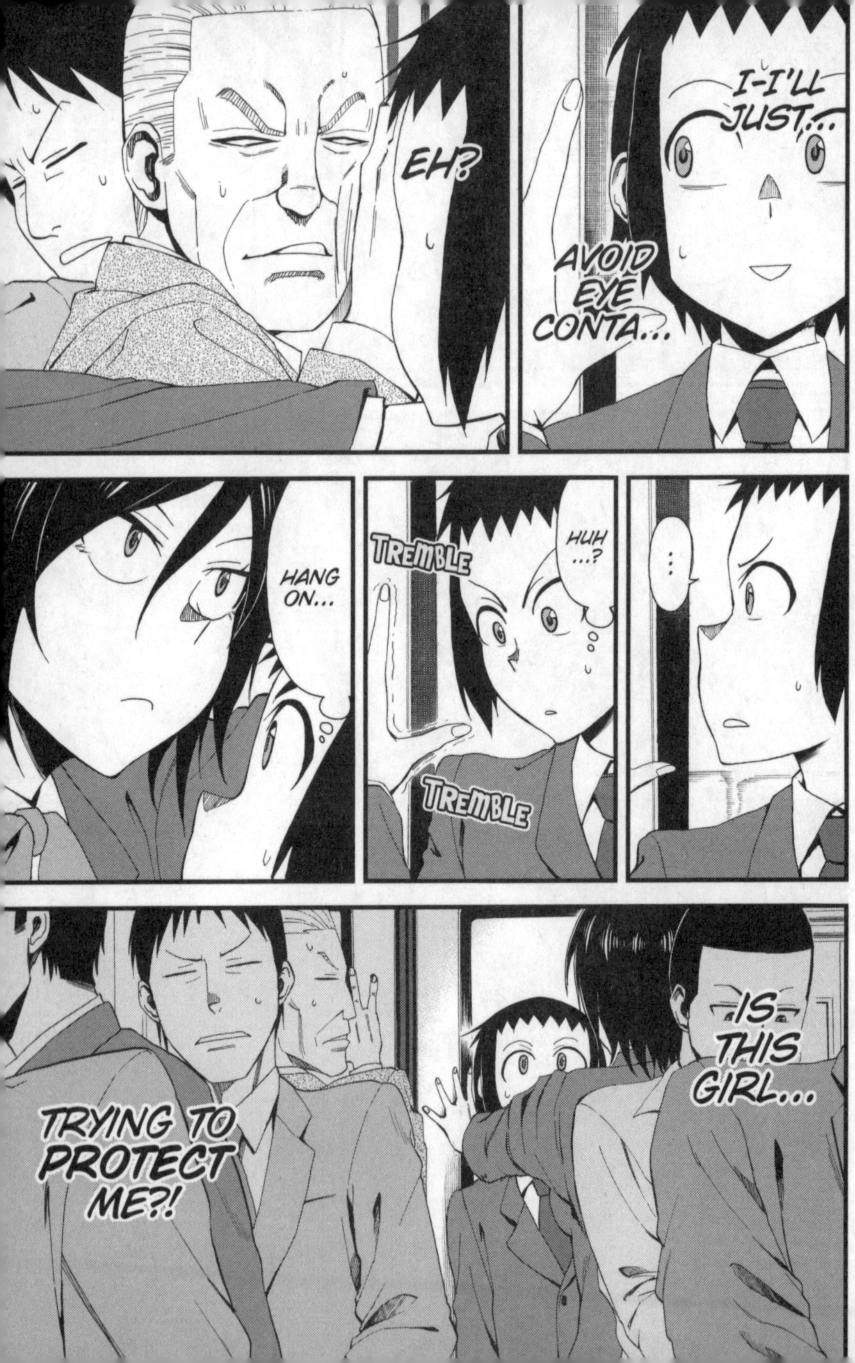
I-I'LL JUST...
AVOID EYE CONTA...
EH?
...
HUH ...?
TREMBLE
TREMBLE
HANG ON...
IS THIS GIRL...
TRYING TO PROTECT ME?!

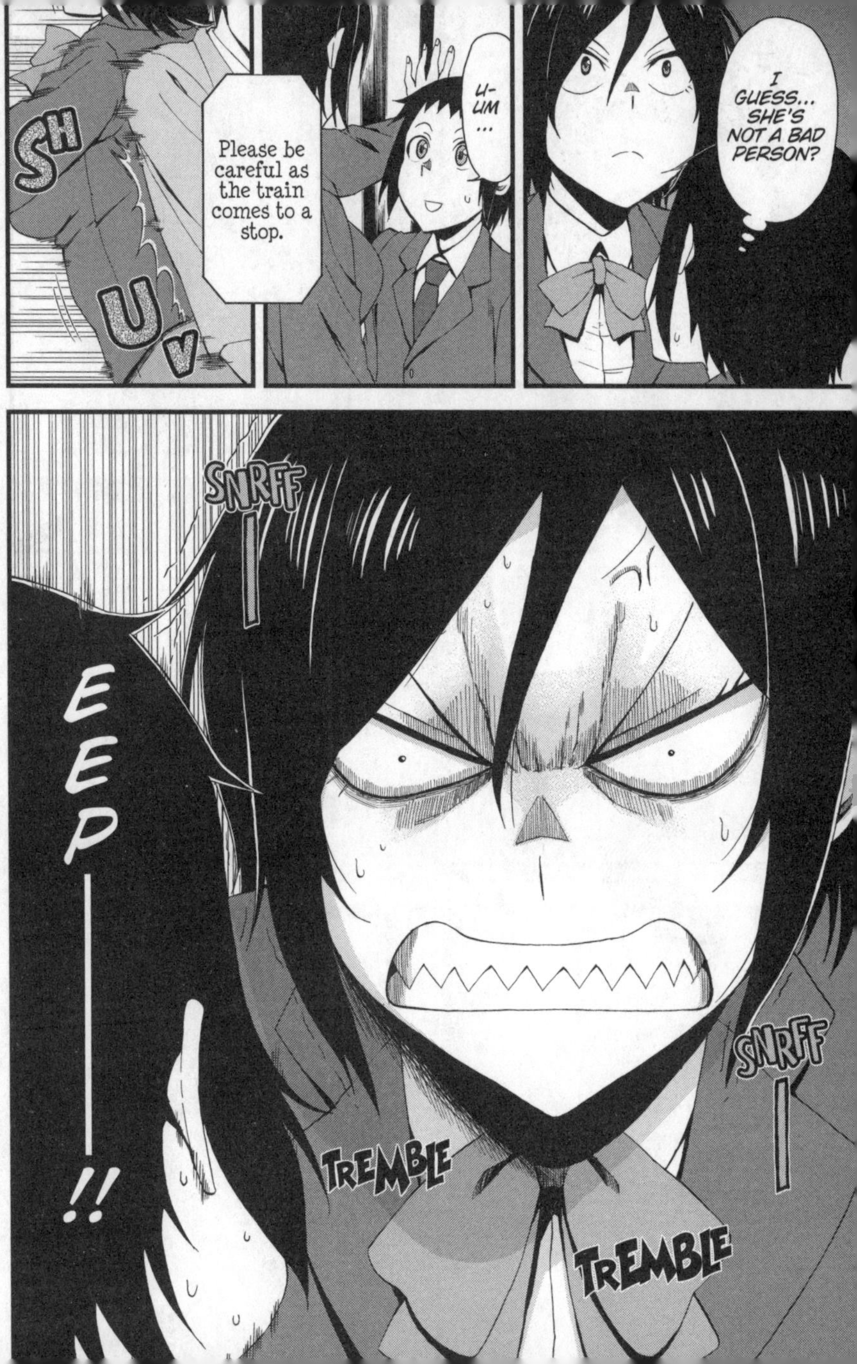
I GUESS... SHE'S NOT A BAD PERSON?
U-UM...
Please be careful as the train comes to a stop.
SHUV
SNRFF
EEP——!!
SNRFF
TREMBLE
TREMBLE

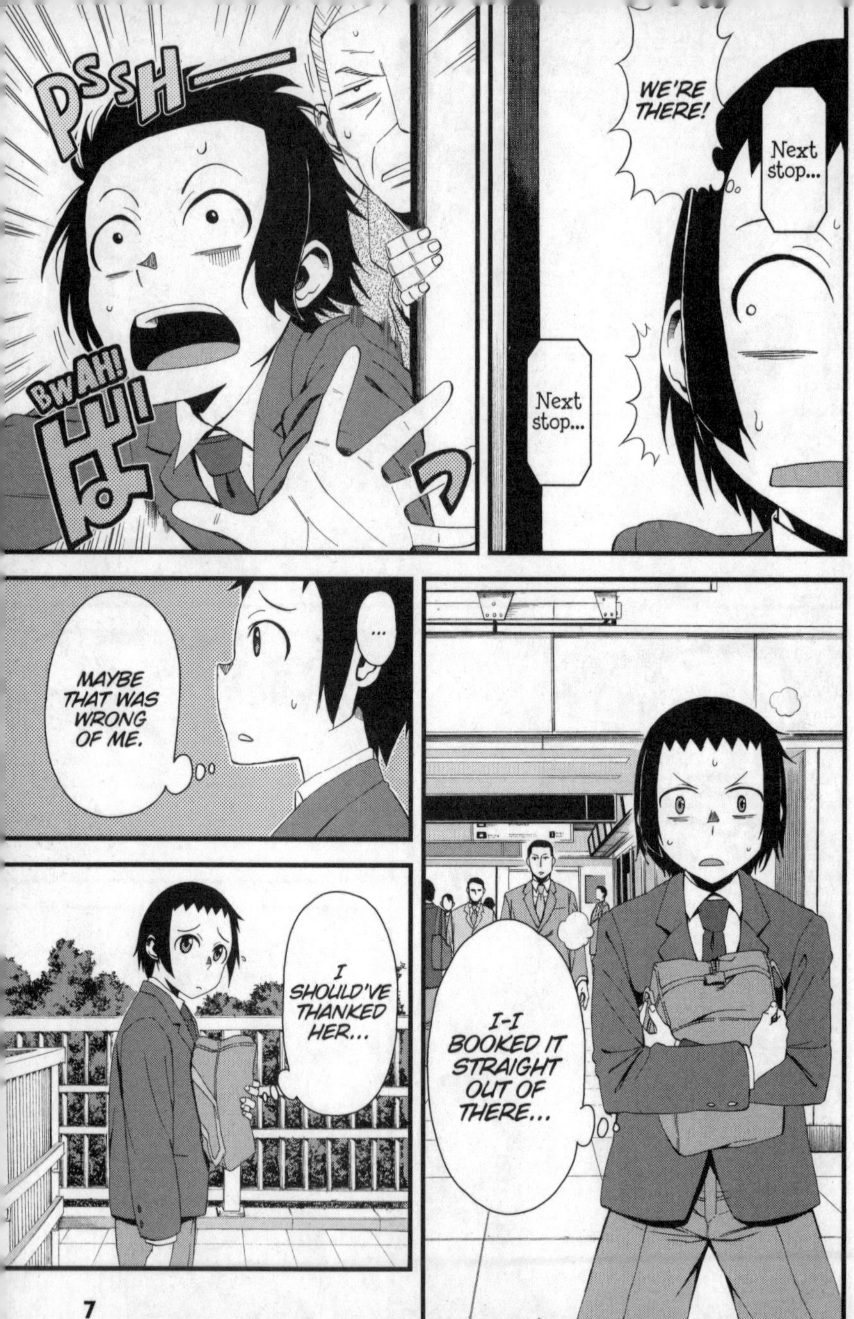
Next stop...
WE'RE THERE!
Next stop...
PSSH—
BWAH!
ぱっ
I-I BOOKED IT STRAIGHT OUT OF THERE...
...
MAYBE THAT WAS WRONG OF ME.
I SHOULD'VE THANKED HER...

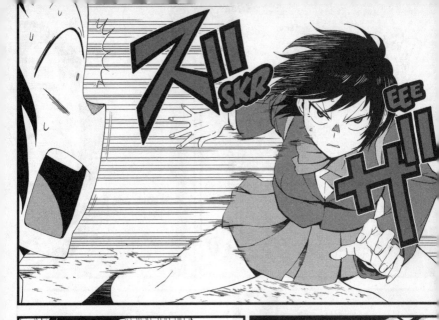

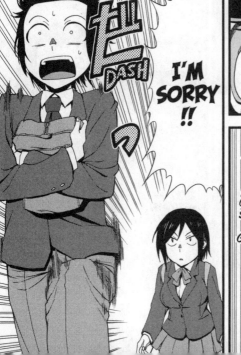

I'M SORRY!!

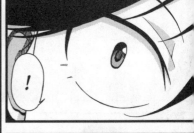

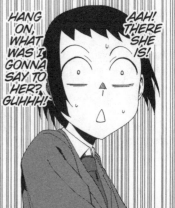

HANG ON, WHAT WAS I GONNA SAY TO HER? GUHHH!

AAH! THERE SHE IS!

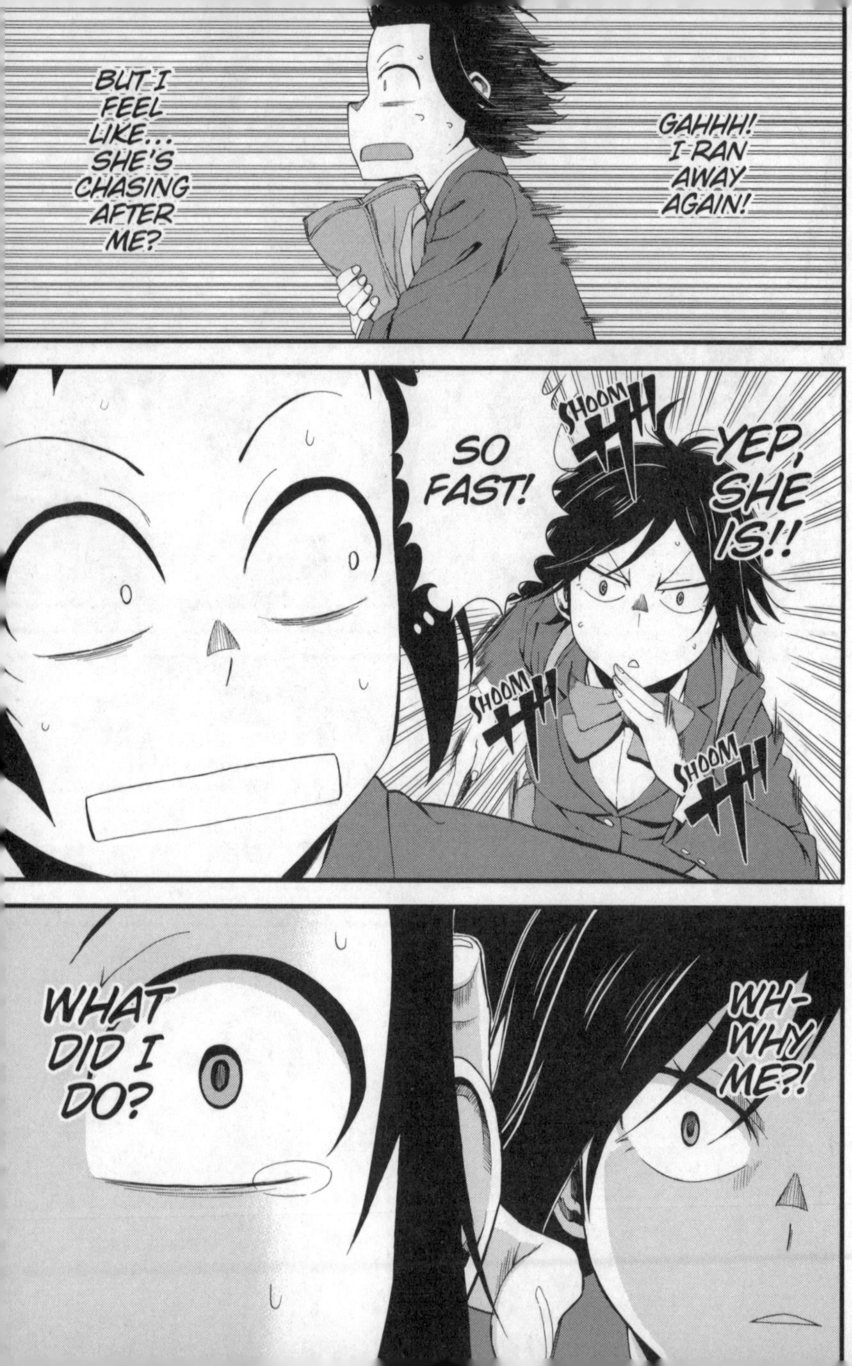
GAHHH! I RAN AWAY AGAIN!
BUT I FEEL LIKE... SHE'S CHASING AFTER ME?
SHOOM
YEP, SHE IS!!
SO FAST!
SHOOM
SHOOM
WH-WHY ME?!
WHAT DID I DO?

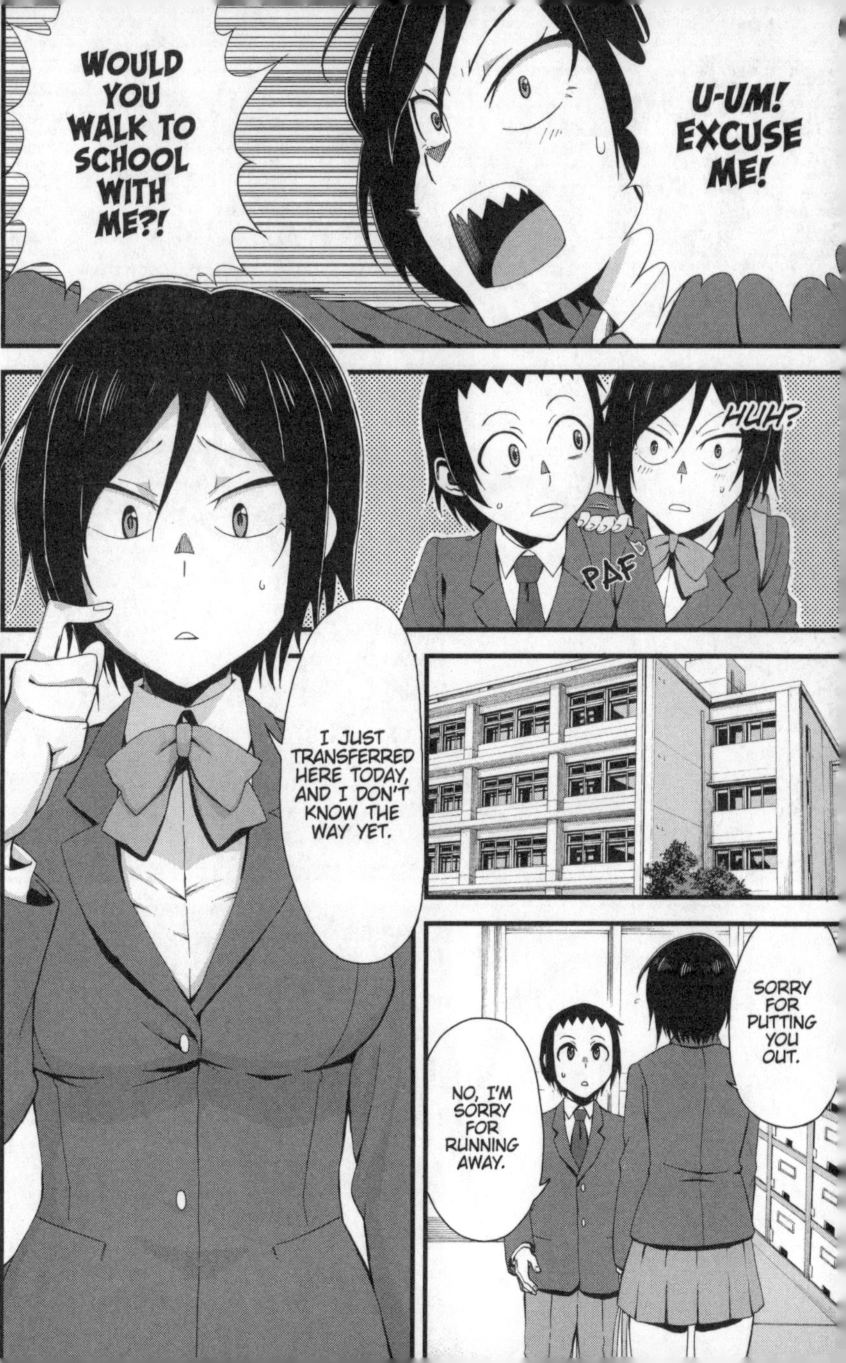
U-UM! EXCUSE ME!
WOULD YOU WALK TO SCHOOL WITH ME?!
HUH?
PAF
SORRY FOR PUTTING YOU OUT.
NO, I'M SORRY FOR RUNNING AWAY.
I JUST TRANSFERRED HERE TODAY, AND I DON'T KNOW THE WAY YET.

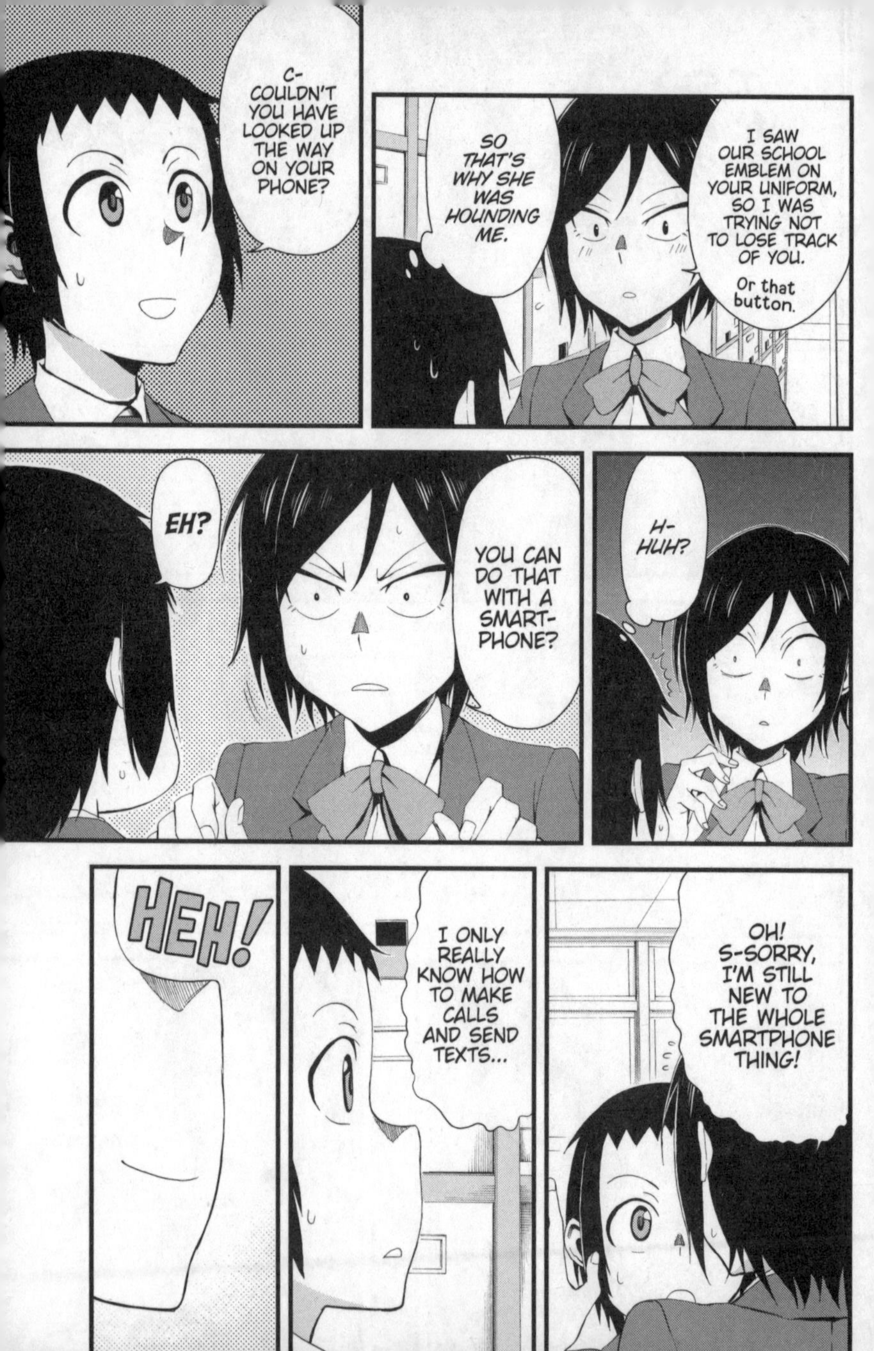
I SAW OUR SCHOOL EMBLEM ON YOUR UNIFORM, SO I WAS TRYING NOT TO LOSE TRACK OF YOU.
Or that button.
SO THAT'S WHY SHE WAS HOUNDING ME.
C-COULDN'T YOU HAVE LOOKED UP THE WAY ON YOUR PHONE?
H-HUH?
YOU CAN DO THAT WITH A SMART-PHONE?
EH?
OH! S-SORRY, I'M STILL NEW TO THE WHOLE SMARTPHONE THING!
I ONLY REALLY KNOW HOW TO MAKE CALLS AND SEND TEXTS...
HEH!

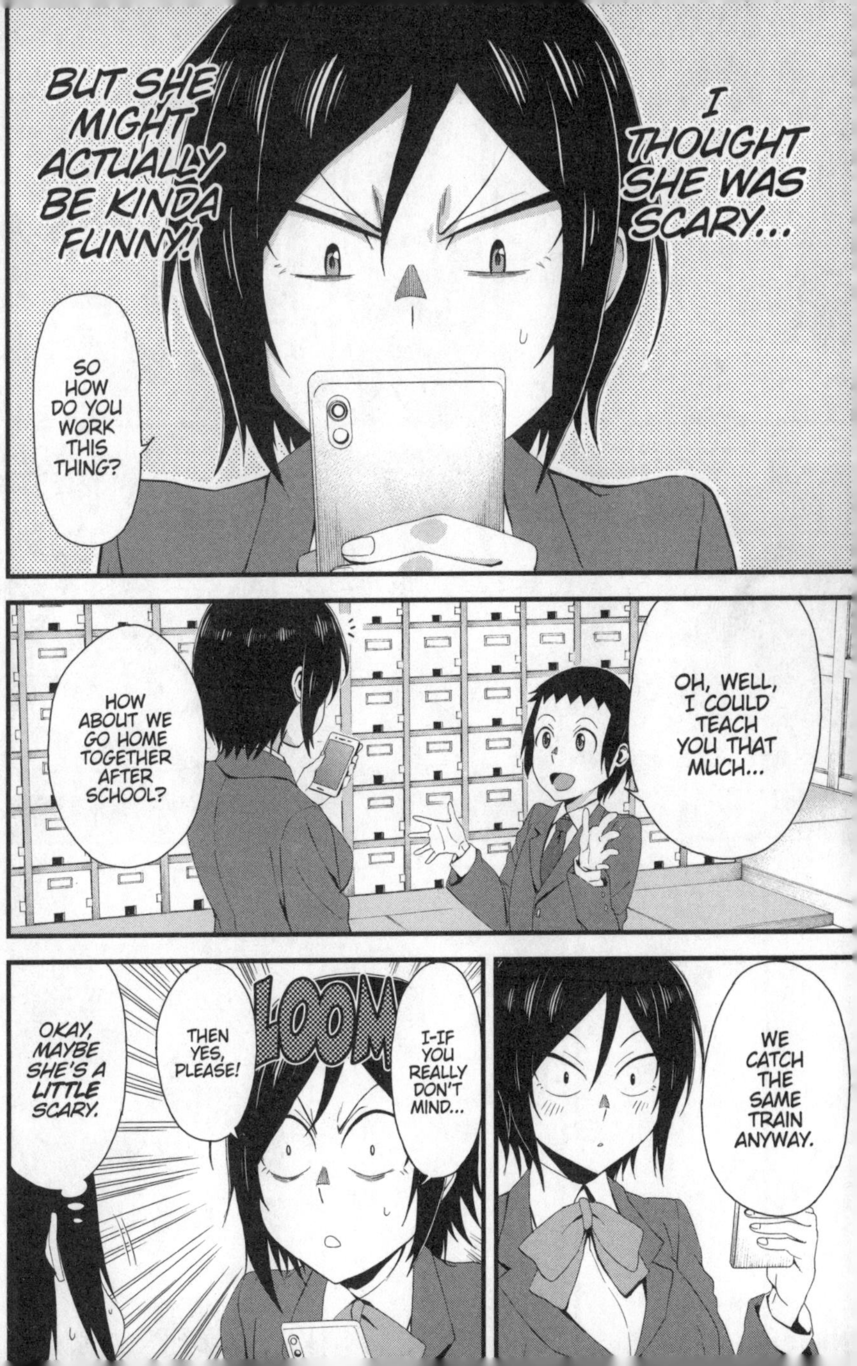
I THOUGHT SHE WAS SCARY...
BUT SHE MIGHT ACTUALLY BE KINDA FUNNY!
SO HOW DO YOU WORK THIS THING?
OH, WELL, I COULD TEACH YOU THAT MUCH...
HOW ABOUT WE GO HOME TOGETHER AFTER SCHOOL?
WE CATCH THE SAME TRAIN ANYWAY.
I-IF YOU REALLY DON'T MIND...
LOOM
THEN YES, PLEASE!
OKAY, MAYBE SHE'S A LITTLE SCARY.

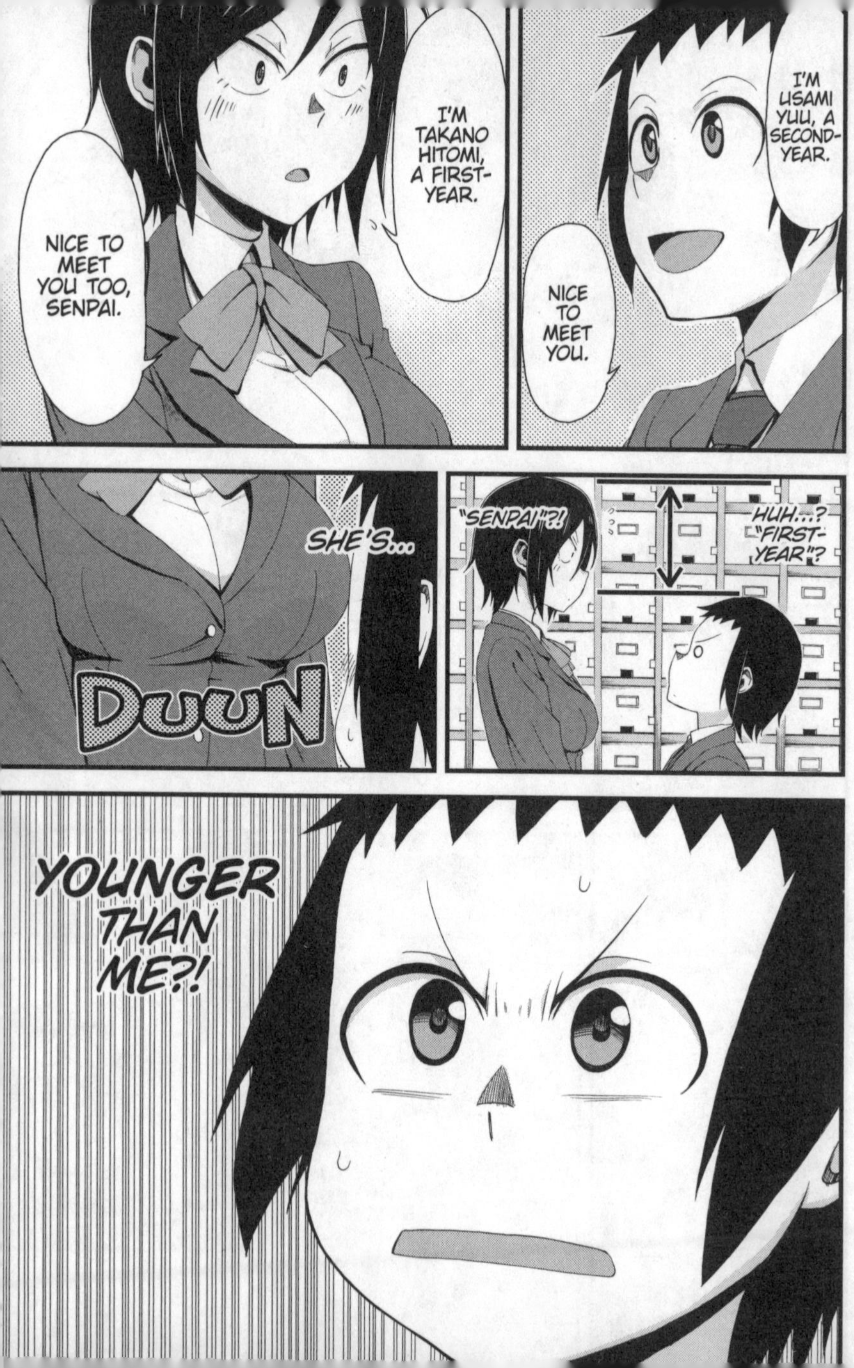
I'M USAMI YUU, A SECOND-YEAR.
NICE TO MEET YOU.
I'M TAKANO HITOMI, A FIRST-YEAR.
NICE TO MEET YOU TOO, SENPAI.
HUH...? "FIRST-YEAR"?
"SENPAI"?!
SHE'S...
DUUN
YOUNGER THAN ME?!

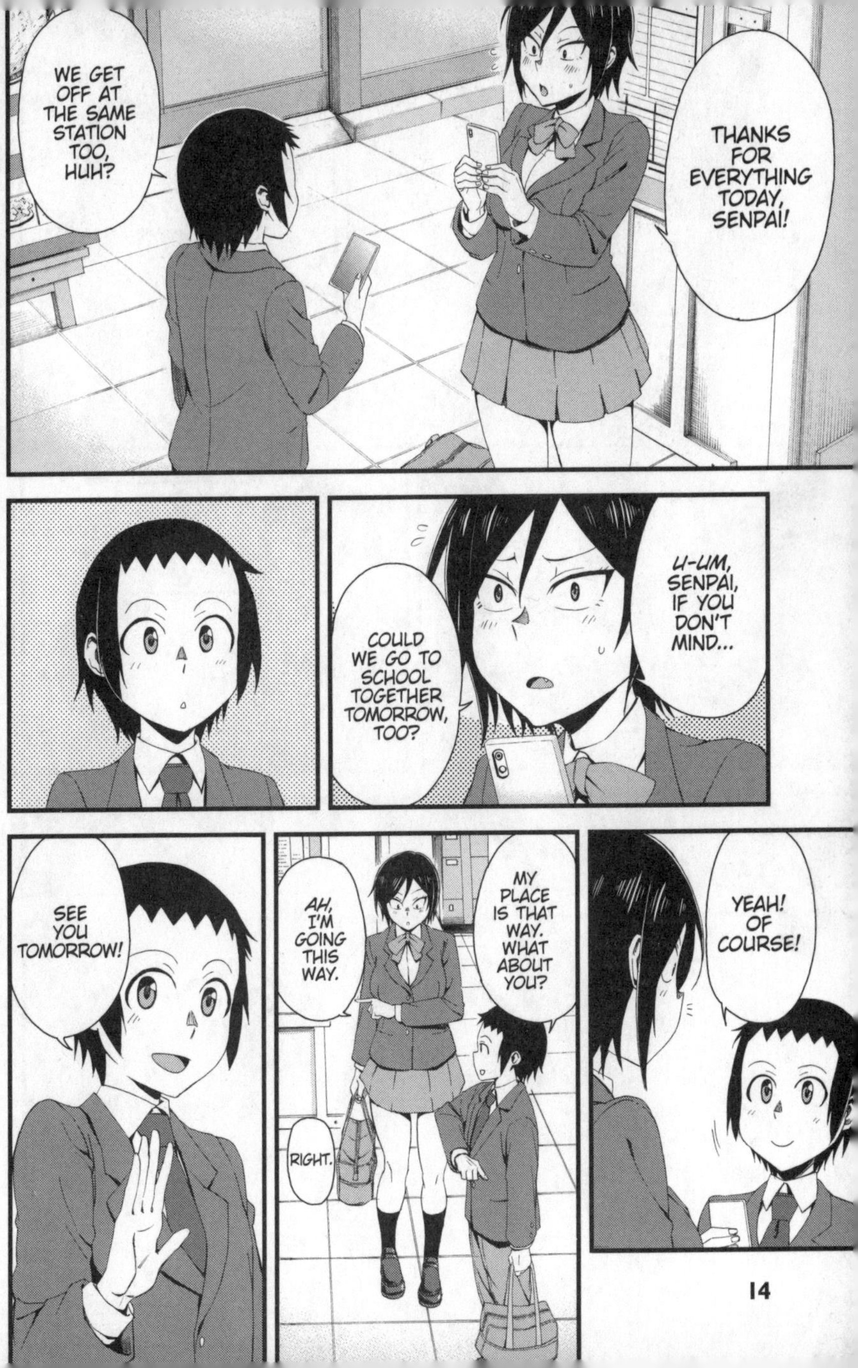
THANKS FOR EVERYTHING TODAY, SENPAI!
WE GET OFF AT THE SAME STATION TOO, HUH?
U-UM, SENPAI, IF YOU DON'T MIND...
COULD WE GO TO SCHOOL TOGETHER TOMORROW, TOO?
YEAH! OF COURSE!
MY PLACE IS THAT WAY. WHAT ABOUT YOU?
AH, I'M GOING THIS WAY.
RIGHT.
SEE YOU TOMORROW!

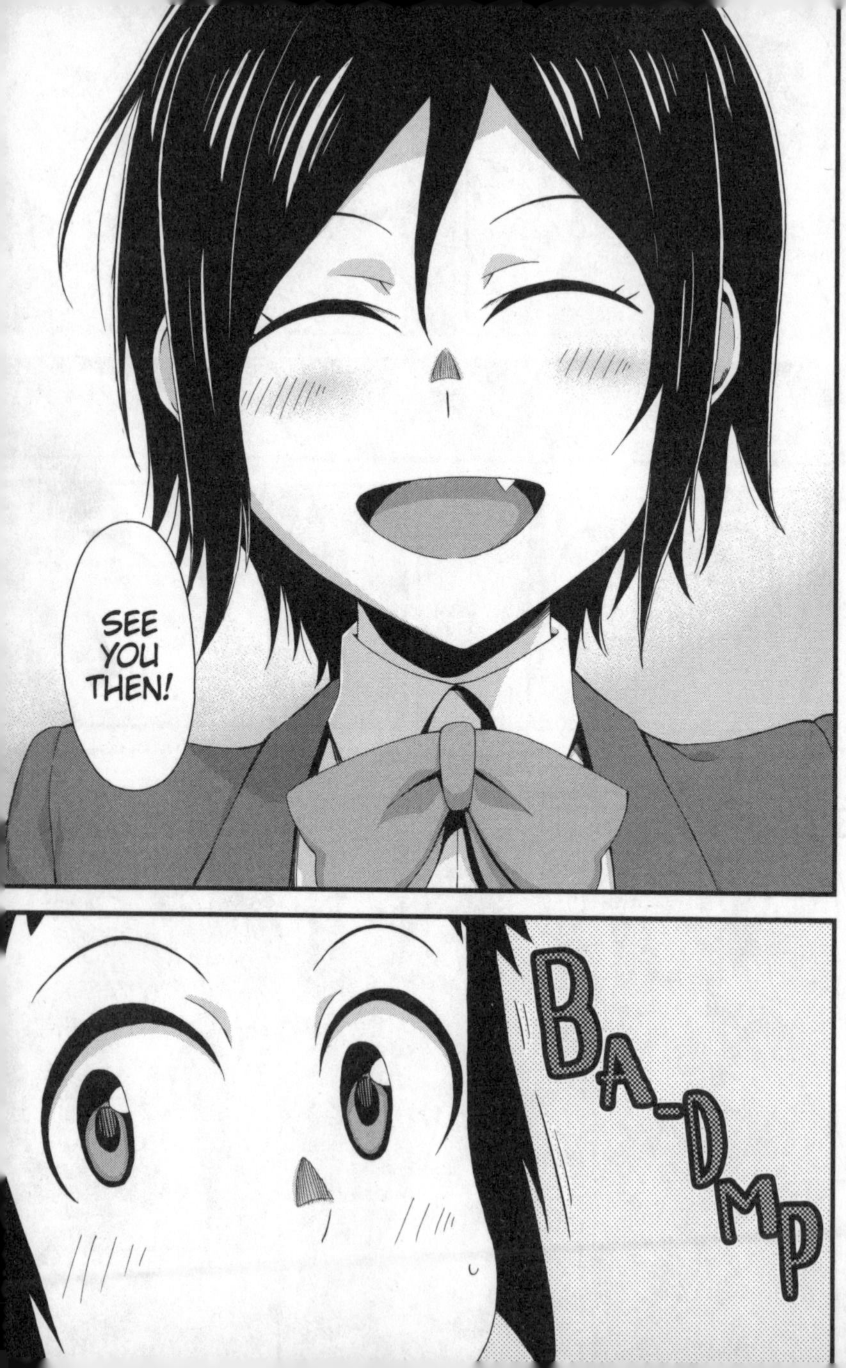
SEE YOU THEN!
BA-DMP

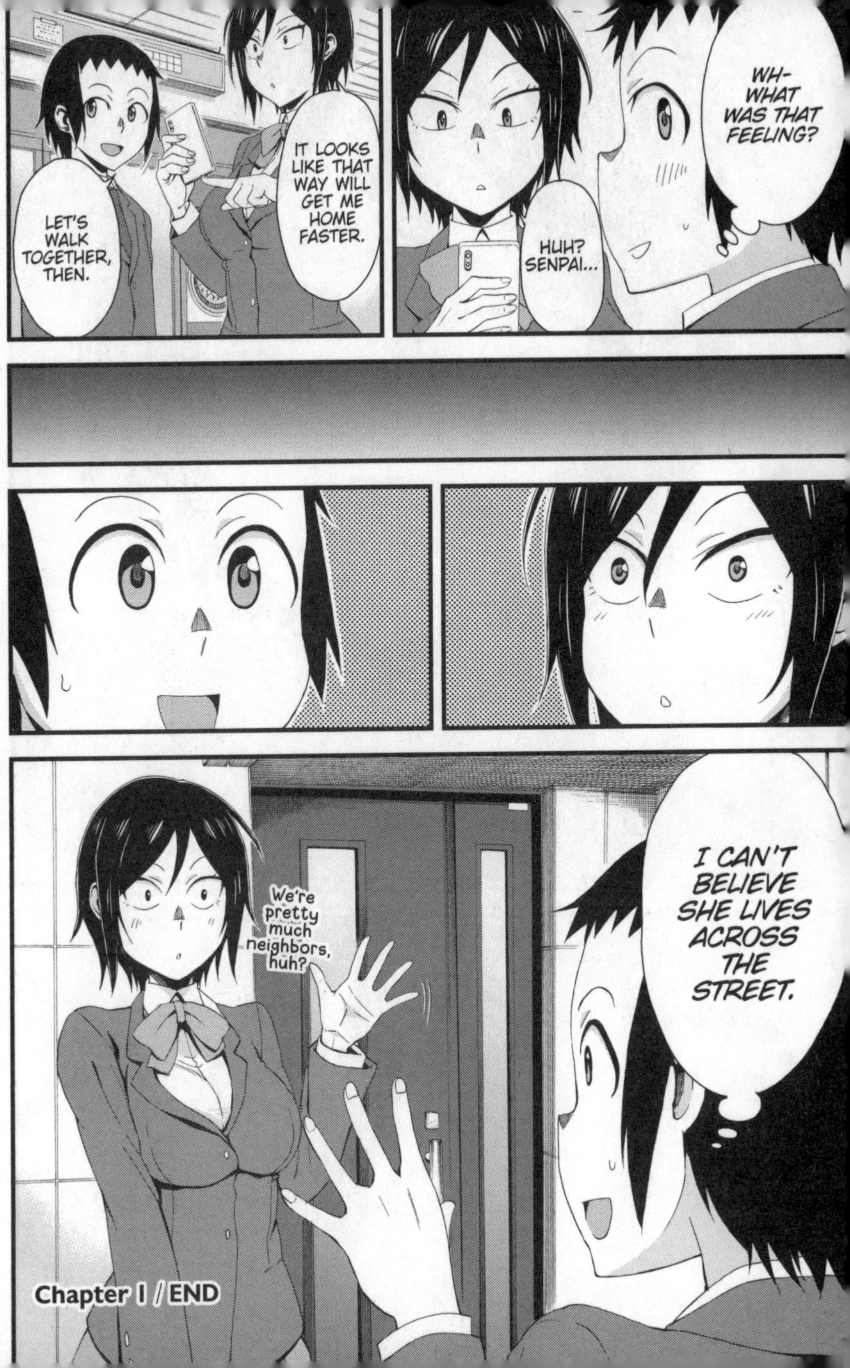
WH- WHAT WAS THAT FEELING?
HUH? SENPAI...
IT LOOKS LIKE THAT WAY WILL GET ME HOME FASTER.
LET'S WALK TOGETHER, THEN.
I CAN'T BELIEVE SHE LIVES ACROSS THE STREET.
We're pretty much neighbors, huh?
Chapter 1 / END

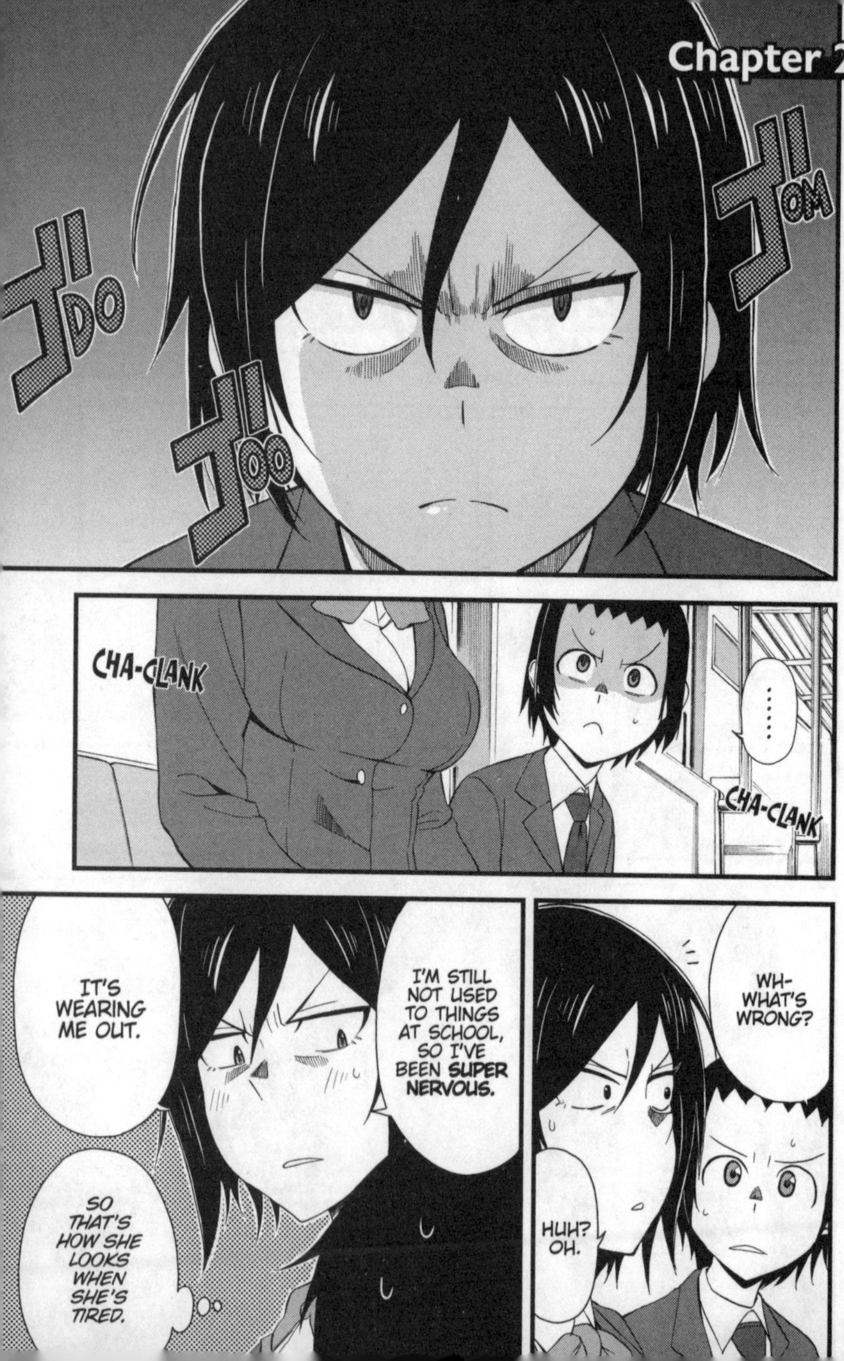
Chapter 2
GOM
DO
DOO
......
CHA-CLANK
CHA-CLANK
WH- WHAT'S WRONG?
HUH? OH.
I'M STILL NOT USED TO THINGS AT SCHOOL, SO I'VE BEEN **SUPER NERVOUS.**
IT'S WEARING ME OUT.
SO THAT'S HOW SHE LOOKS WHEN SHE'S TIRED.

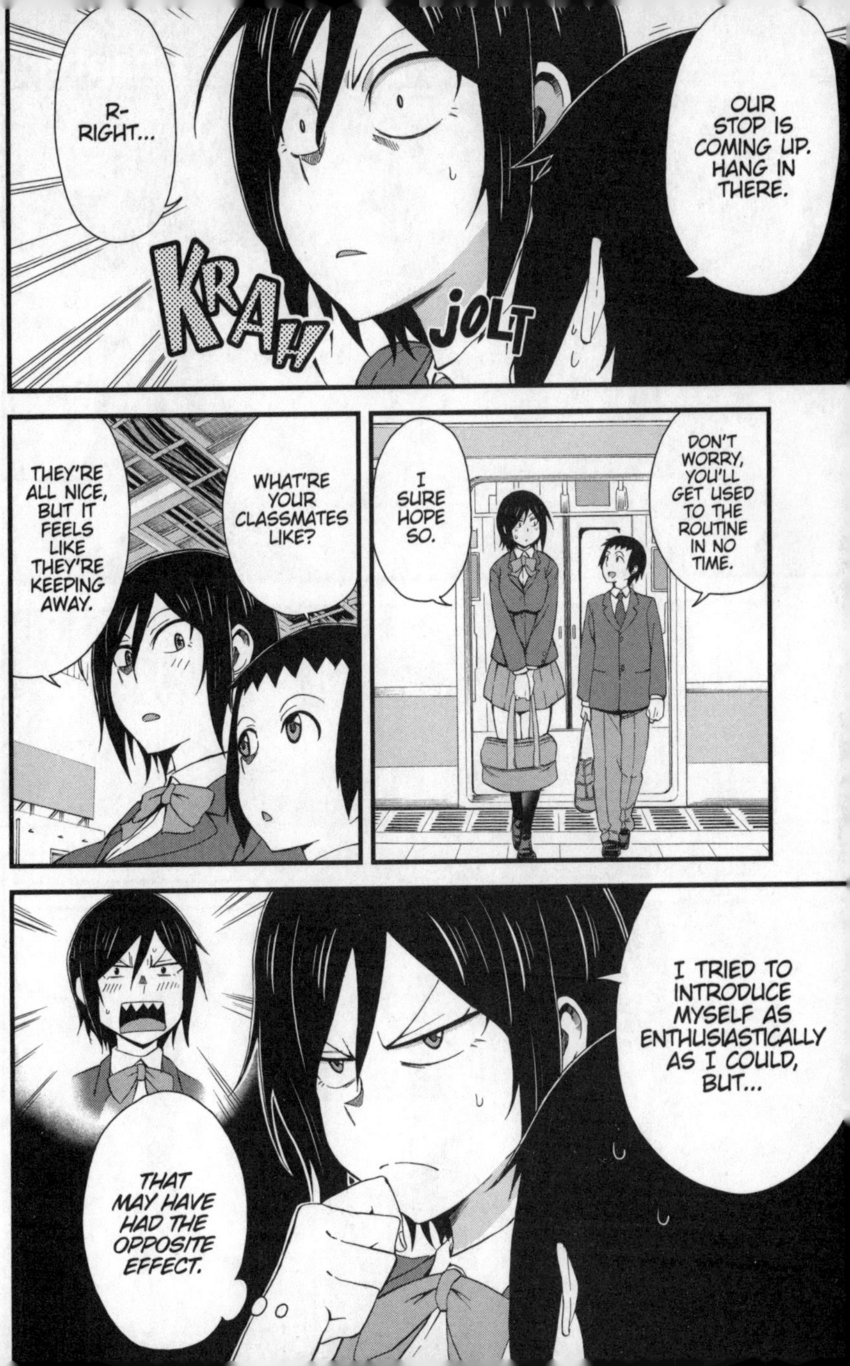
OUR STOP IS COMING UP. HANG IN THERE.
R-RIGHT...
JOLT
KRAH
DON'T WORRY, YOU'LL GET USED TO THE ROUTINE IN NO TIME.
I SURE HOPE SO.
WHAT'RE YOUR CLASSMATES LIKE?
THEY'RE ALL NICE, BUT IT FEELS LIKE THEY'RE KEEPING AWAY.
I TRIED TO INTRODUCE MYSELF AS ENTHUSIASTICALLY AS I COULD, BUT...
THAT MAY HAVE HAD THE OPPOSITE EFFECT.

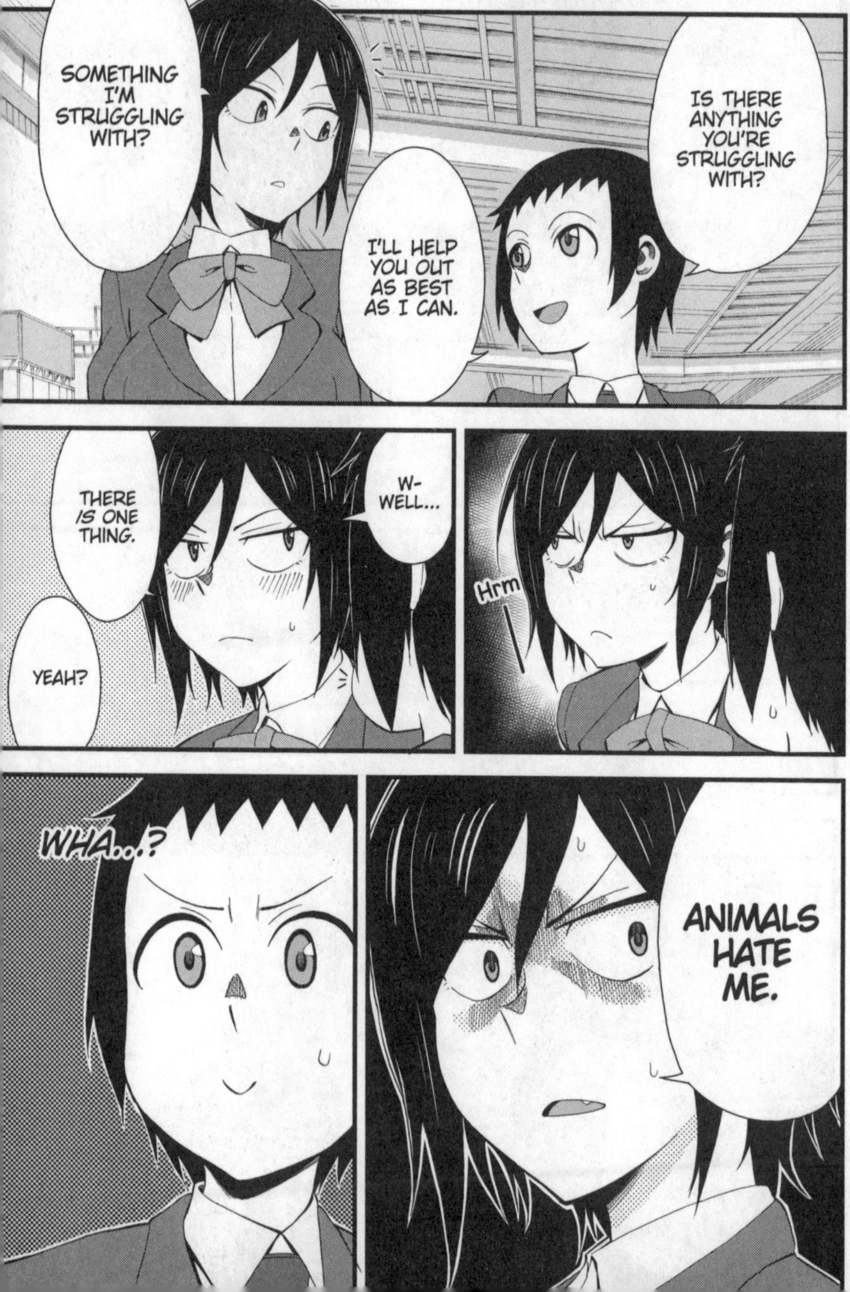
IS THERE ANYTHING YOU'RE STRUGGLING WITH?
I'LL HELP YOU OUT AS BEST AS I CAN.
SOMETHING I'M STRUGGLING WITH?
Hrm
W-WELL...
THERE *IS* ONE THING.
YEAH?
ANIMALS HATE ME.
WHA...?

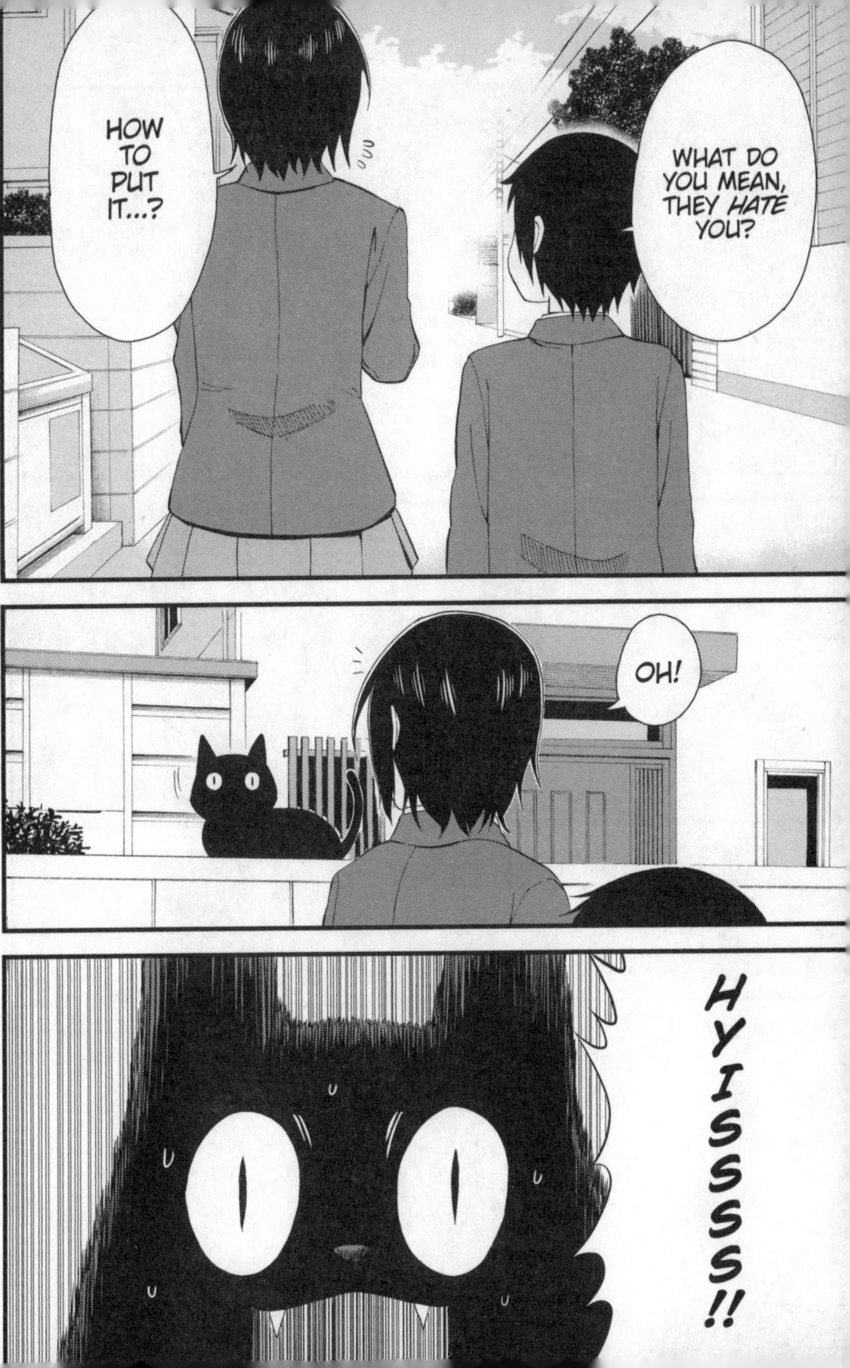
WHAT DO YOU MEAN, THEY *HATE* YOU?
HOW TO PUT IT...?
OH!
HYISSSS!!

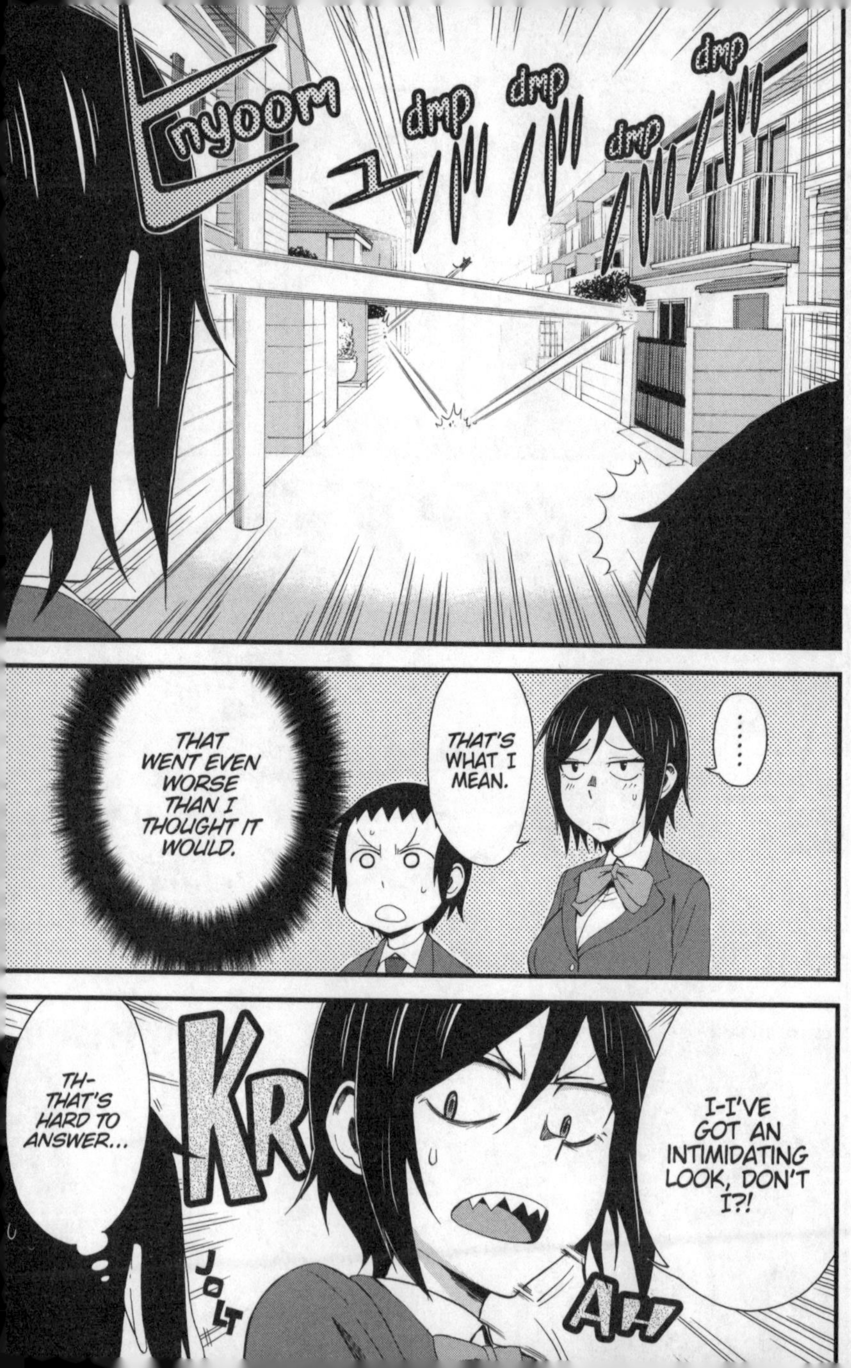
drp
drp
drp
drp
Enyoom
......
THAT'S WHAT I MEAN.
THAT WENT EVEN WORSE THAN I THOUGHT IT WOULD.
I-I'VE GOT AN INTIMIDATING LOOK, DON'T I?!
KR
TH- THAT'S HARD TO ANSWER...
AH
JOLT

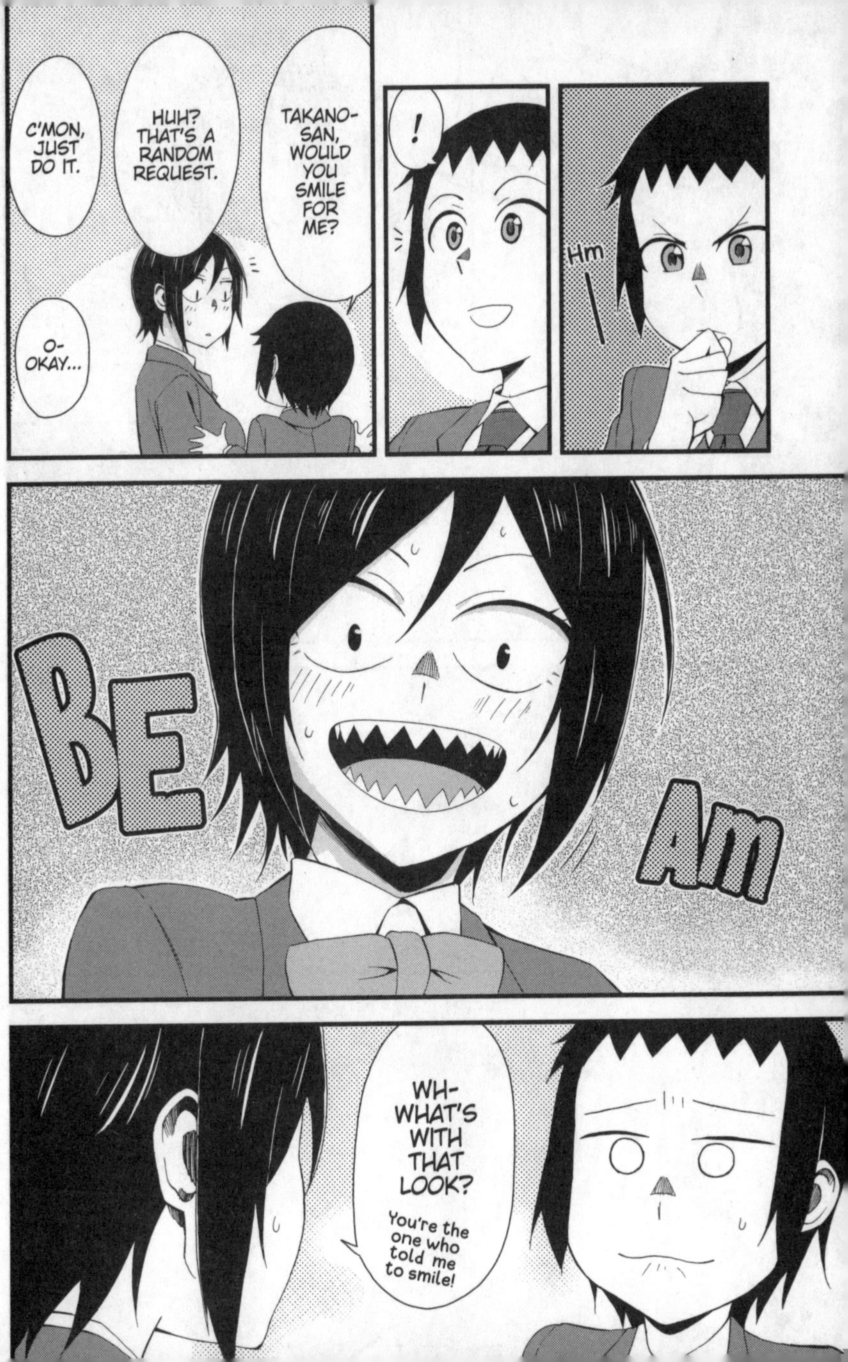
Hm
!
TAKANO-SAN, WOULD YOU SMILE FOR ME?
HUH? THAT'S A RANDOM REQUEST.
C'MON, JUST DO IT.
O-OKAY...
BE
Am
WH-WHAT'S WITH THAT LOOK?
You're the one who told me to smile!

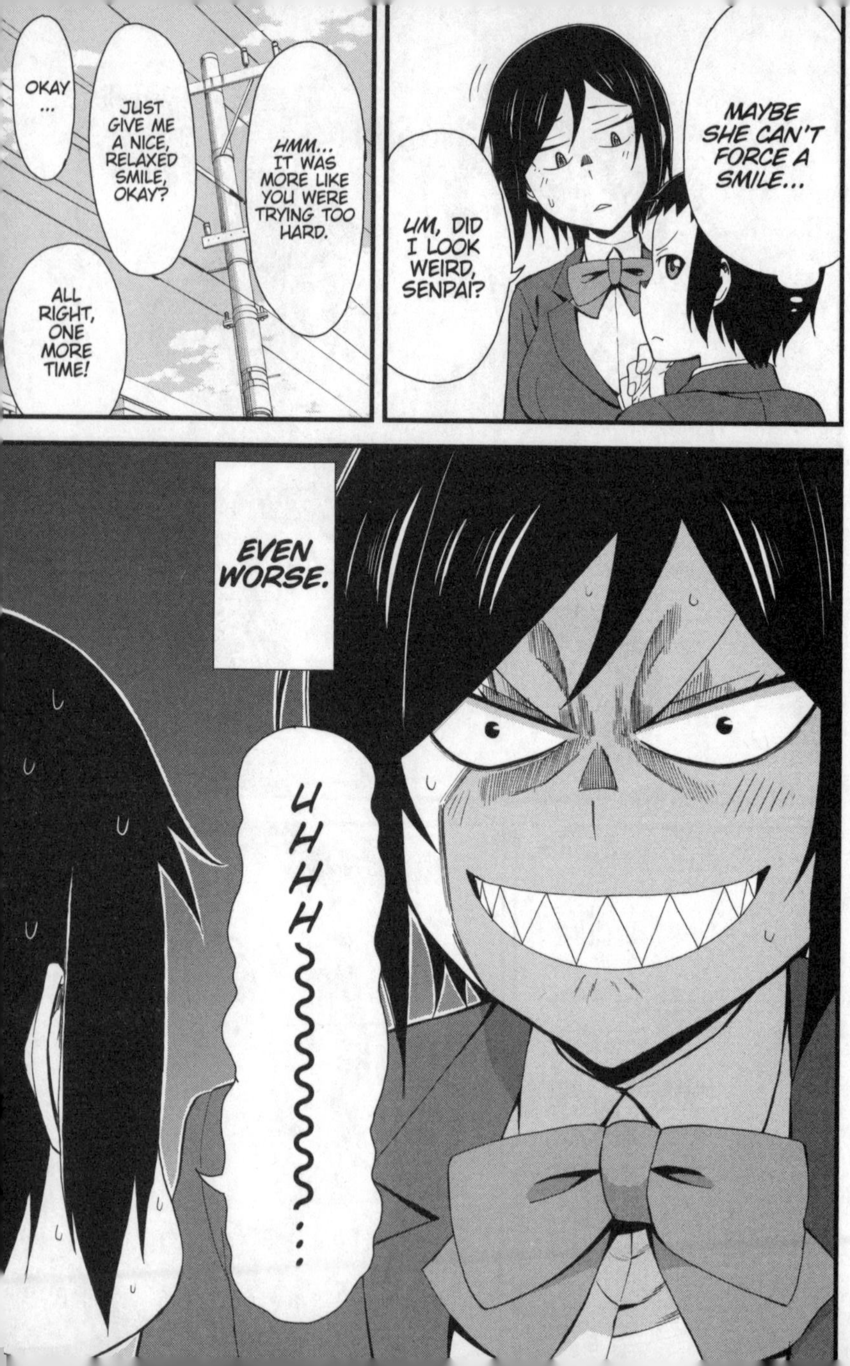
MAYBE SHE CAN'T FORCE A SMILE...
UM, DID I LOOK WEIRD, SENPAI?
HMM... IT WAS MORE LIKE YOU WERE TRYING TOO HARD.
JUST GIVE ME A NICE, RELAXED SMILE, OKAY?
OKAY...
ALL RIGHT, ONE MORE TIME!
EVEN WORSE.
UHHH~...

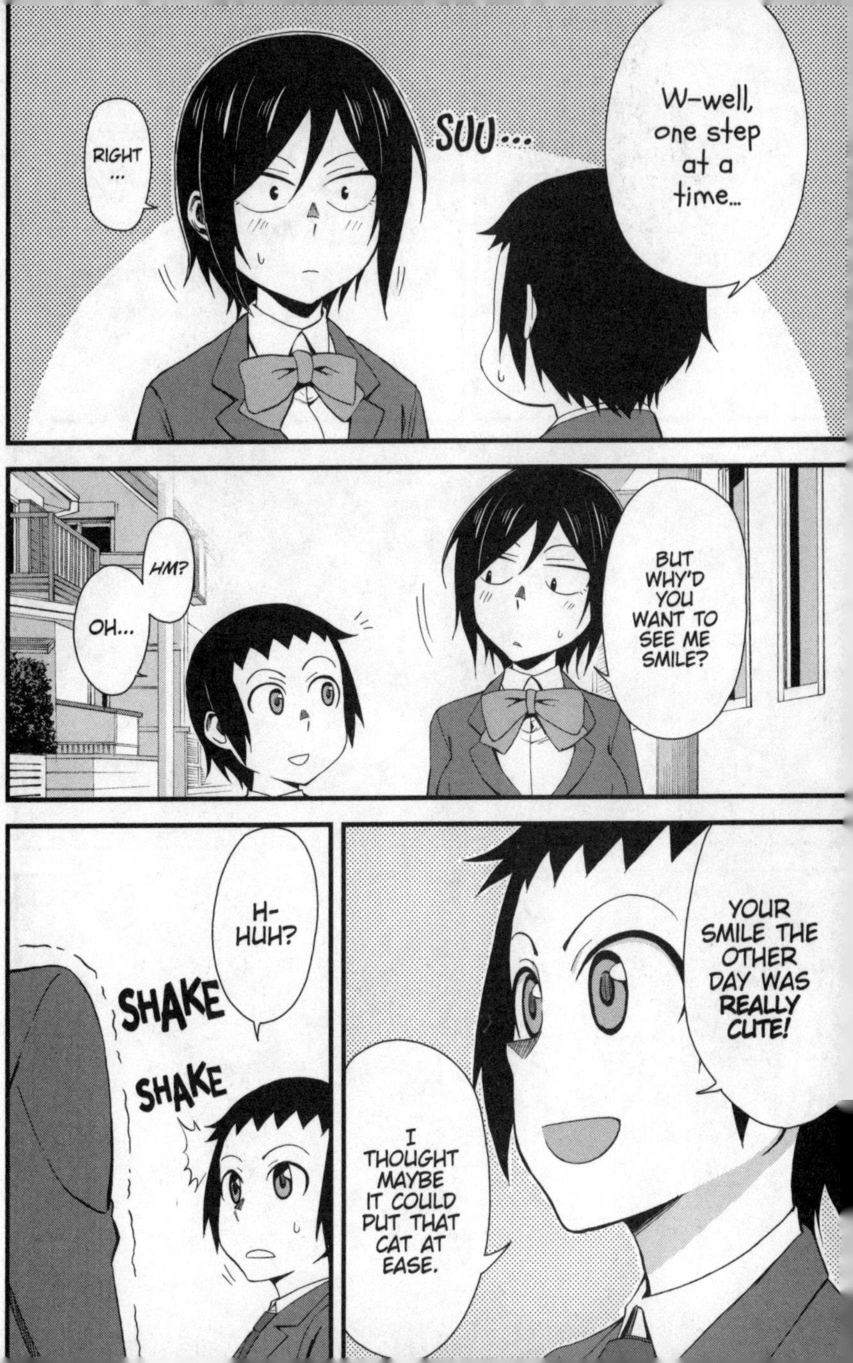
W-well, one step at a time...
SUU...
RIGHT ...
BUT WHY'D YOU WANT TO SEE ME SMILE?
HM?
OH...
YOUR SMILE THE OTHER DAY WAS REALLY CUTE!
I THOUGHT MAYBE IT COULD PUT THAT CAT AT EASE.
H-HUH?
SHAKE
SHAKE

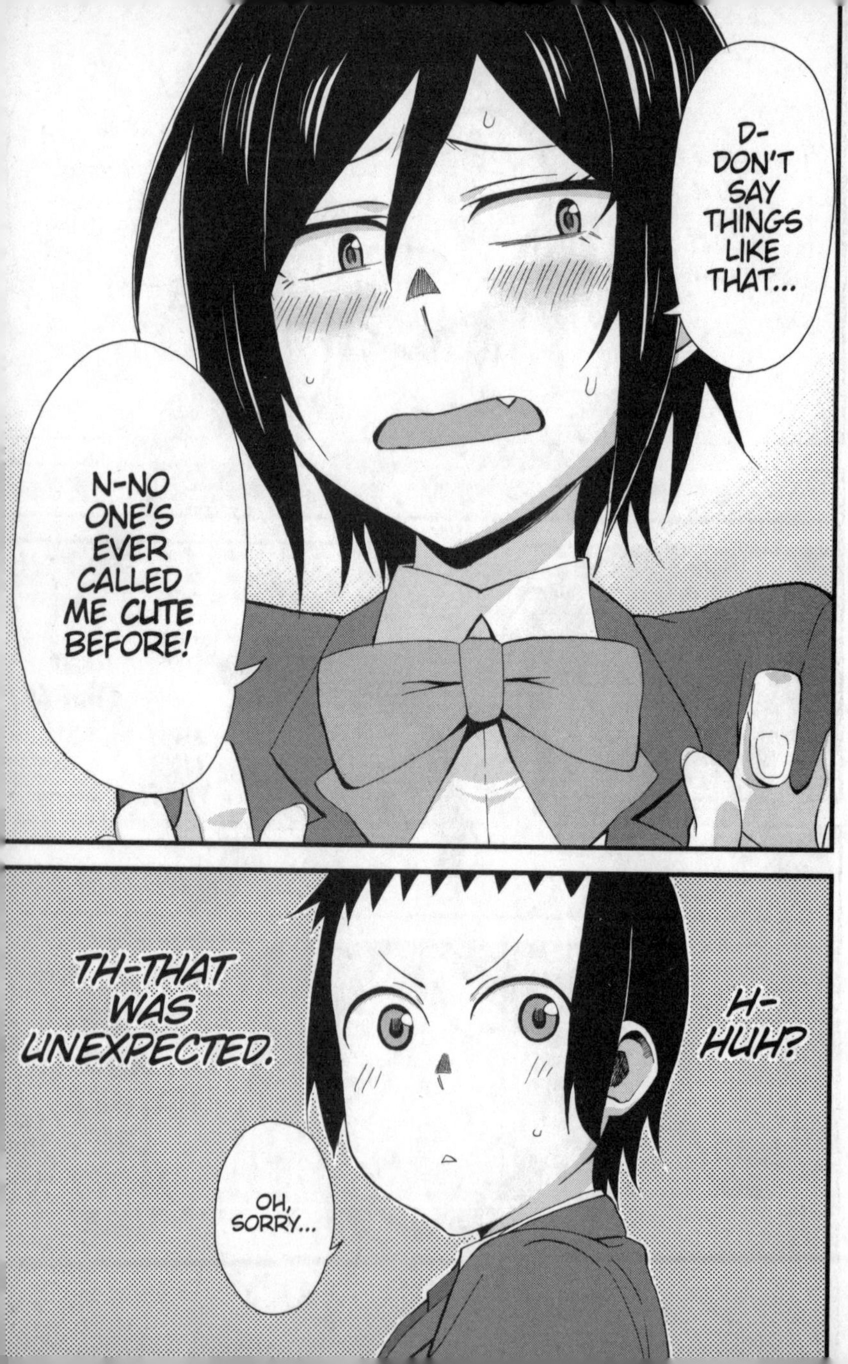
D-DON'T SAY THINGS LIKE THAT...
N-NO ONE'S EVER CALLED ME CUTE BEFORE!
H-HUH?
TH-THAT WAS UNEXPECTED.
OH, SORRY...

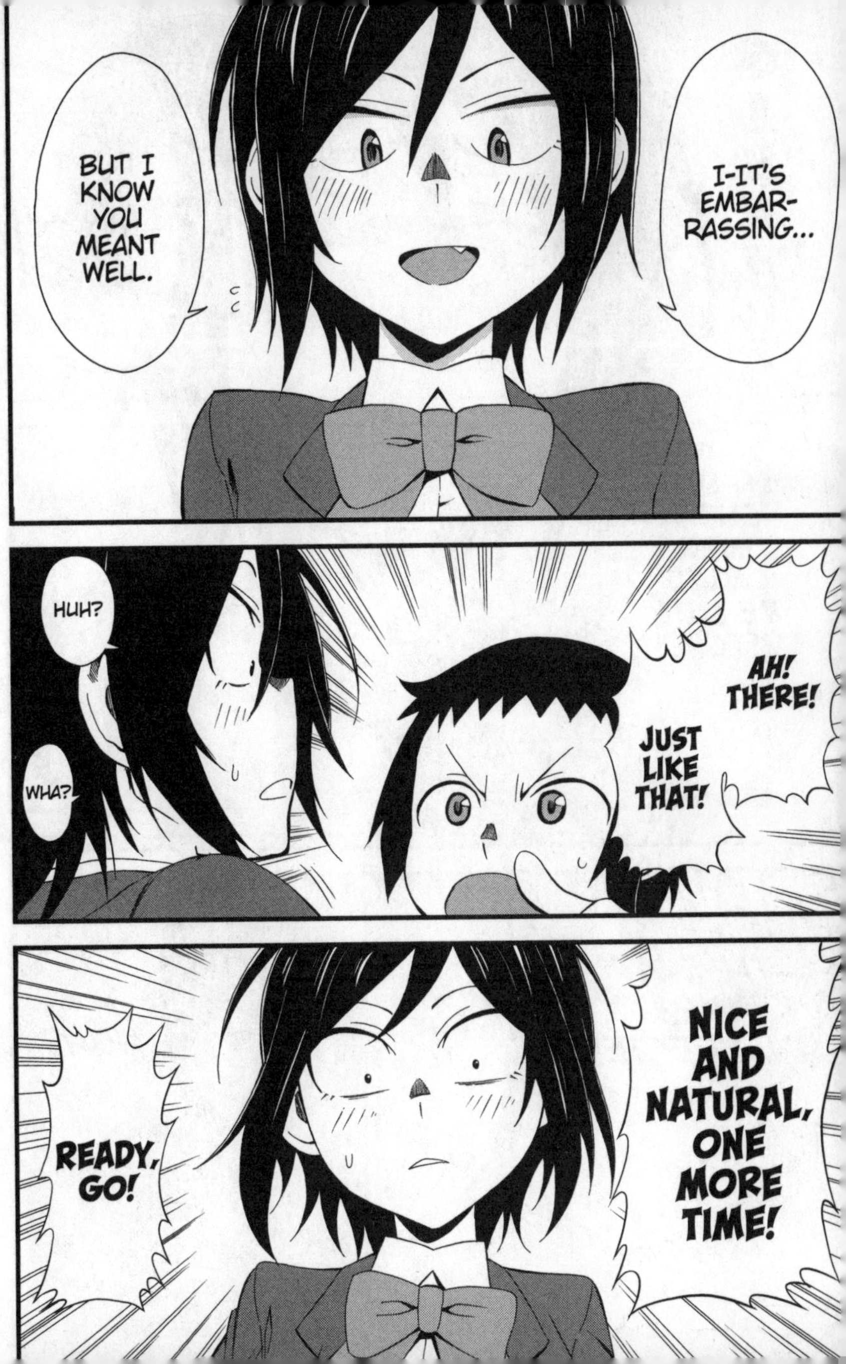
I-IT'S EMBAR-RASSING...
BUT I KNOW YOU MEANT WELL.
AH! THERE!
JUST LIKE THAT!
HUH?
WHA?
NICE AND NATURAL, ONE MORE TIME!
READY, GO!

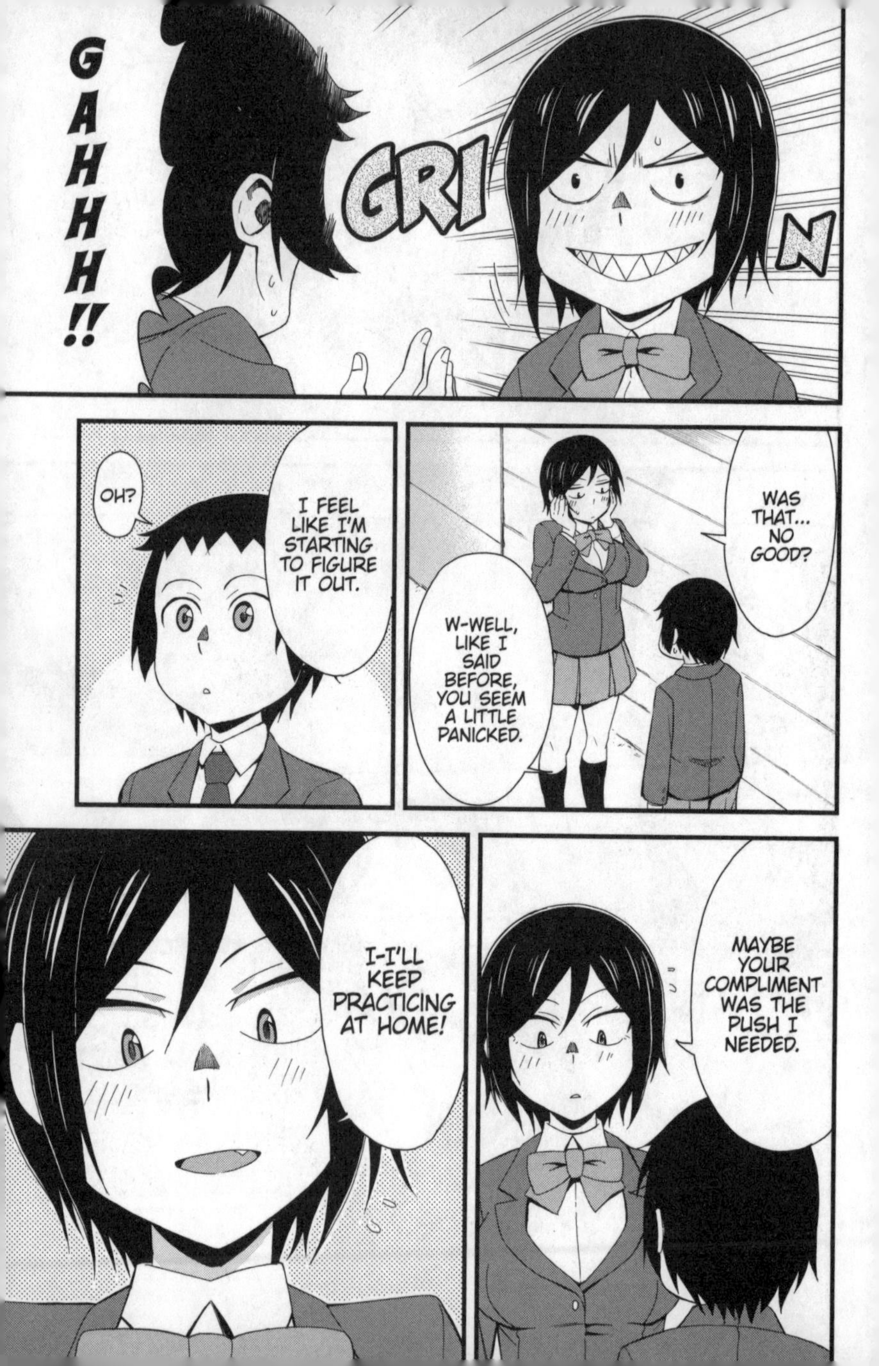
GRI
N
GAHHHH!!
WAS THAT... NO GOOD?
W-WELL, LIKE I SAID BEFORE, YOU SEEM A LITTLE PANICKED.
I FEEL LIKE I'M STARTING TO FIGURE IT OUT.
OH?
MAYBE YOUR COMPLIMENT WAS THE PUSH I NEEDED.
I-I'LL KEEP PRACTICING AT HOME!

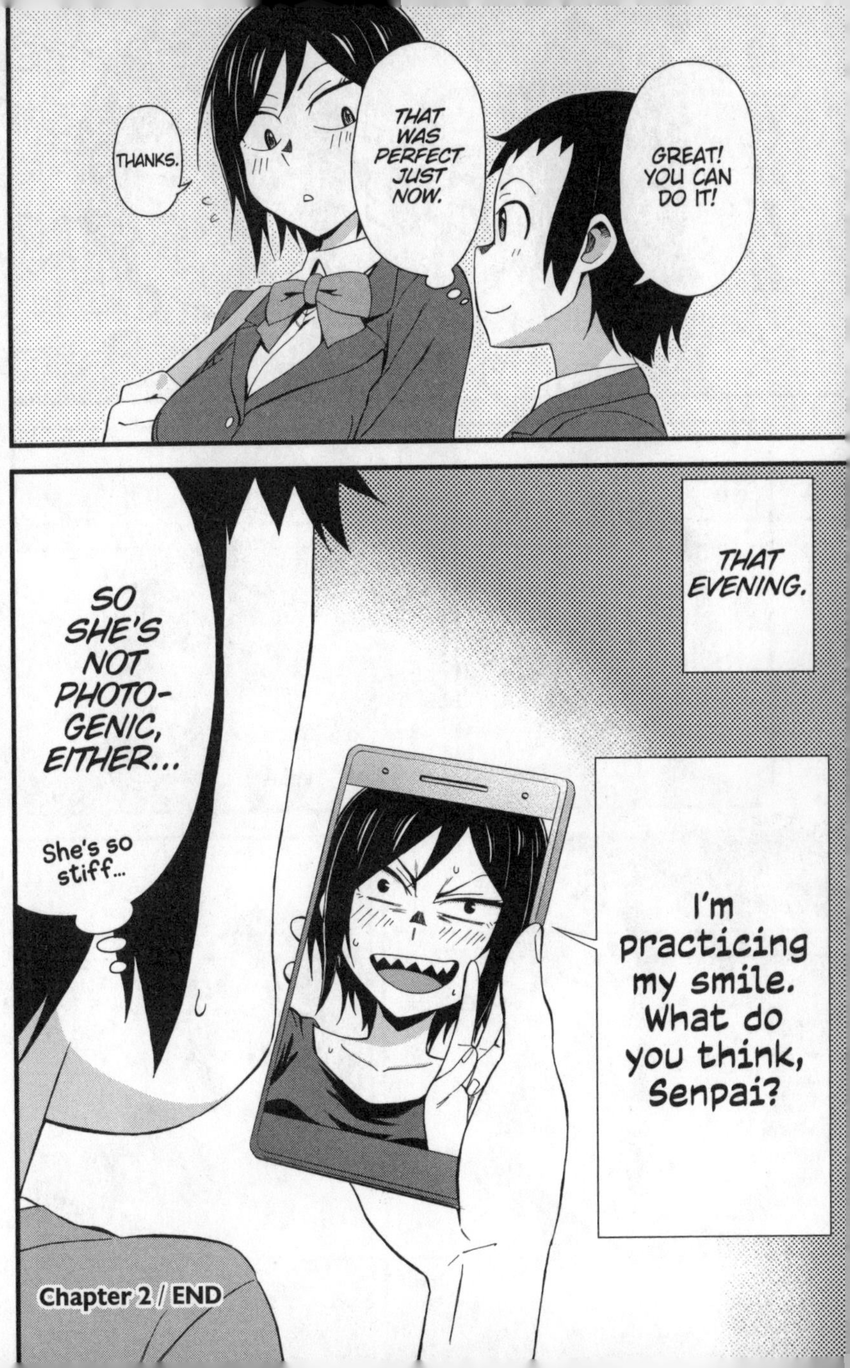
GREAT! YOU CAN DO IT!
THAT WAS PERFECT JUST NOW.
THANKS.
THAT EVENING.
I'm practicing my smile. What do you think, Senpai?
SO SHE'S NOT PHOTOGENIC, EITHER...
She's so stiff...
Chapter 2 / END

Chapter 3

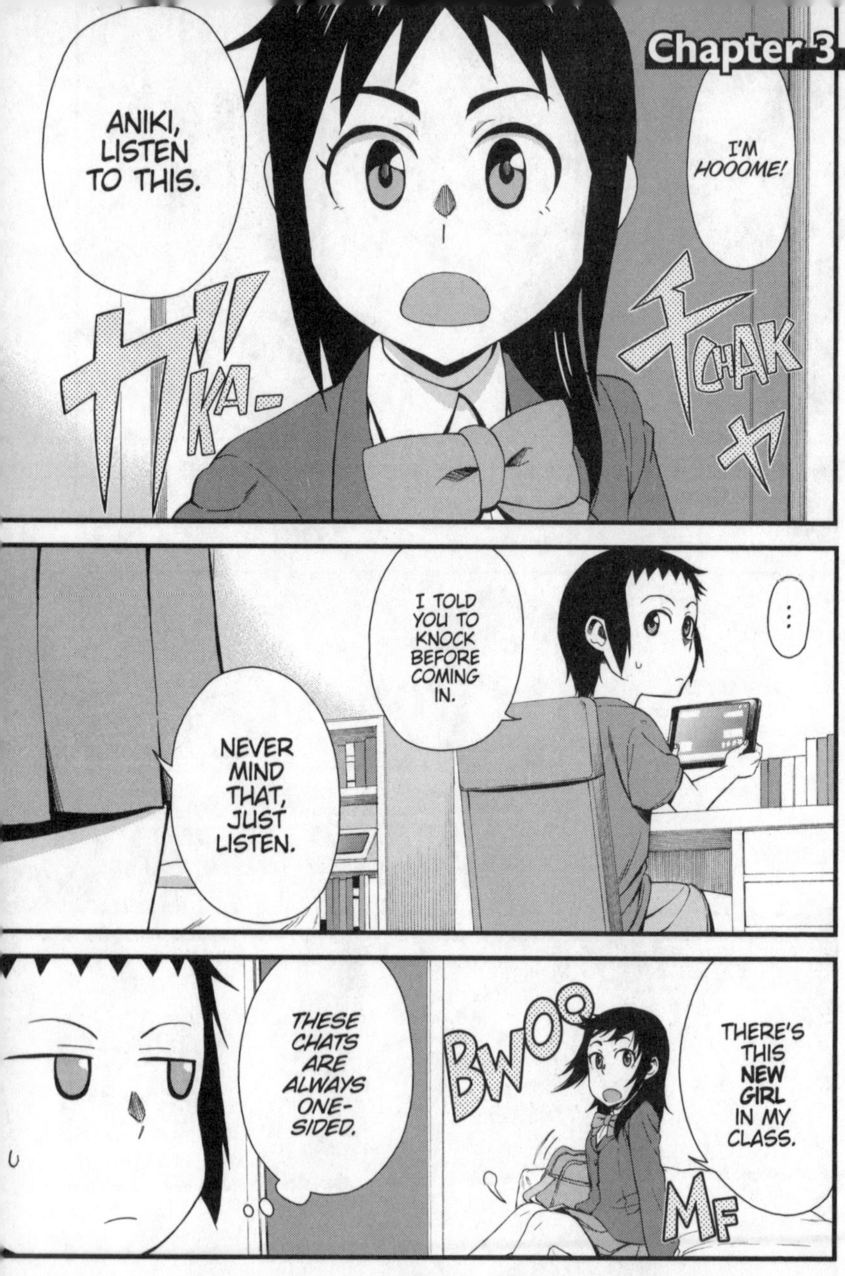
I'M HOOOME!
CHAK
ANIKI, LISTEN TO THIS.
KA-
...
I TOLD YOU TO KNOCK BEFORE COMING IN.
NEVER MIND THAT, JUST LISTEN.
THERE'S THIS NEW GIRL IN MY CLASS.
BWOO
MF
THESE CHATS ARE ALWAYS ONE-SIDED.

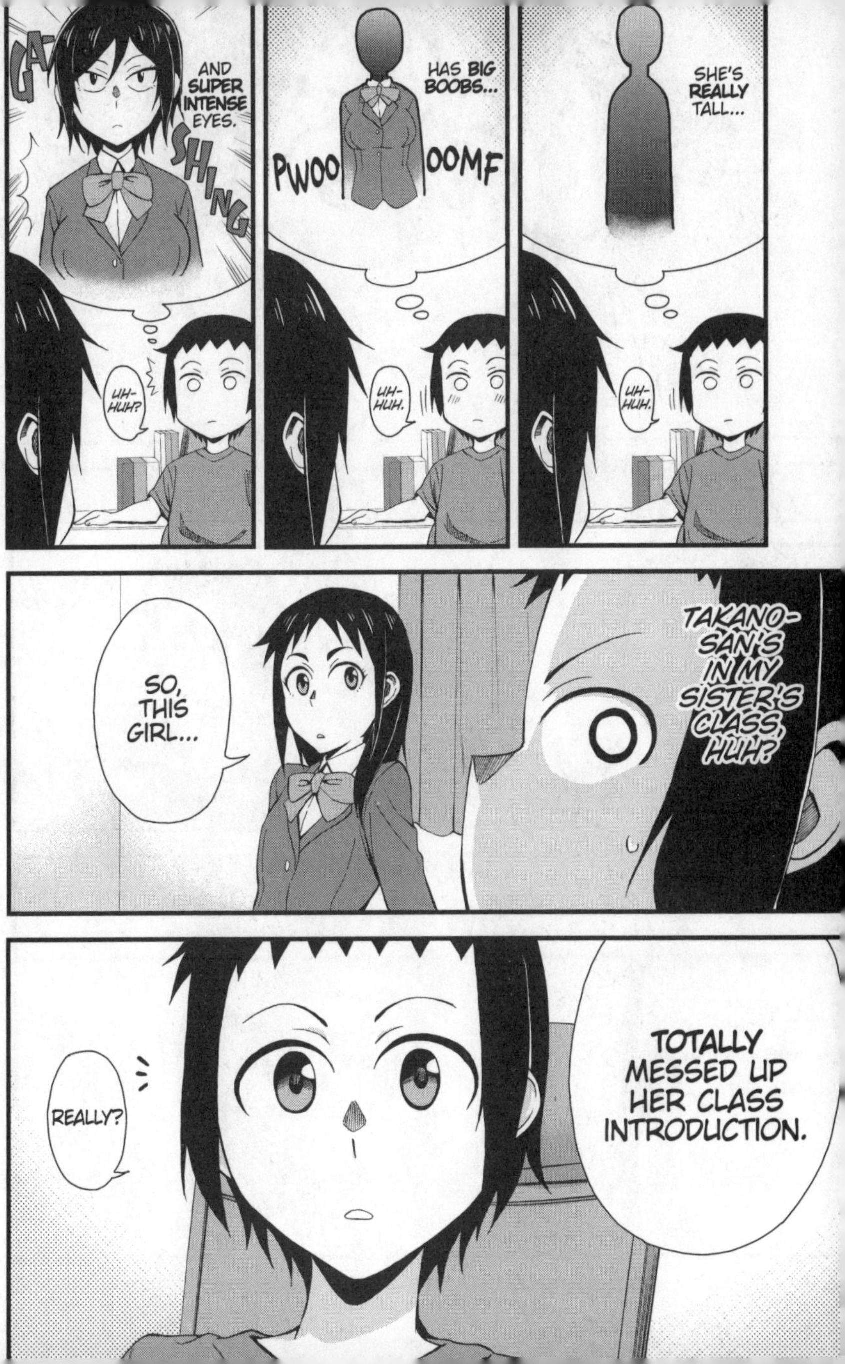
SHE'S REALLY TALL...
UH-HUH.
HAS BIG BOOBS...
PWOO OOMF
UH-HUH.
GA-
AND SUPER INTENSE EYES.
SHING
UH-HUH?
TAKANO-SAN'S IN MY SISTER'S CLASS, HUH?
SO, THIS GIRL...
TOTALLY MESSED UP HER CLASS INTRODUCTION.
REALLY?

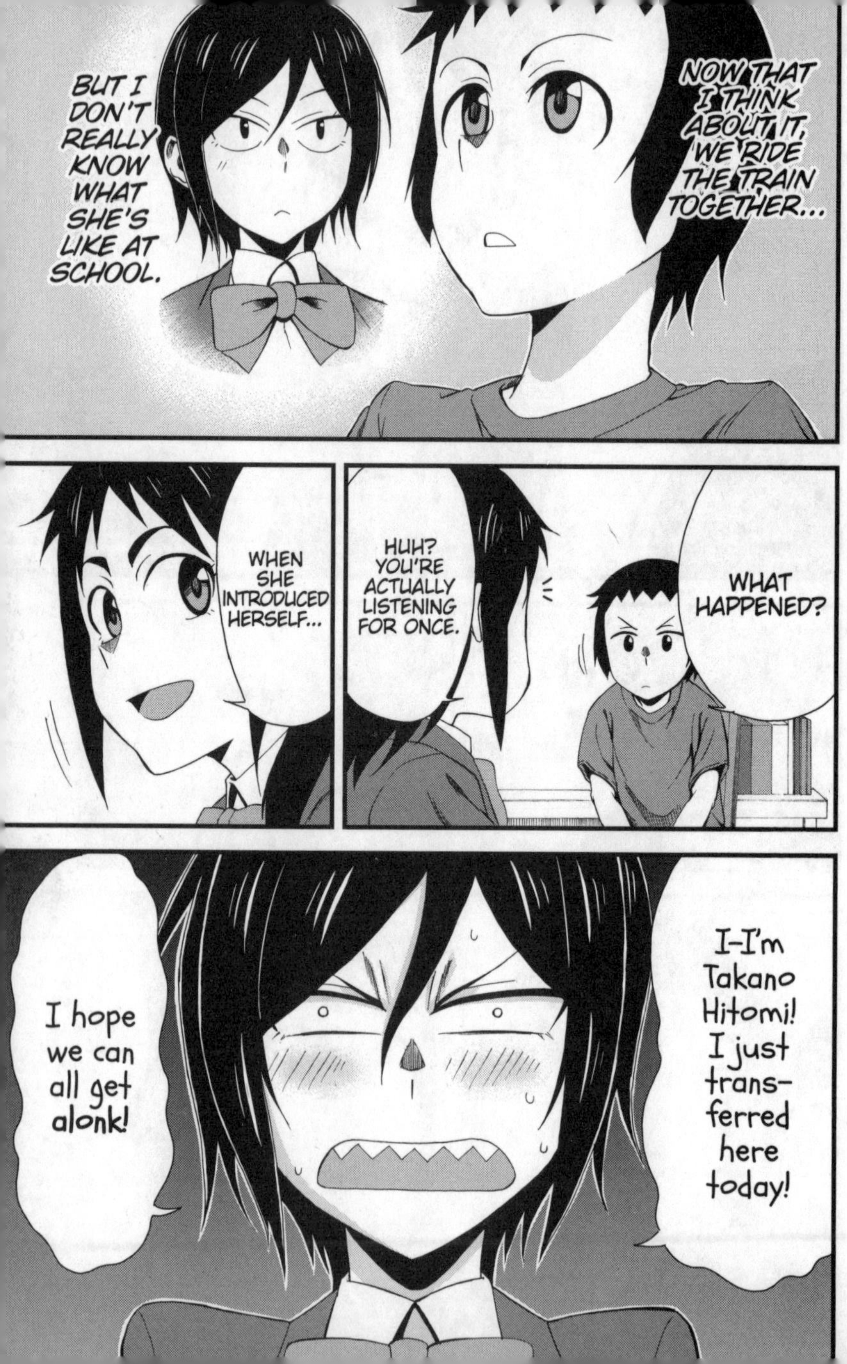
NOW THAT I THINK ABOUT IT, WE RIDE THE TRAIN TOGETHER...
BUT I DON'T REALLY KNOW WHAT SHE'S LIKE AT SCHOOL.
WHAT HAPPENED?
HUH? YOU'RE ACTUALLY LISTENING FOR ONCE.
WHEN SHE INTRODUCED HERSELF...
I-I'm Takano Hitomi! I just trans-ferred here today!
I hope we can all get alonk!

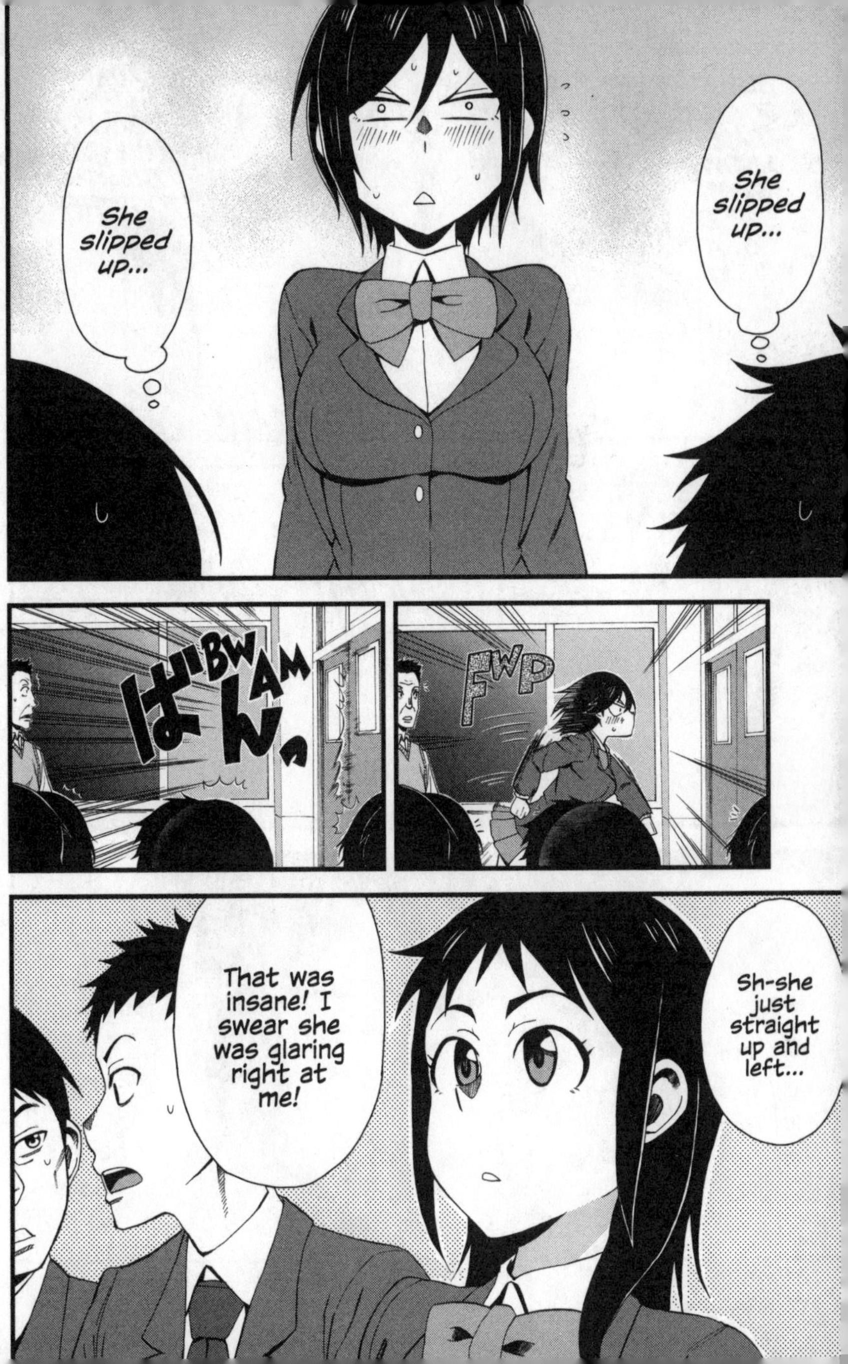

She slipped up...
She slipped up...
FWP
BWAM
ばんっ
Sh-she just straight up and left...
That was insane! I swear she was glaring right at me!

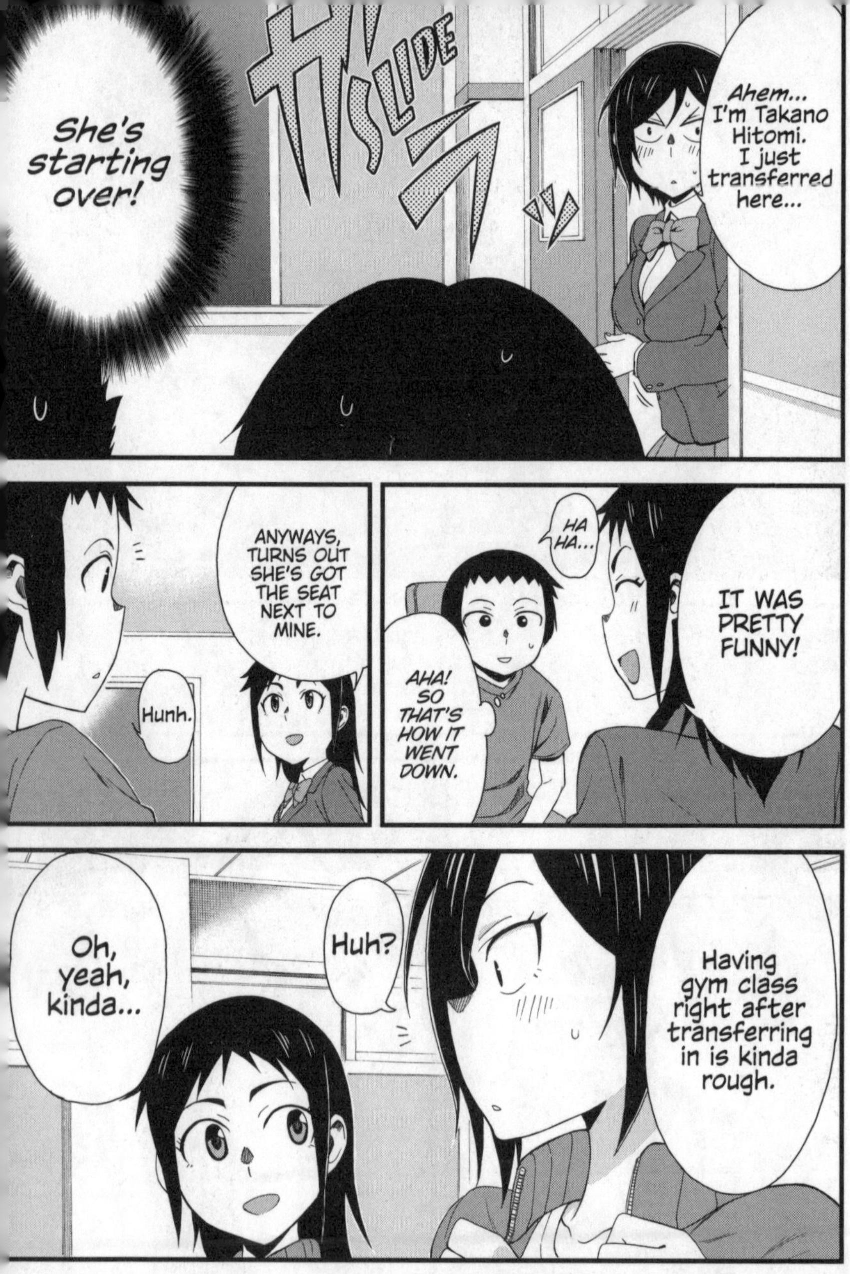
Ahem... I'm Takano Hitomi. I just transferred here...
SLIDE
She's starting over!
IT WAS PRETTY FUNNY!
HA HA...
AHA! SO THAT'S HOW IT WENT DOWN.
ANYWAYS, TURNS OUT SHE'S GOT THE SEAT NEXT TO MINE.
Hunh.
Having gym class right after transferring in is kinda rough.
Huh?
Oh, yeah, kinda...

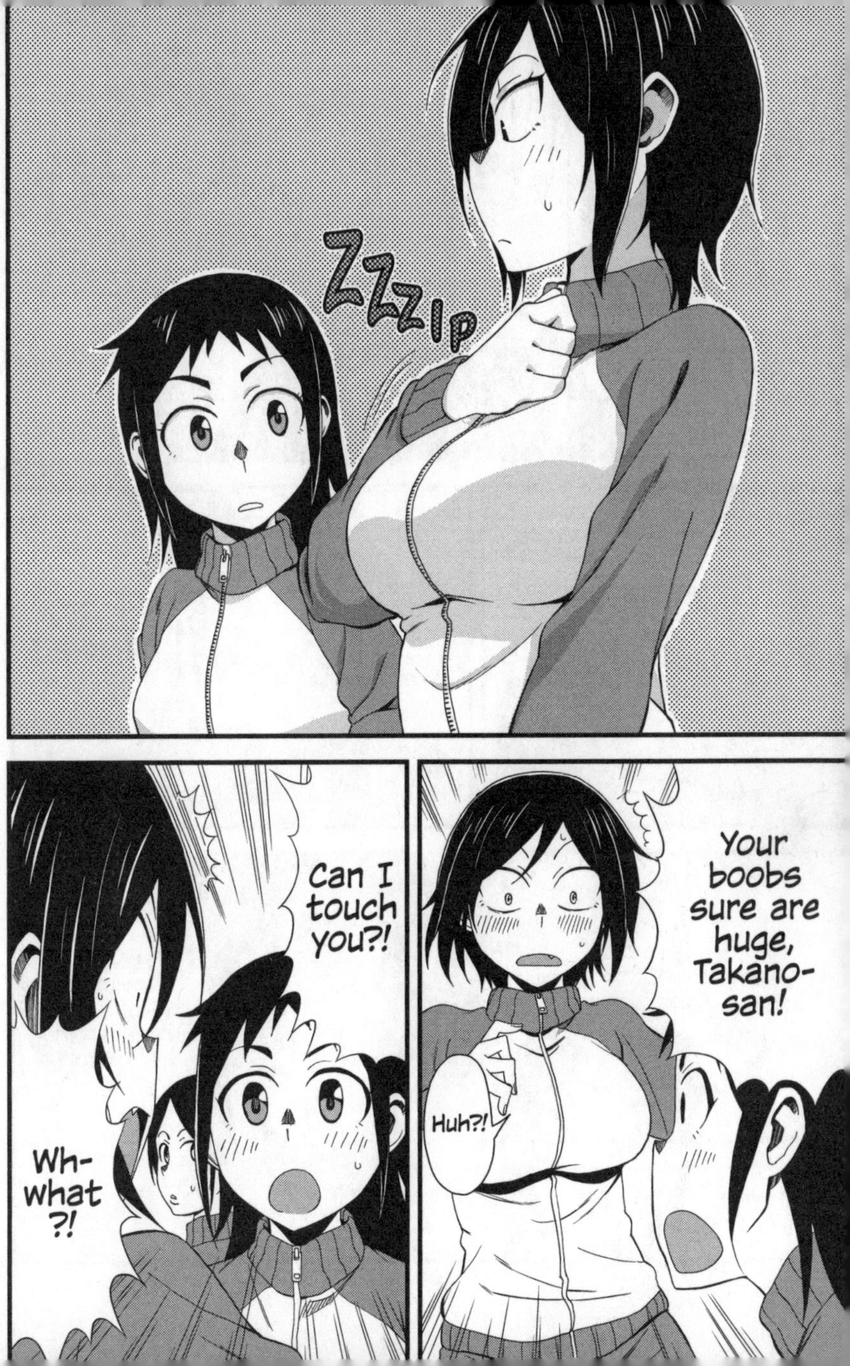
ZZZip
Your boobs sure are huge, Takano-san!
Huh?!
Can I touch you?!
Wh-what?!

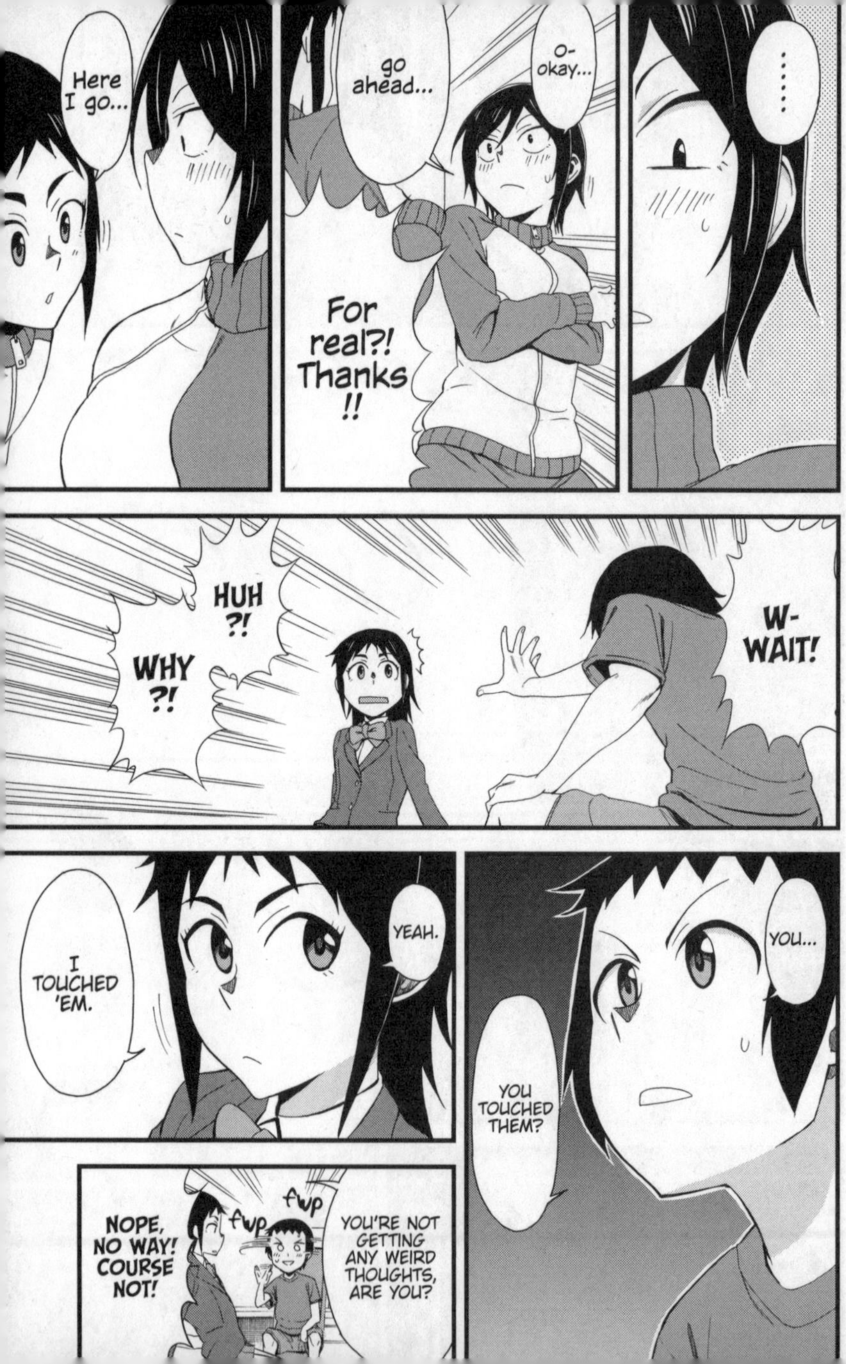
......
O-okay...
go ahead...
For real?! Thanks !!
Here I go...
W-WAIT!
HUH ?!
WHY ?!
YOU...
YOU TOUCHED THEM?
YEAH.
I TOUCHED 'EM.
YOU'RE NOT GETTING ANY WEIRD THOUGHTS, ARE YOU?
fwp
fwp
NOPE, NO WAY! COURSE NOT!

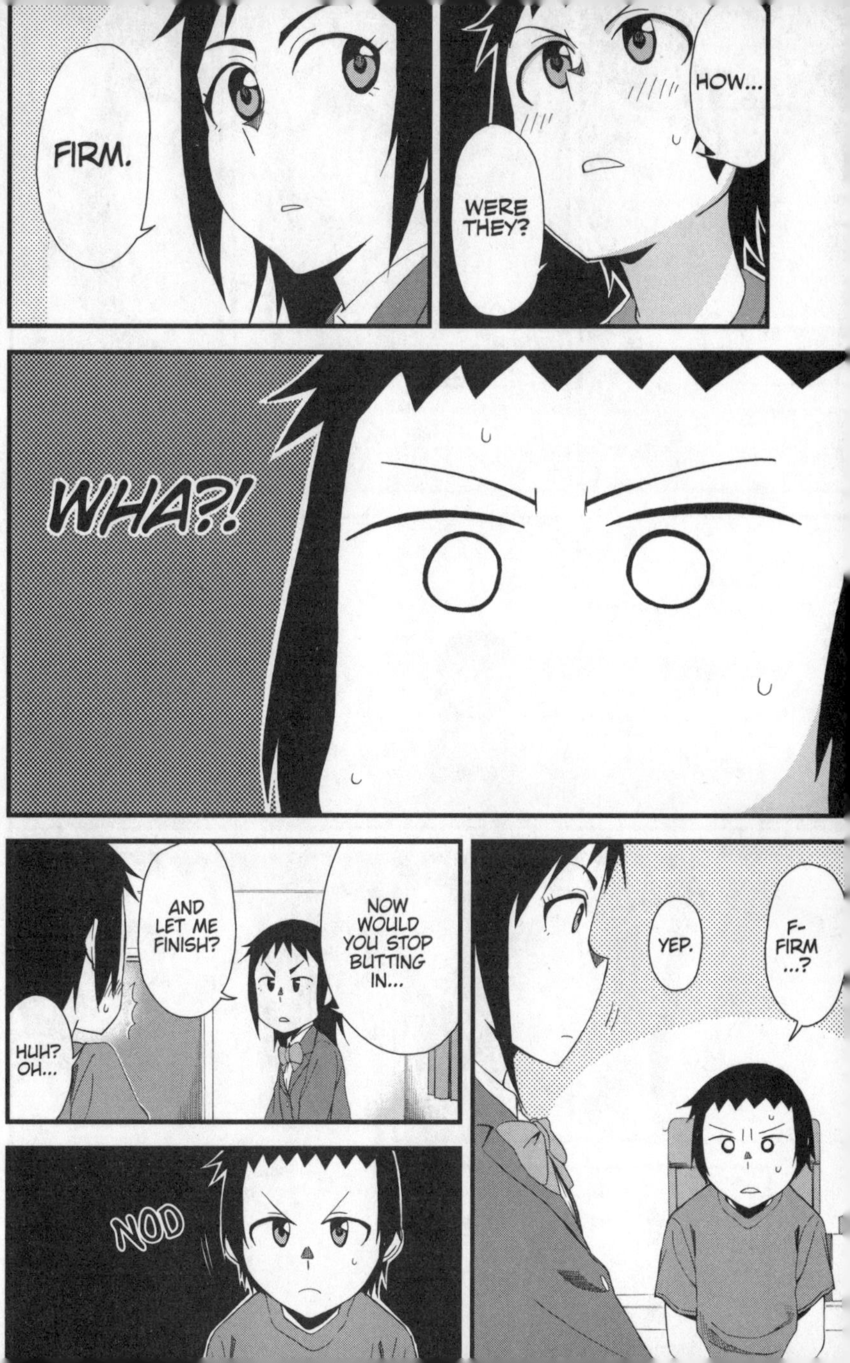
HOW...
WERE THEY?
FIRM.
WHA?!
F-FIRM...?
YEP.
NOW WOULD YOU STOP BUTTING IN...
AND LET ME FINISH?
HUH? OH...
NOD

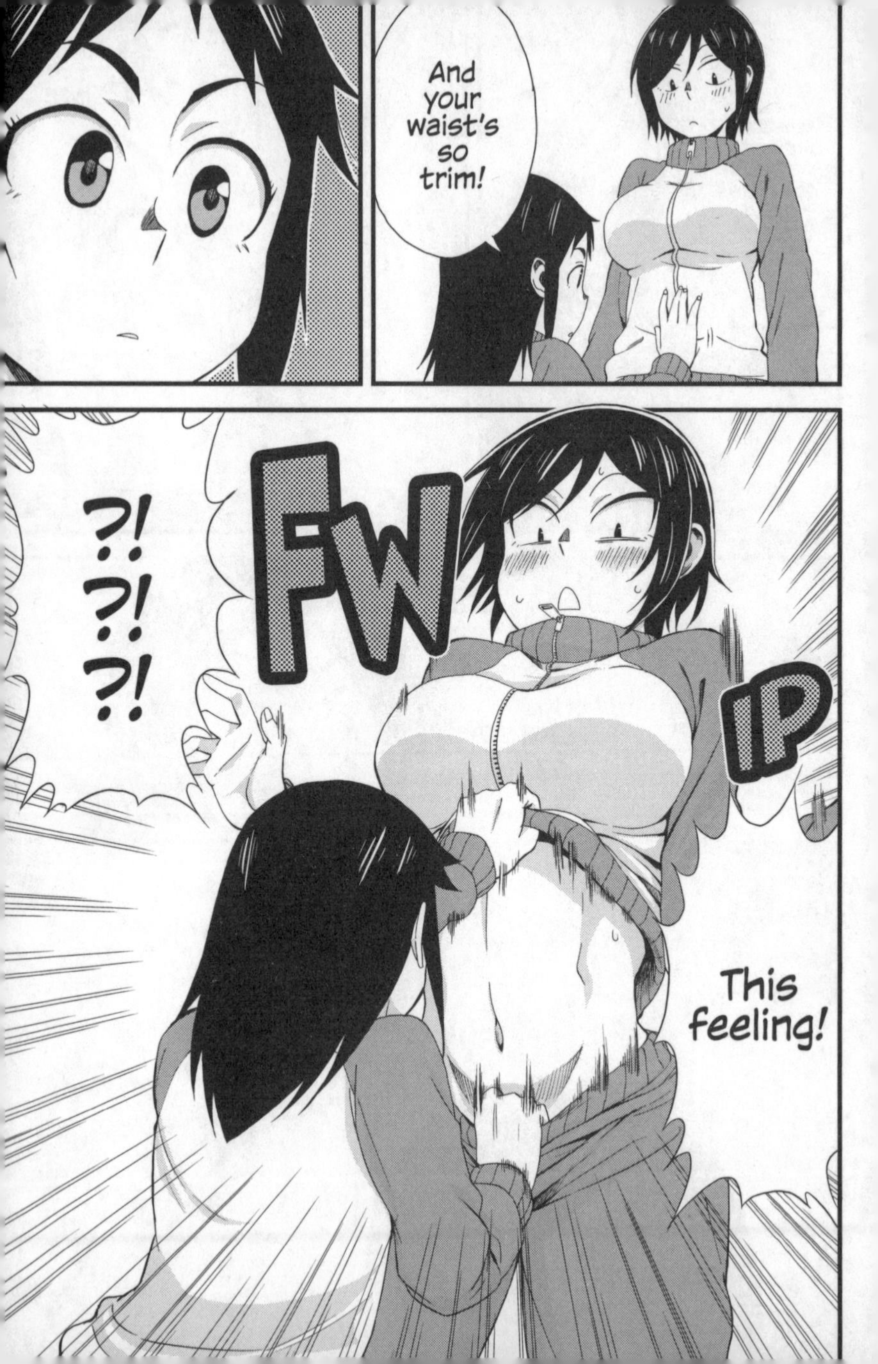
And your waist's so trim!
FW
IP
?!?!?!
This feeling!

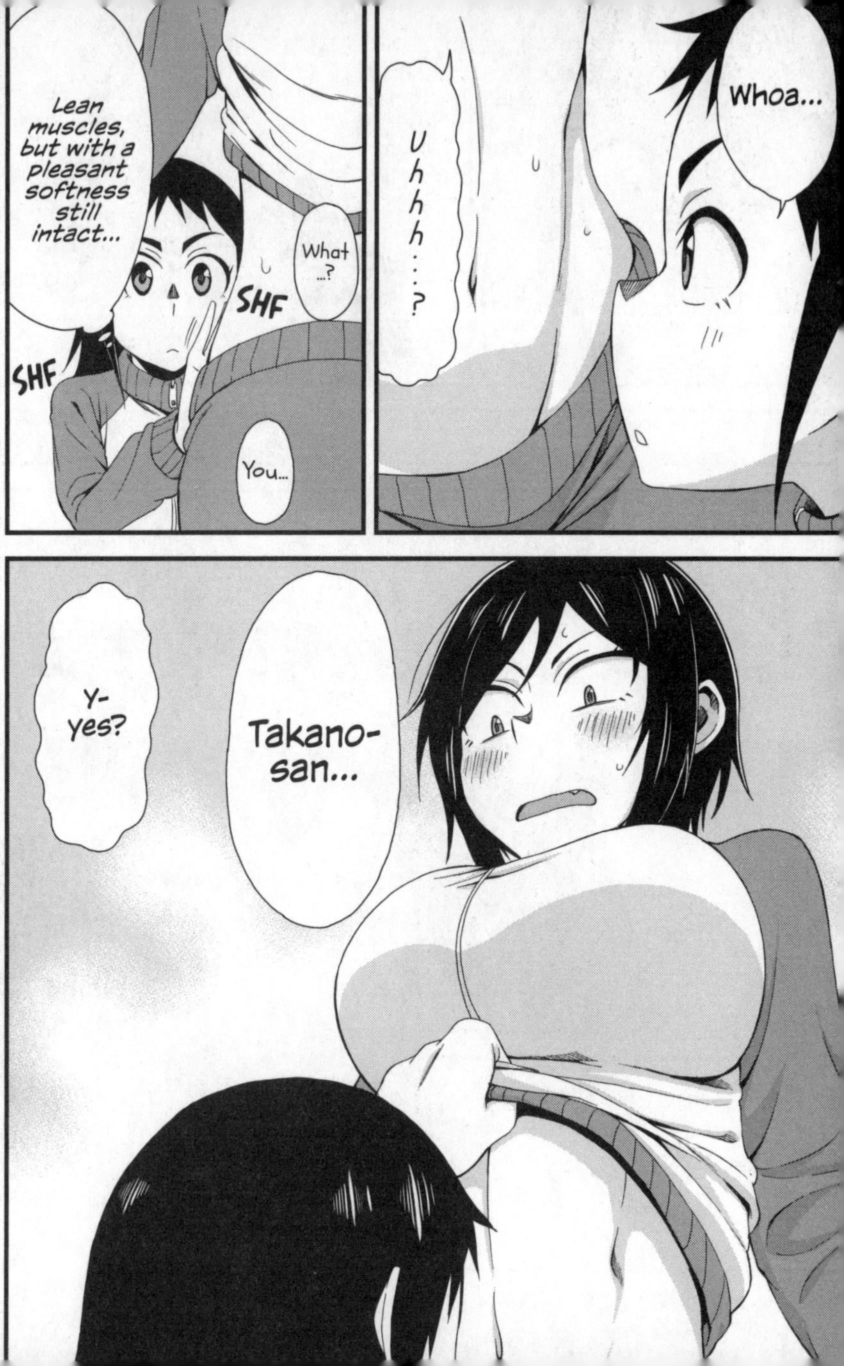
Whoa...
Uhhh...?
Lean muscles, but with a pleasant softness still intact...
SHF
SHF
What...?
You...
Takano-san...
Y- yes?

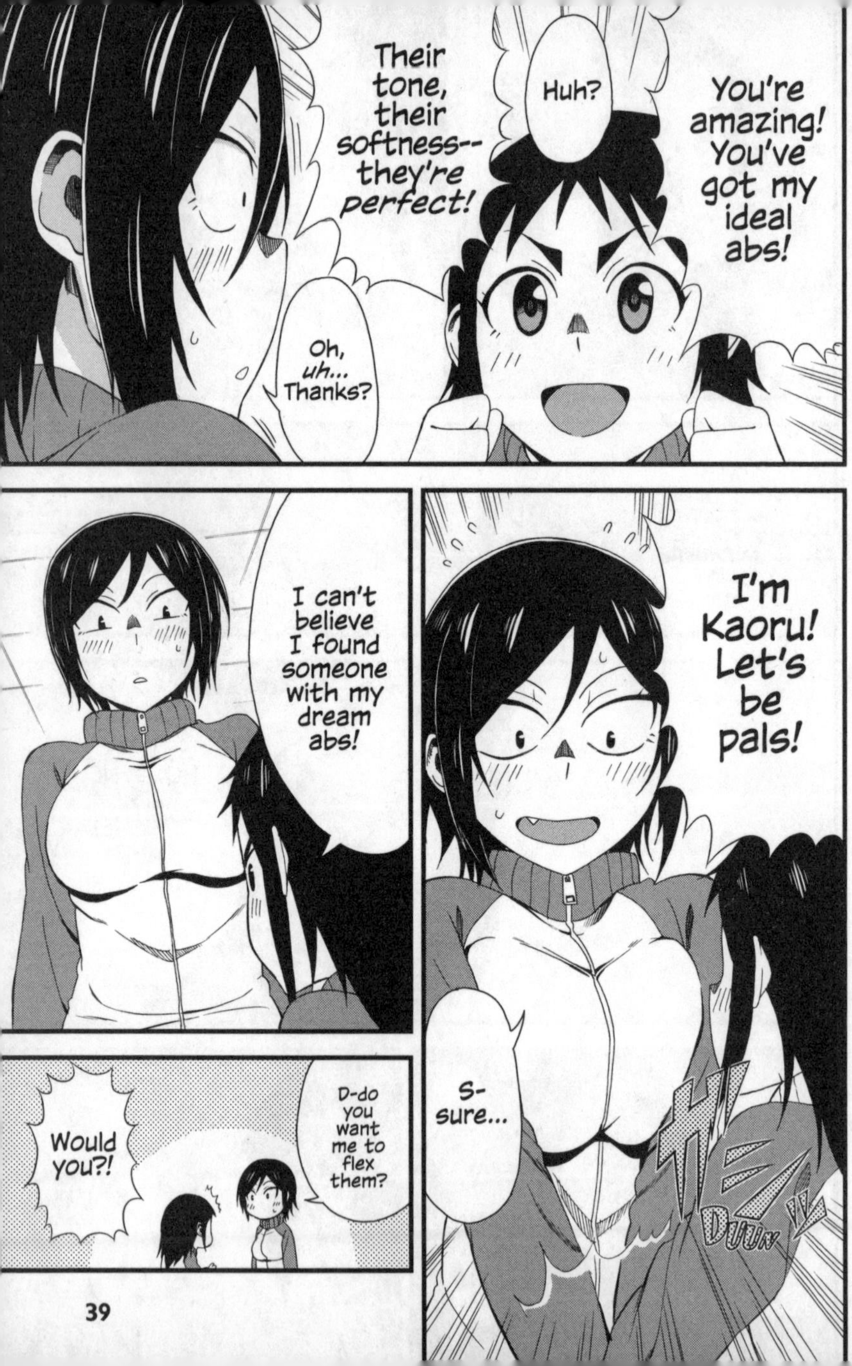
You're amazing! You've got my ideal abs!
Huh?
Their tone, their softness-- they're perfect!
Oh, uh... Thanks?
I'm Kaoru! Let's be pals!
S-sure...
DUUN
I can't believe I found someone with my dream abs!
D-do you want me to flex them?
Would you?!

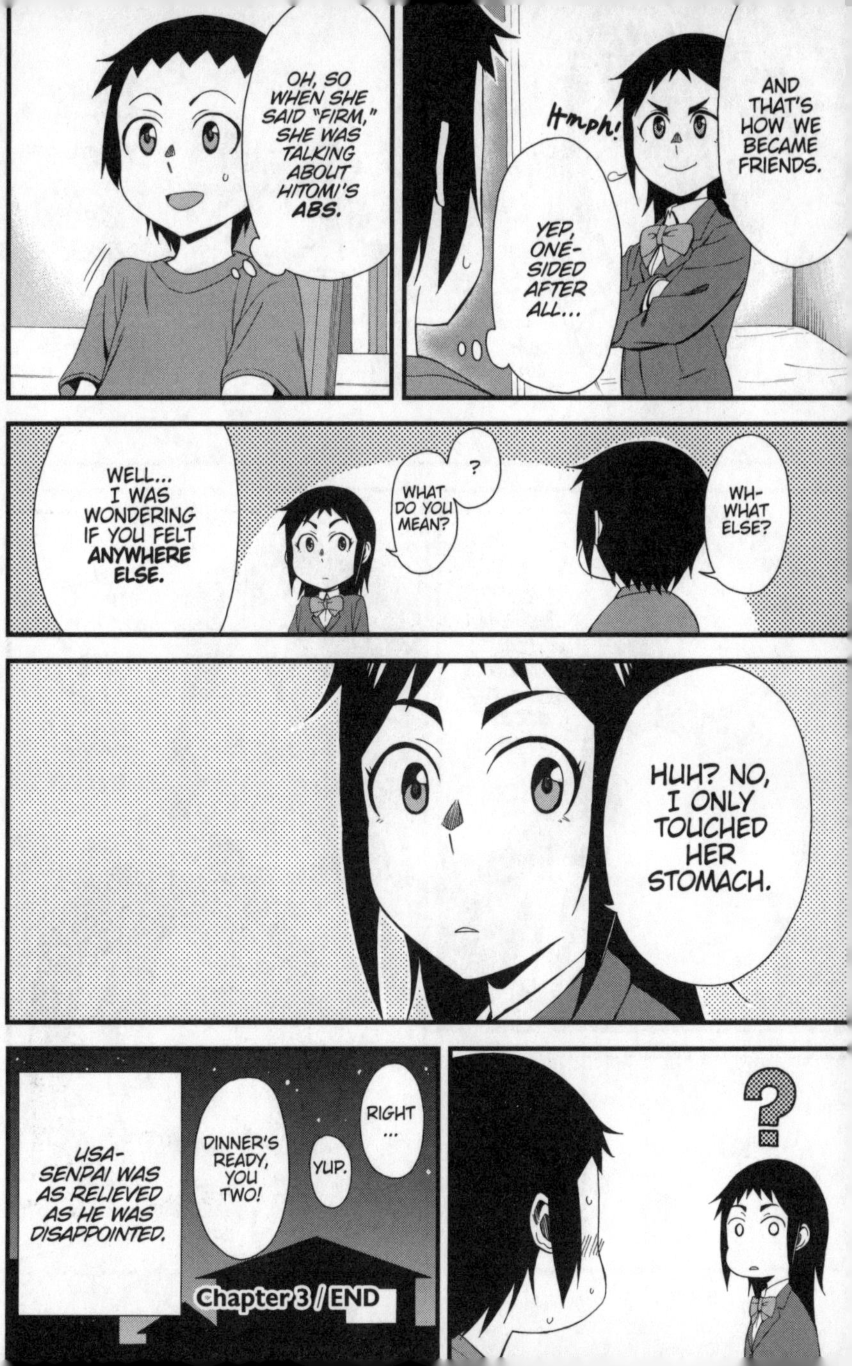
AND THAT'S HOW WE BECAME FRIENDS.
Hmph!
YEP, ONE-SIDED AFTER ALL...
OH, SO WHEN SHE SAID "FIRM," SHE WAS TALKING ABOUT HITOMI'S ABS.
WH-WHAT ELSE?
?
WHAT DO YOU MEAN?
WELL... I WAS WONDERING IF YOU FELT ANYWHERE ELSE.
HUH? NO, I ONLY TOUCHED HER STOMACH.
?
RIGHT...
YUP.
DINNER'S READY, YOU TWO!
USA-SENPAI WAS AS RELIEVED AS HE WAS DISAPPOINTED.
Chapter 3 / END

Hitomi-chan is Shy With Strangers

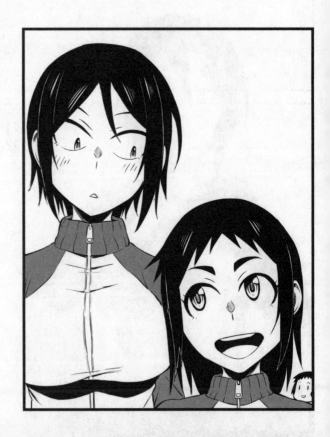

Hitomi-chan is Shy With Strangers

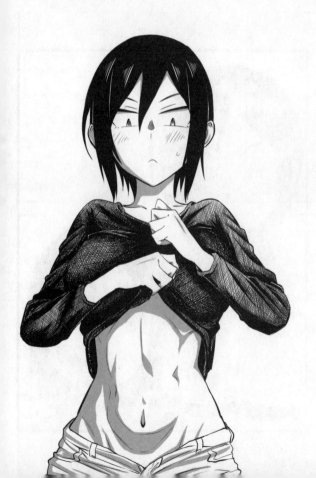

Chapter 4

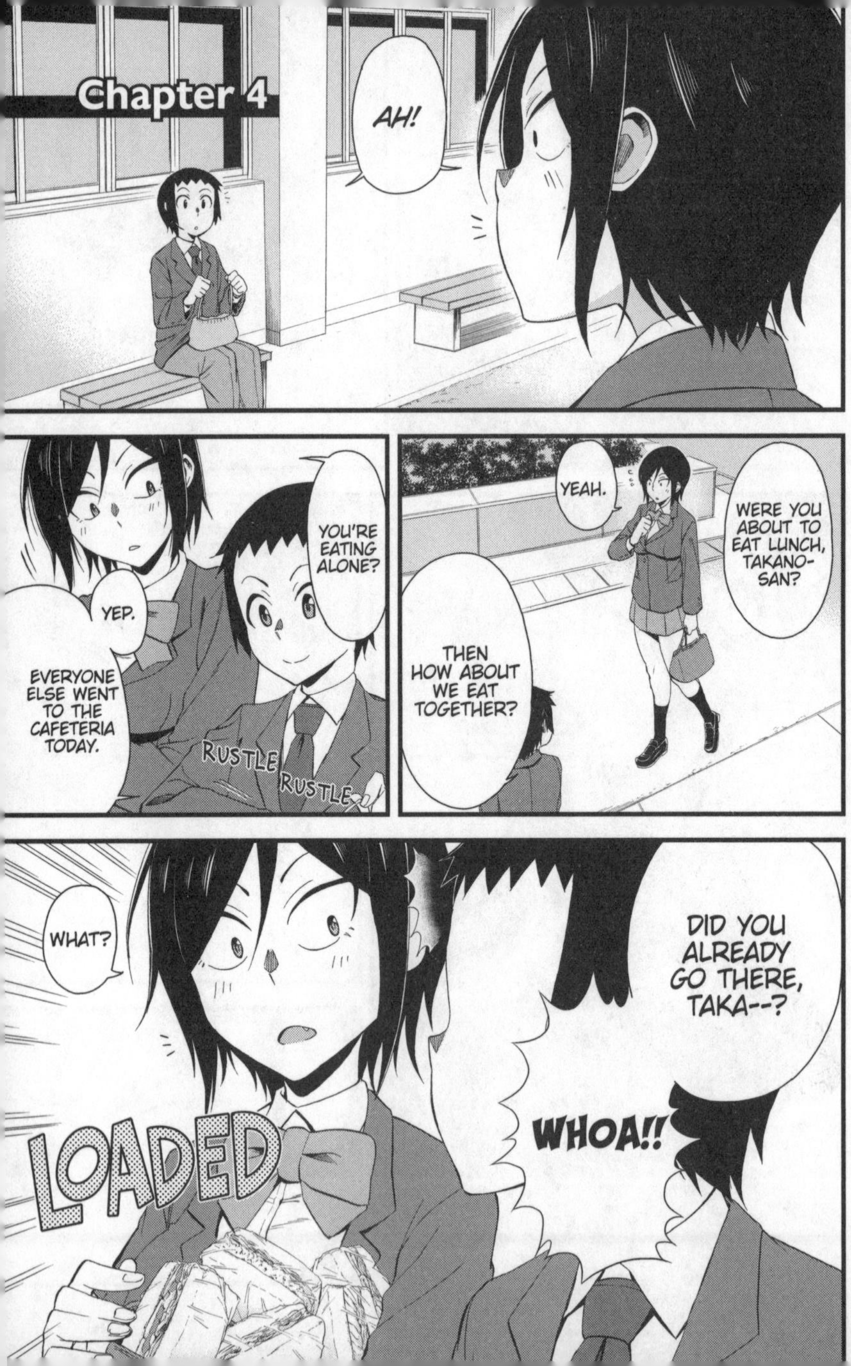

AH!
WERE YOU ABOUT TO EAT LUNCH, TAKANO-SAN?
YEAH.
THEN HOW ABOUT WE EAT TOGETHER?
YOU'RE EATING ALONE?
YEP.
EVERYONE ELSE WENT TO THE CAFETERIA TODAY.
RUSTLE RUSTLE
DID YOU ALREADY GO THERE, TAKA--?
WHOA!!
WHAT?
LOADED

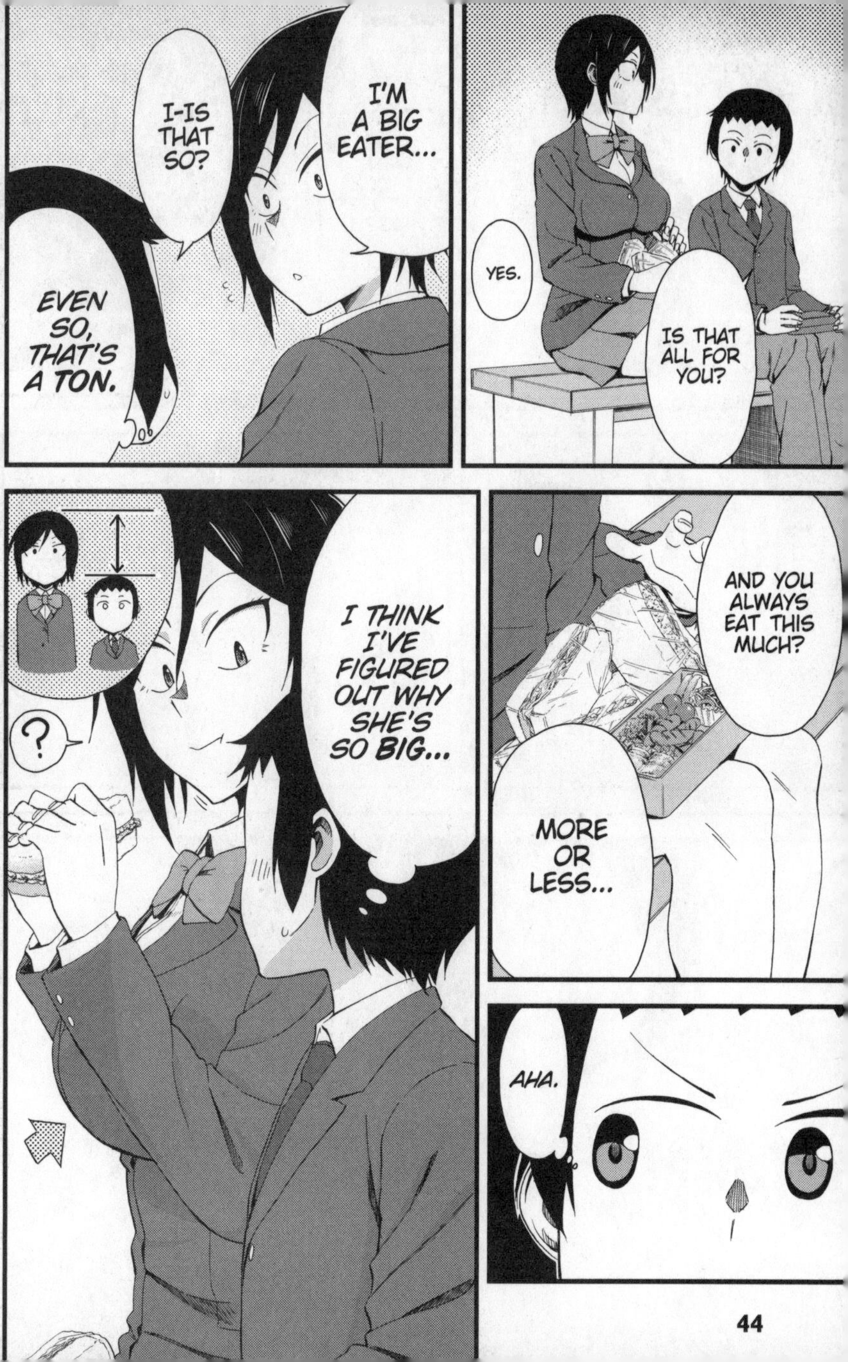
IS THAT ALL FOR YOU?
YES.
I'M A BIG EATER...
I-IS THAT SO?
EVEN SO, THAT'S A TON.
AND YOU ALWAYS EAT THIS MUCH?
MORE OR LESS...
AHA.
I THINK I'VE FIGURED OUT WHY SHE'S SO BIG...
?

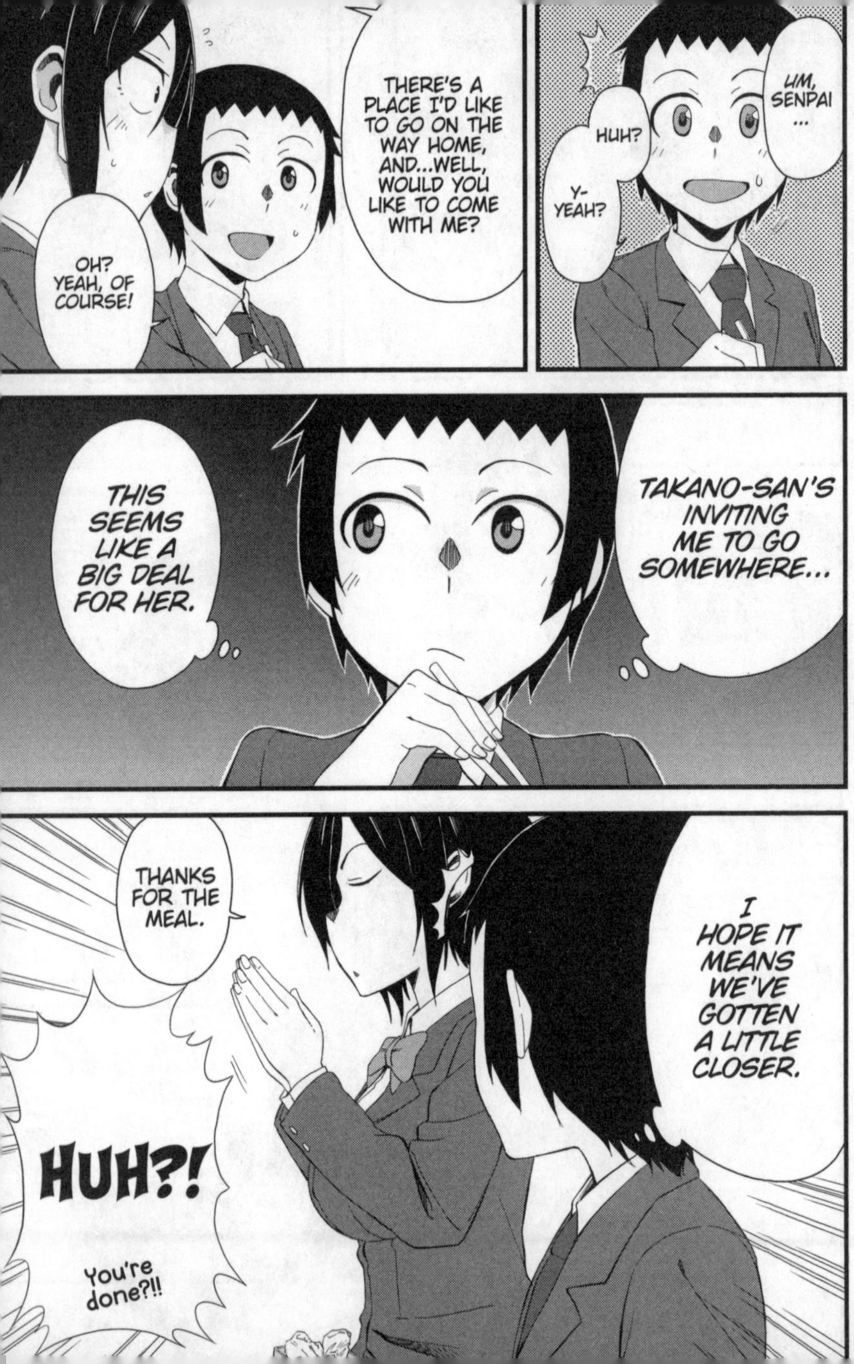
UM, SENPAI ...
HUH?
Y-YEAH?
THERE'S A PLACE I'D LIKE TO GO ON THE WAY HOME, AND...WELL, WOULD YOU LIKE TO COME WITH ME?
OH? YEAH, OF COURSE!
TAKANO-SAN'S INVITING ME TO GO SOMEWHERE...
THIS SEEMS LIKE A BIG DEAL FOR HER.
I HOPE IT MEANS WE'VE GOTTEN A LITTLE CLOSER.
THANKS FOR THE MEAL.
HUH?!
You're done?!!

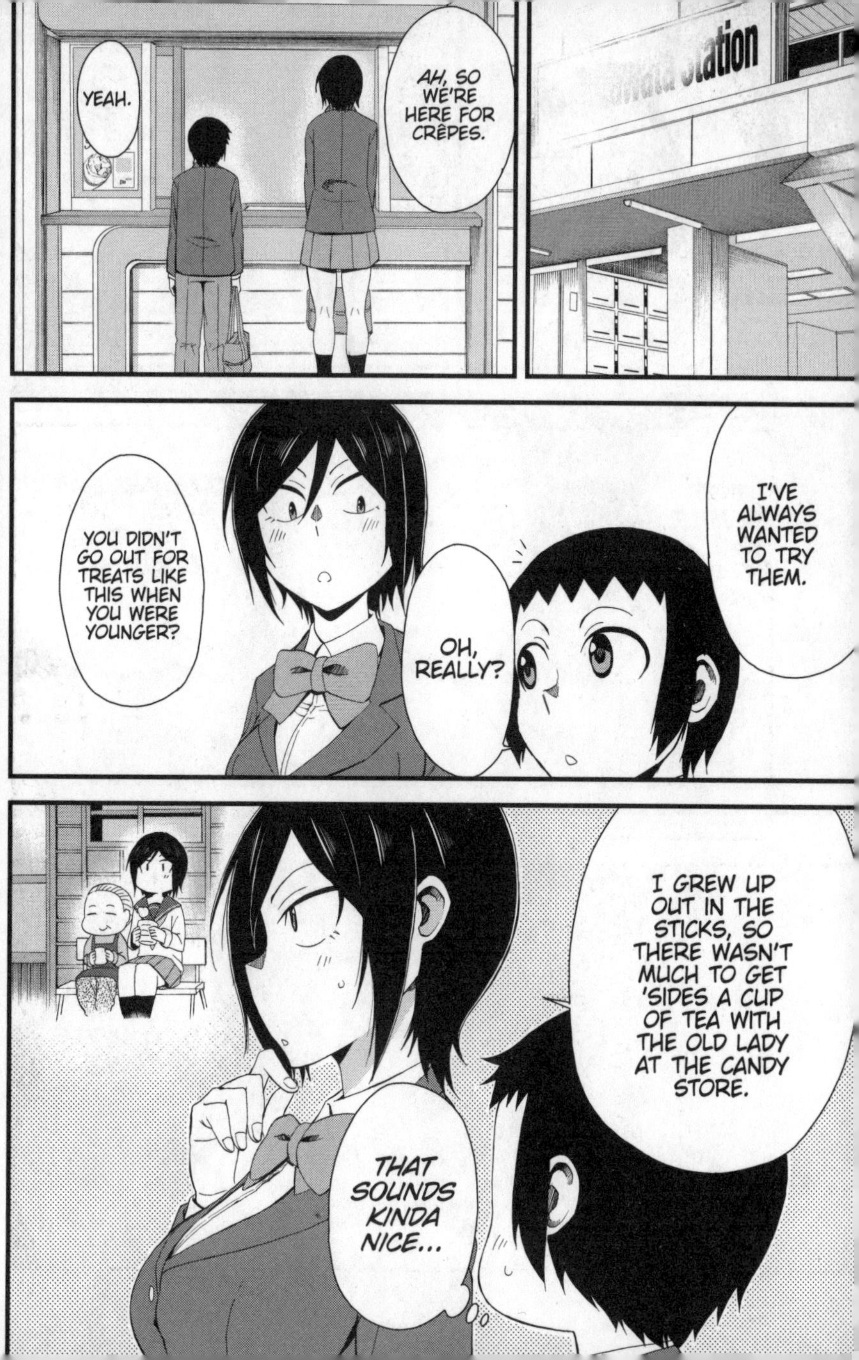
AH, SO WE'RE HERE FOR CRÊPES.
YEAH.
I'VE ALWAYS WANTED TO TRY THEM.
OH, REALLY?
YOU DIDN'T GO OUT FOR TREATS LIKE THIS WHEN YOU WERE YOUNGER?
I GREW UP OUT IN THE STICKS, SO THERE WASN'T MUCH TO GET 'SIDES A CUP OF TEA WITH THE OLD LADY AT THE CANDY STORE.
THAT SOUNDS KINDA NICE...

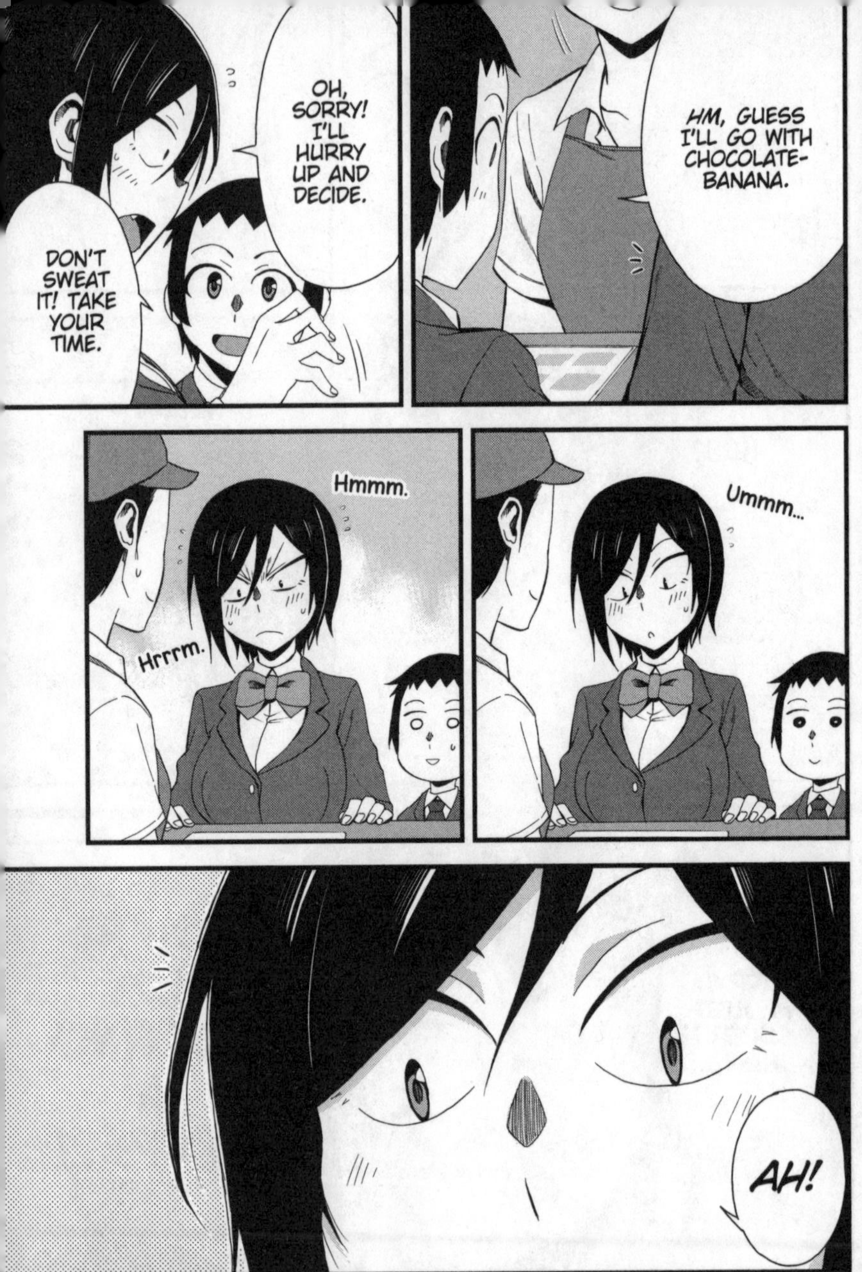
HM, GUESS I'LL GO WITH CHOCOLATE-BANANA.
OH, SORRY! I'LL HURRY UP AND DECIDE.
DON'T SWEAT IT! TAKE YOUR TIME.
Ummm...
Hmmm.
Hrrrm.
AH!

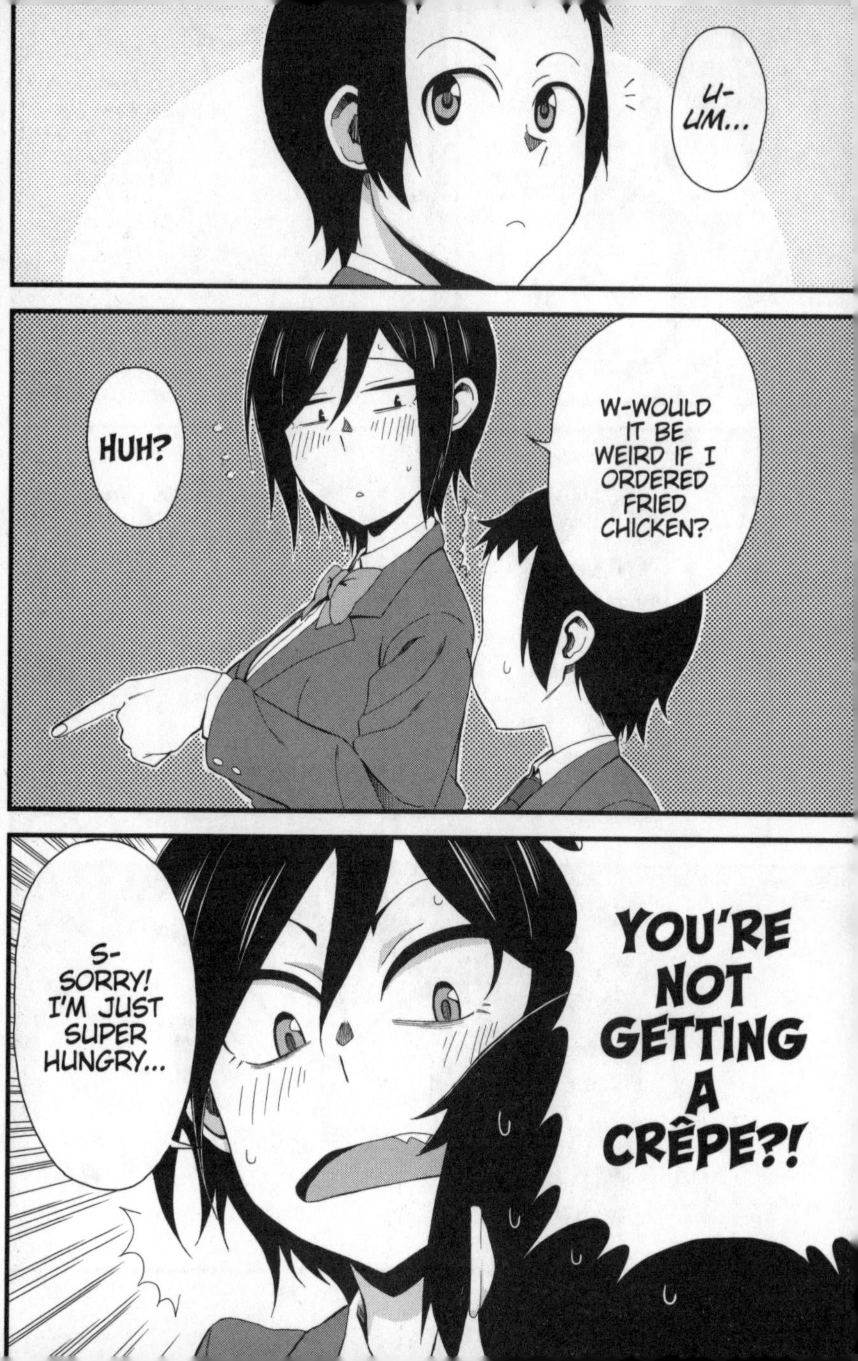
U-UM...
W-WOULD IT BE WEIRD IF I ORDERED FRIED CHICKEN?
HUH?
YOU'RE NOT GETTING A CRÊPE?!
S-SORRY! I'M JUST SUPER HUNGRY...

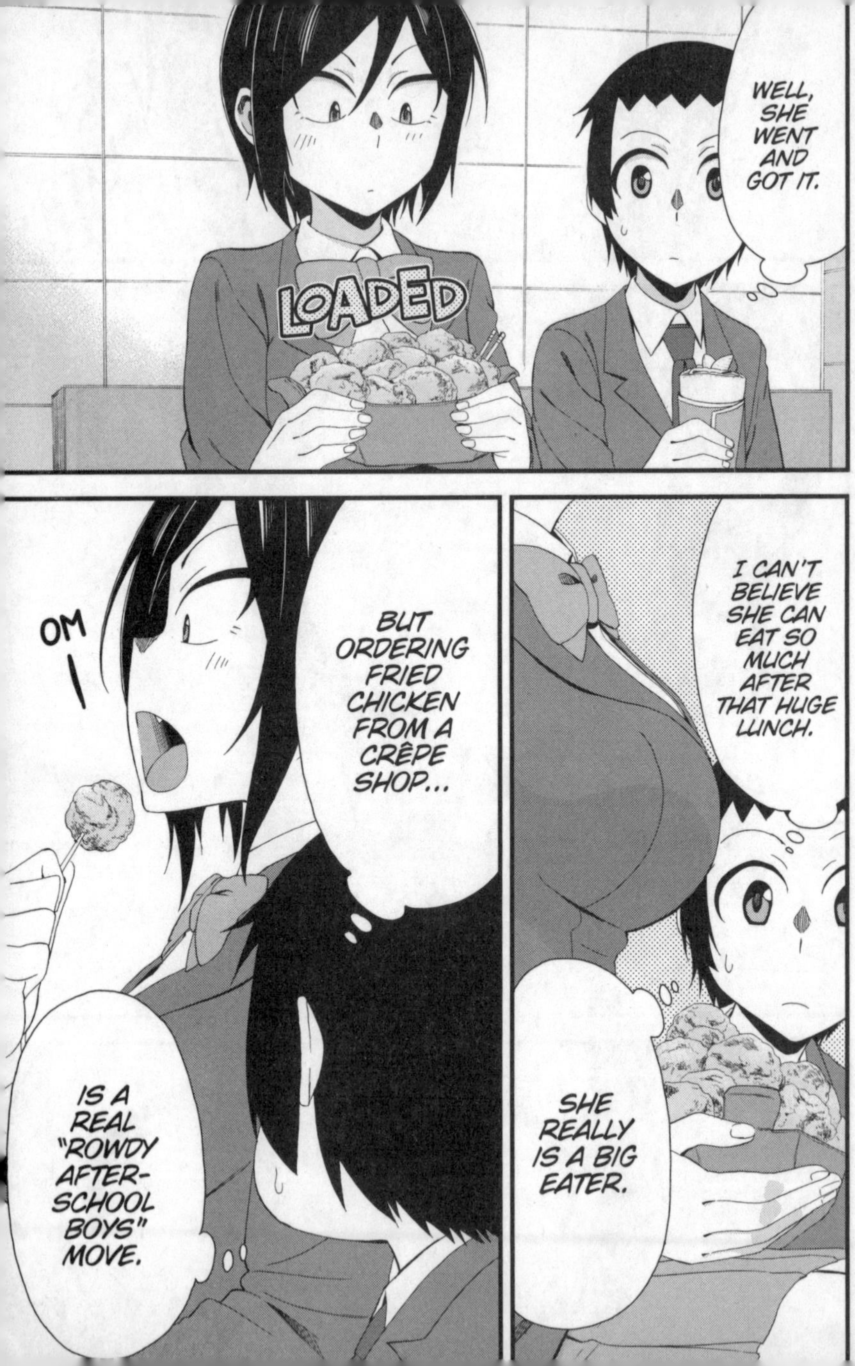
WELL, SHE WENT AND GOT IT.
LOADED
I CAN'T BELIEVE SHE CAN EAT SO MUCH AFTER THAT HUGE LUNCH.
SHE REALLY IS A BIG EATER.
BUT ORDERING FRIED CHICKEN FROM A CRÊPE SHOP...
OM
IS A REAL "ROWDY AFTER-SCHOOL BOYS" MOVE.

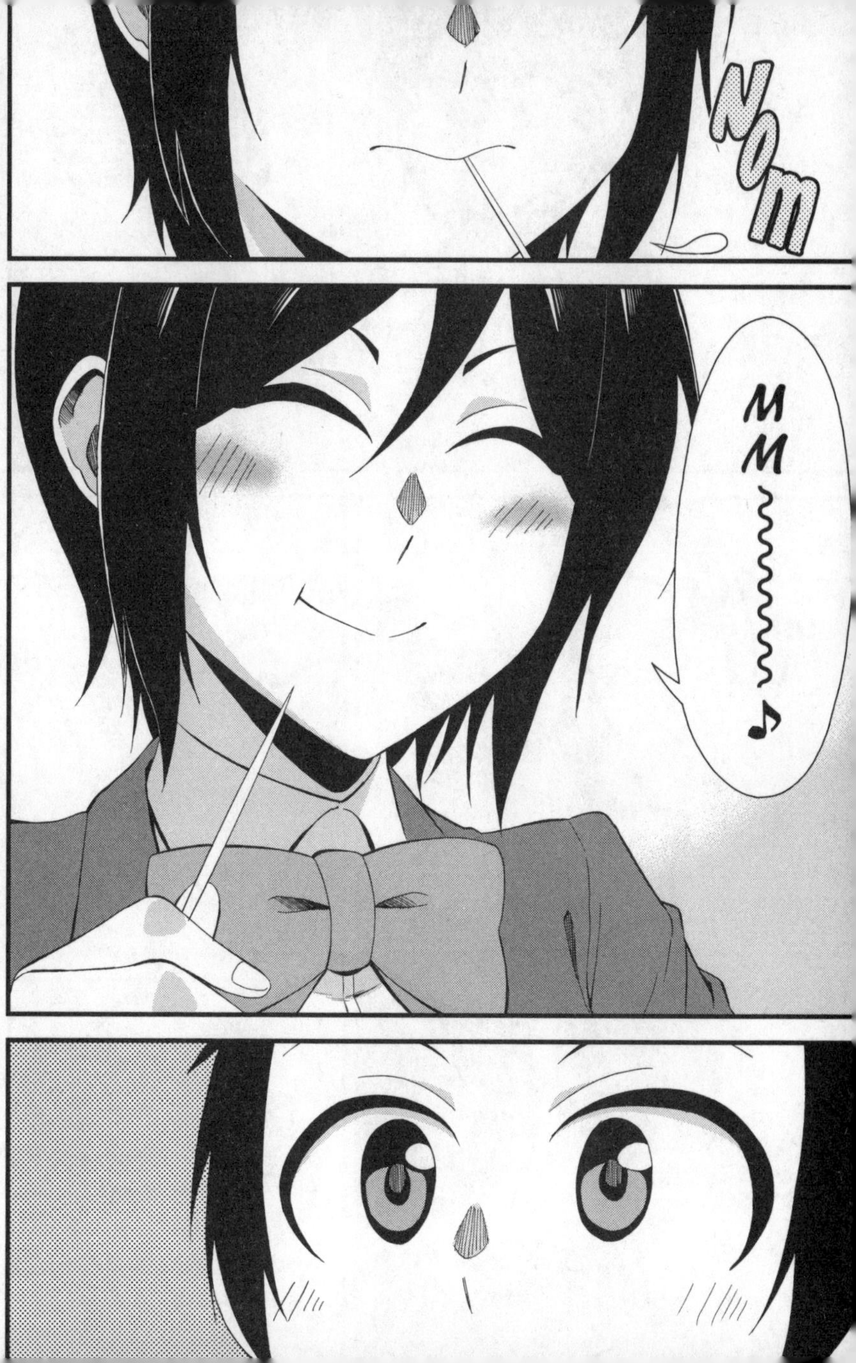
NOM
MM~~~♪

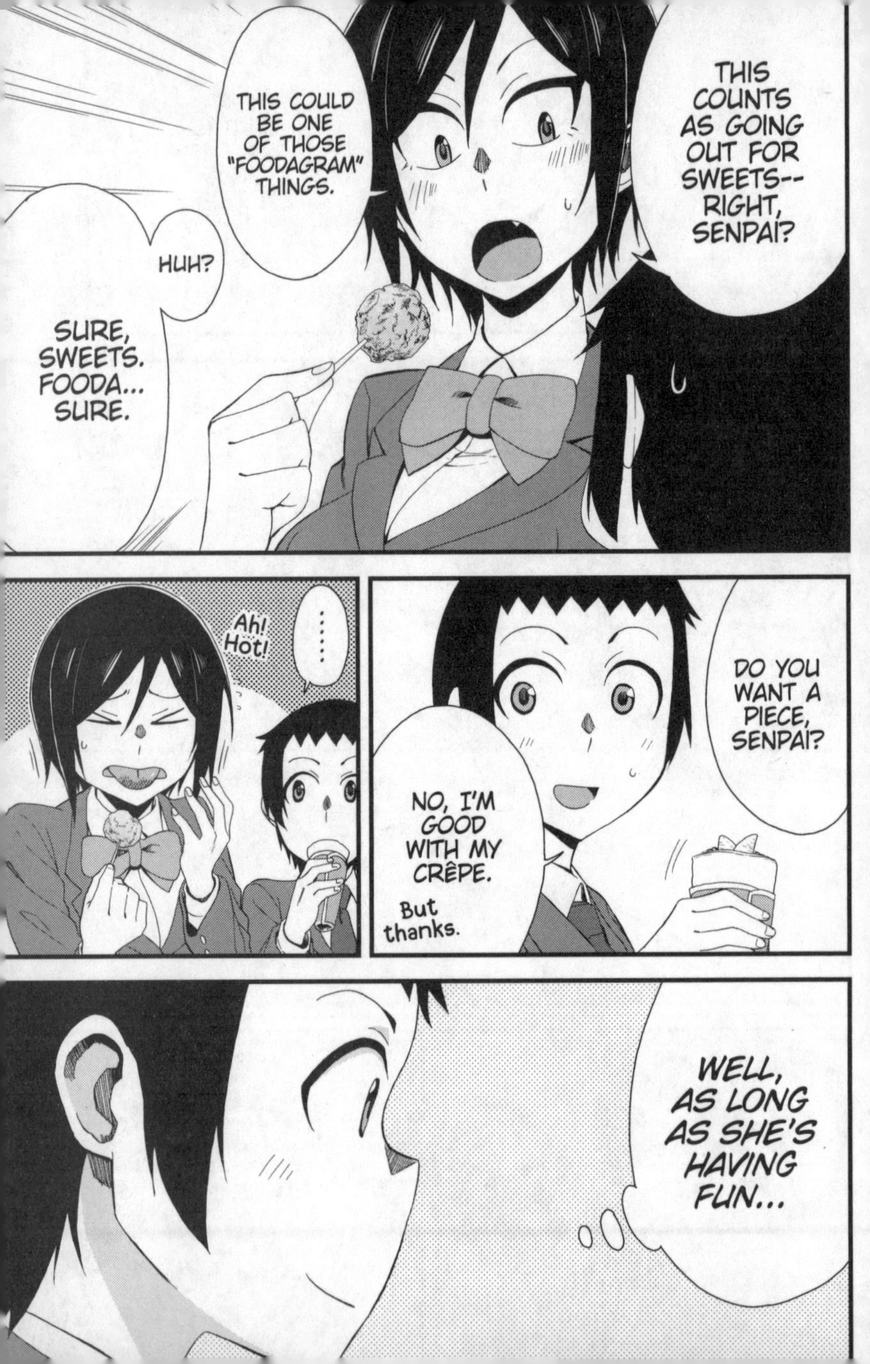
THIS COUNTS AS GOING OUT FOR SWEETS-- RIGHT, SENPAI?
THIS COULD BE ONE OF THOSE "FOODAGRAM" THINGS.
HUH?
SURE, SWEETS. FOODA... SURE.
DO YOU WANT A PIECE, SENPAI?
NO, I'M GOOD WITH MY CRÊPE.
But thanks.
......
Ah! Hot!
WELL, AS LONG AS SHE'S HAVING FUN...

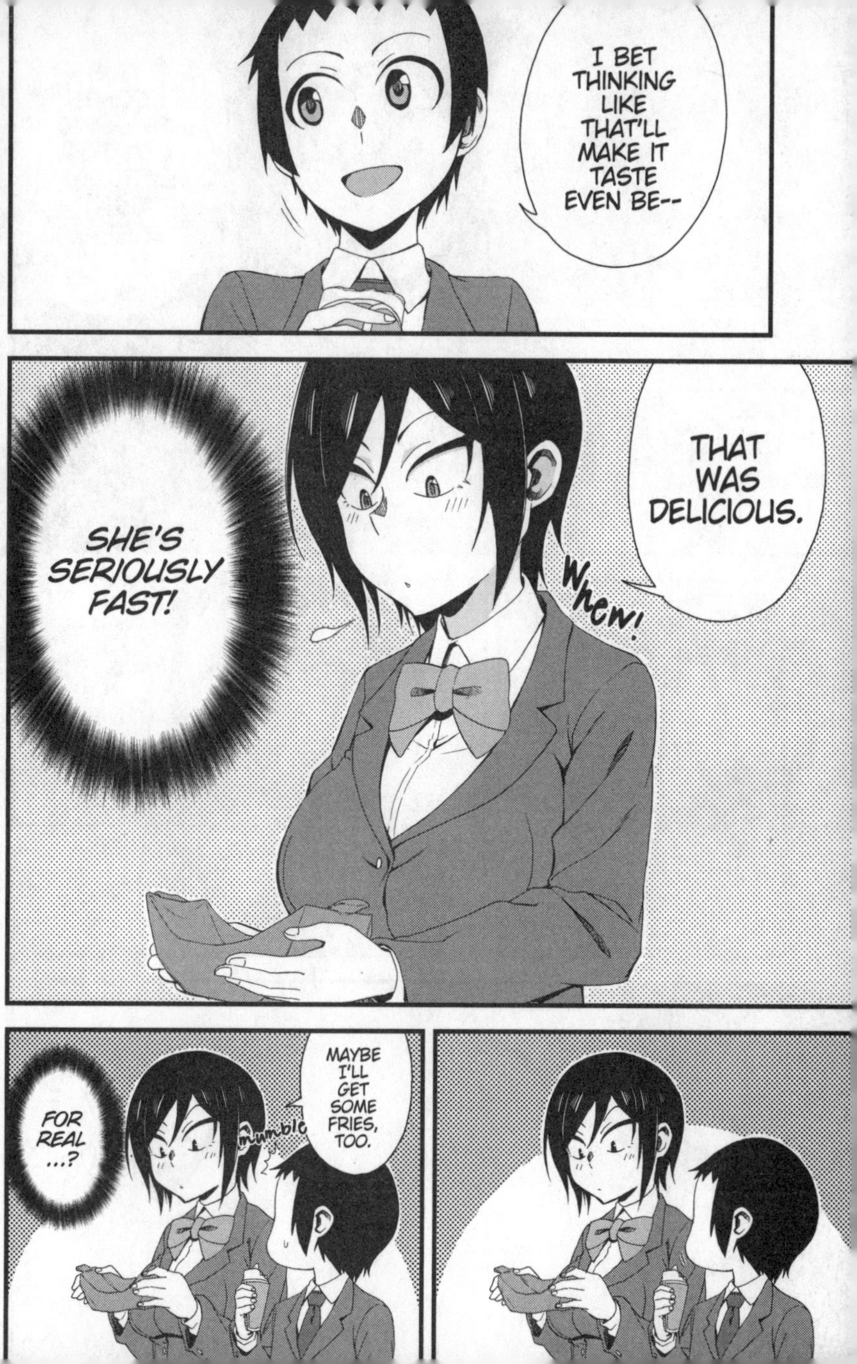

I BET THINKING LIKE THAT'LL MAKE IT TASTE EVEN BE--
THAT WAS DELICIOUS.
Whew!
SHE'S SERIOUSLY FAST!
MAYBE I'LL GET SOME FRIES, TOO.
mumble
FOR REAL ...?

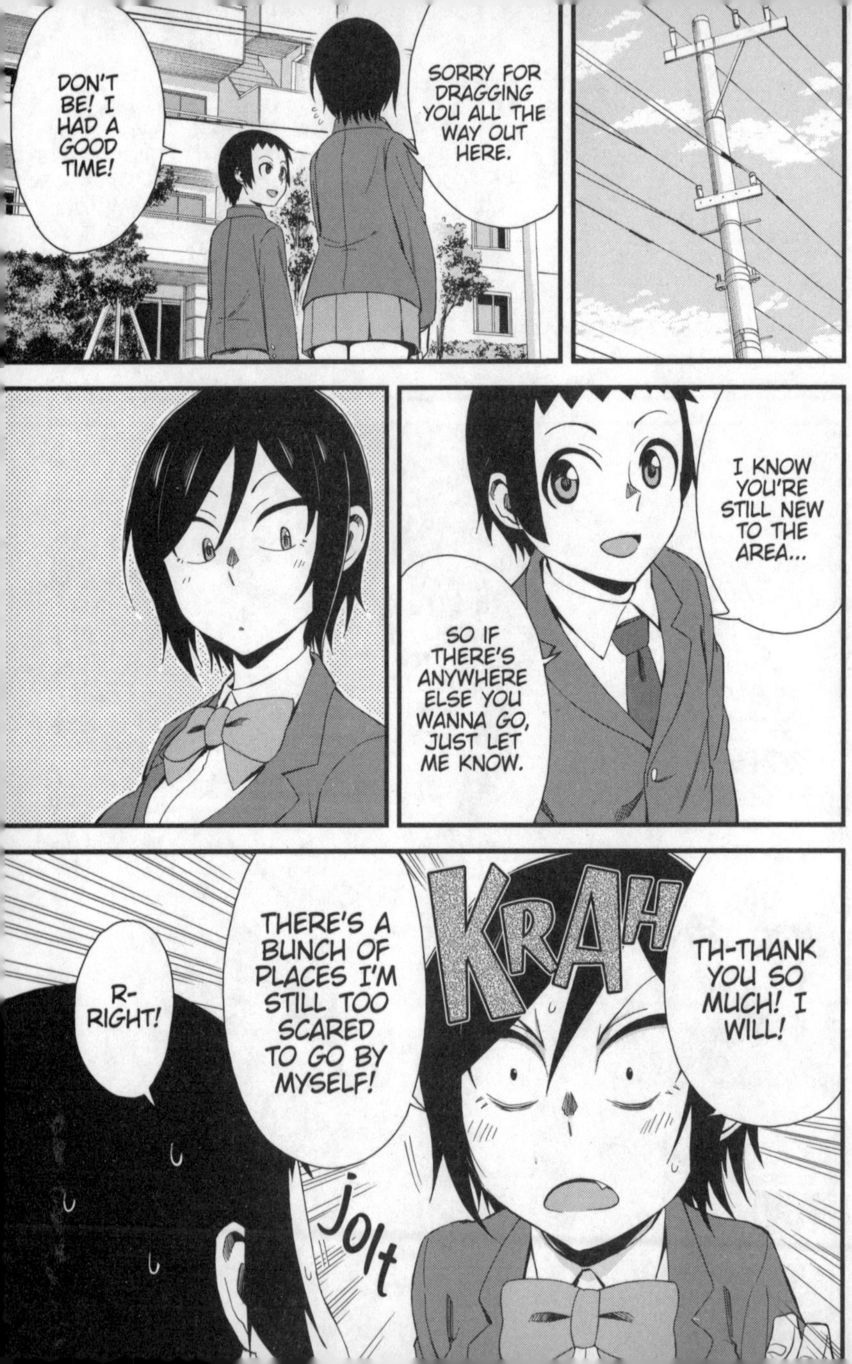
SORRY FOR DRAGGING YOU ALL THE WAY OUT HERE.
DON'T BE! I HAD A GOOD TIME!
I KNOW YOU'RE STILL NEW TO THE AREA...
SO IF THERE'S ANYWHERE ELSE YOU WANNA GO, JUST LET ME KNOW.
TH-THANK YOU SO MUCH! I WILL!
KRAH
THERE'S A BUNCH OF PLACES I'M STILL TOO SCARED TO GO BY MYSELF!
R-RIGHT!
jolt

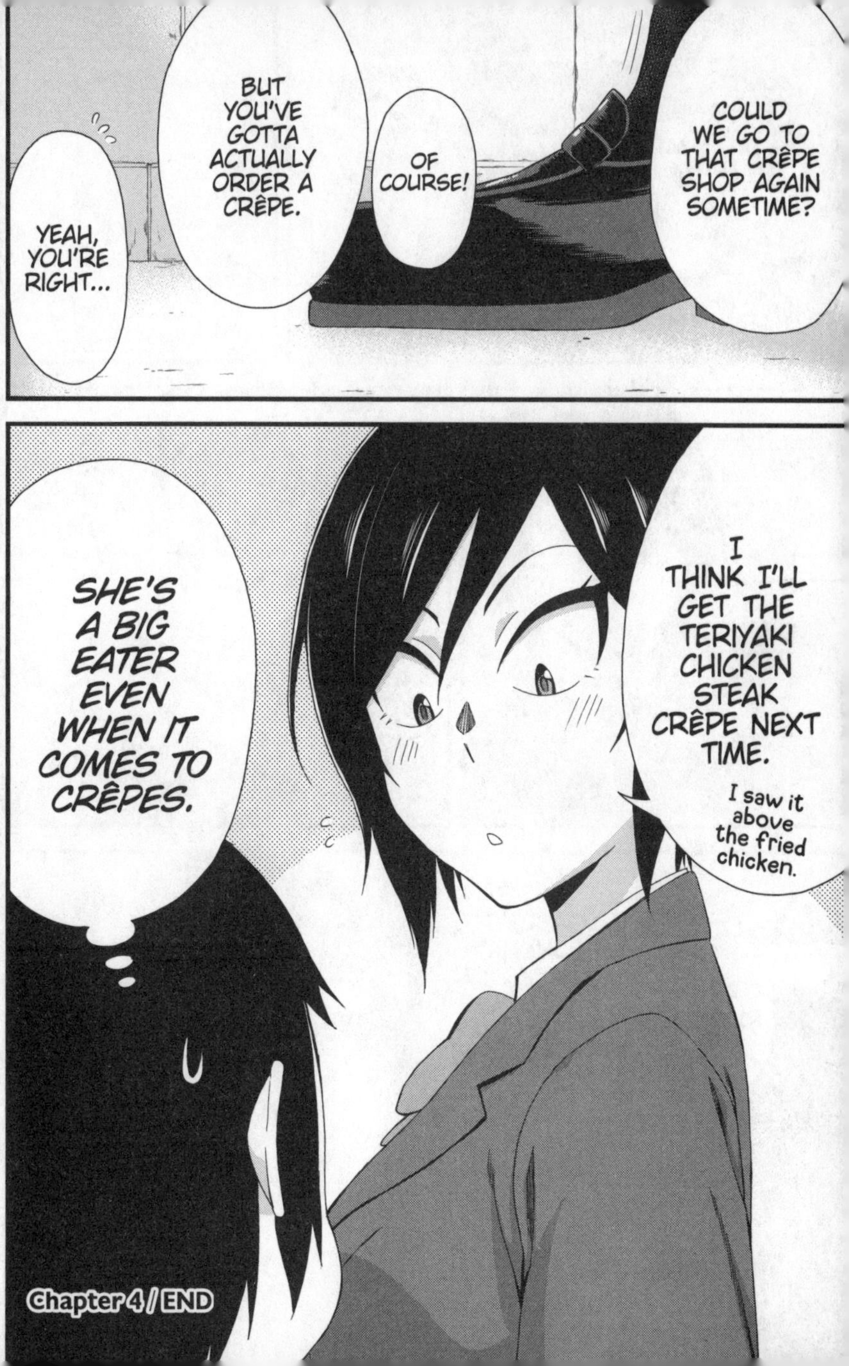
COULD WE GO TO THAT CRÊPE SHOP AGAIN SOMETIME?
OF COURSE!
BUT YOU'VE GOTTA ACTUALLY ORDER A CRÊPE.
YEAH, YOU'RE RIGHT...
I THINK I'LL GET THE TERIYAKI CHICKEN STEAK CRÊPE NEXT TIME.
I saw it above the fried chicken.
SHE'S A BIG EATER EVEN WHEN IT COMES TO CRÊPES.
Chapter 4 / END

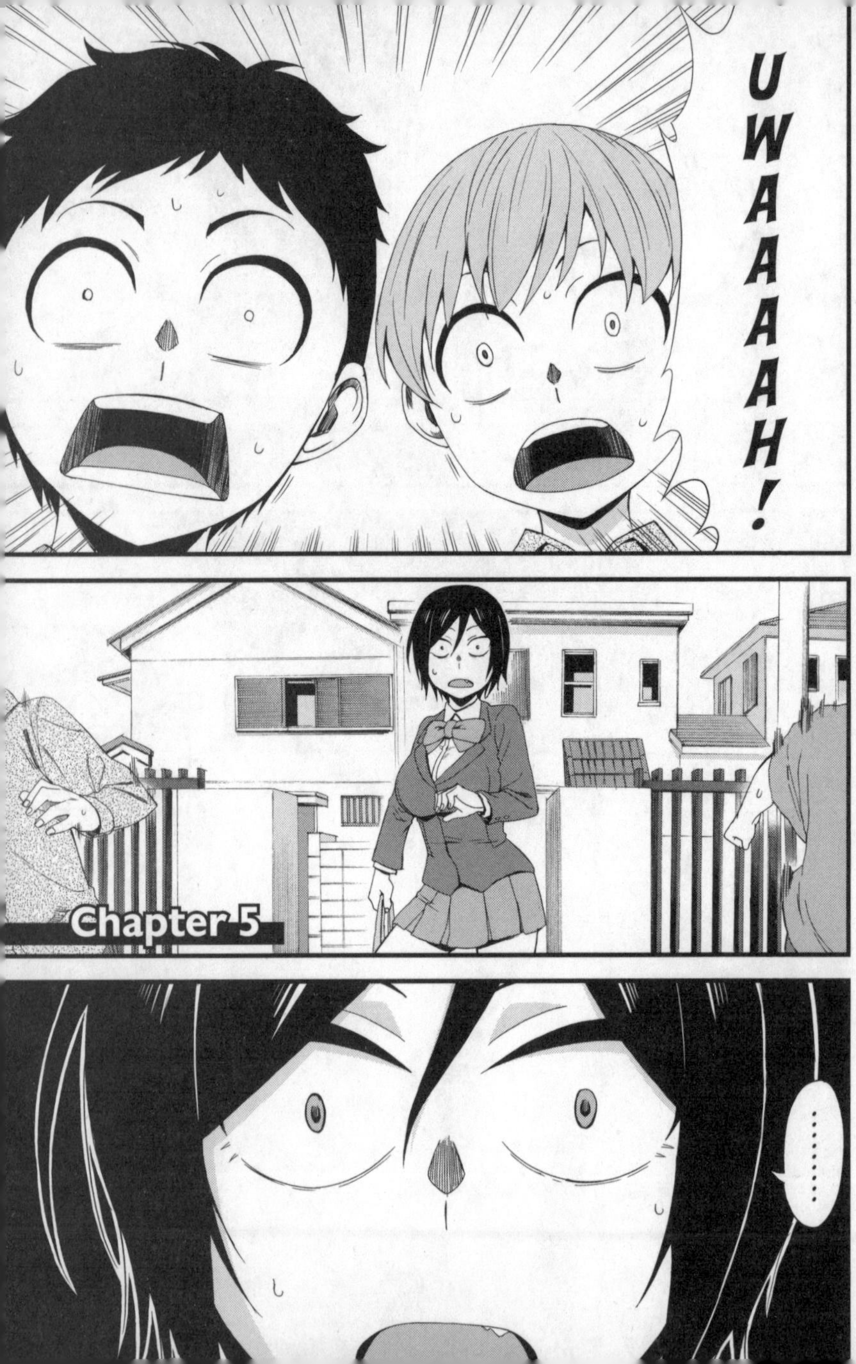
UWAAAAH!
Chapter 5
......

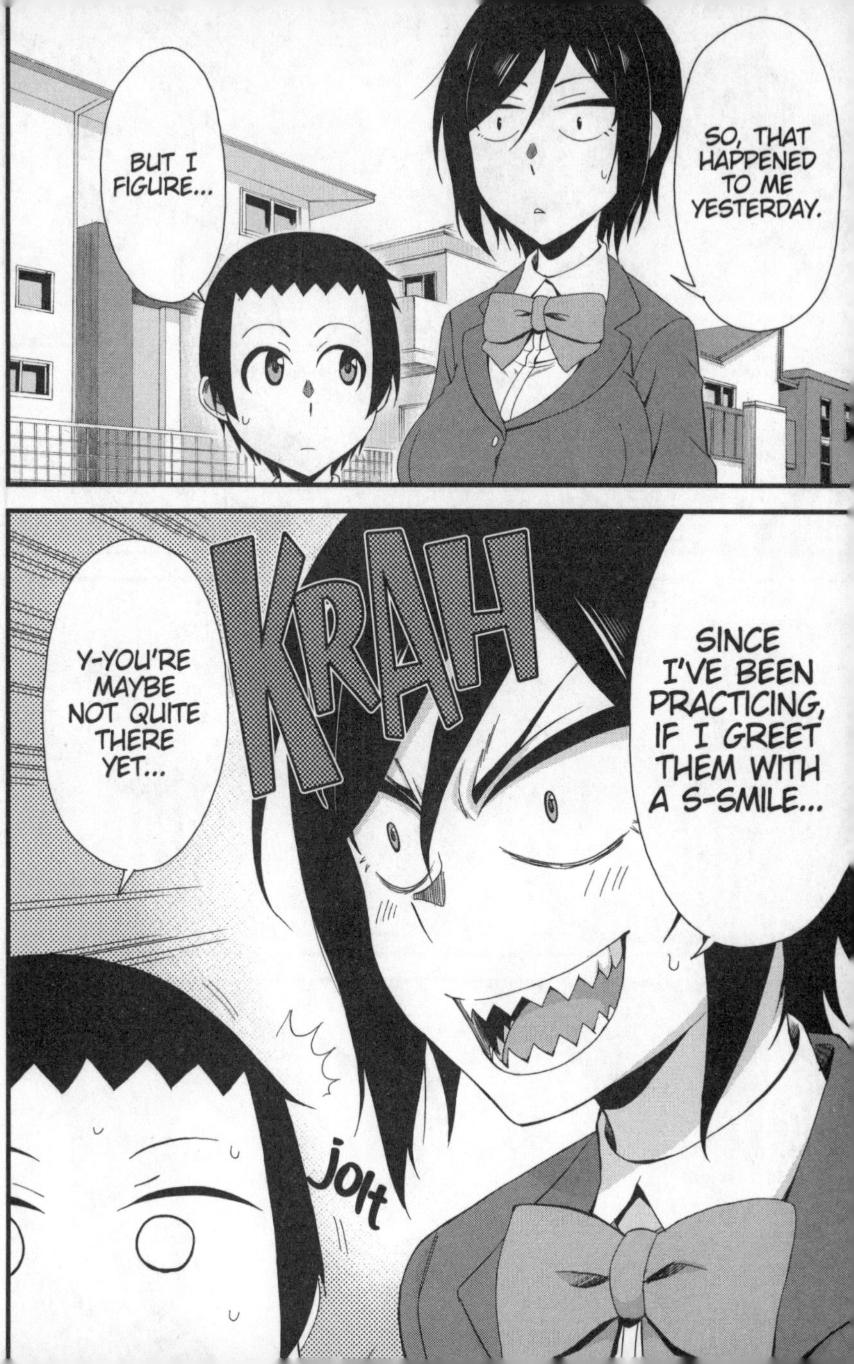
SO, THAT HAPPENED TO ME YESTERDAY.
BUT I FIGURE...
SINCE I'VE BEEN PRACTICING, IF I GREET THEM WITH A S-SMILE...
KRAH
Y-YOU'RE MAYBE NOT QUITE THERE YET...
jolt

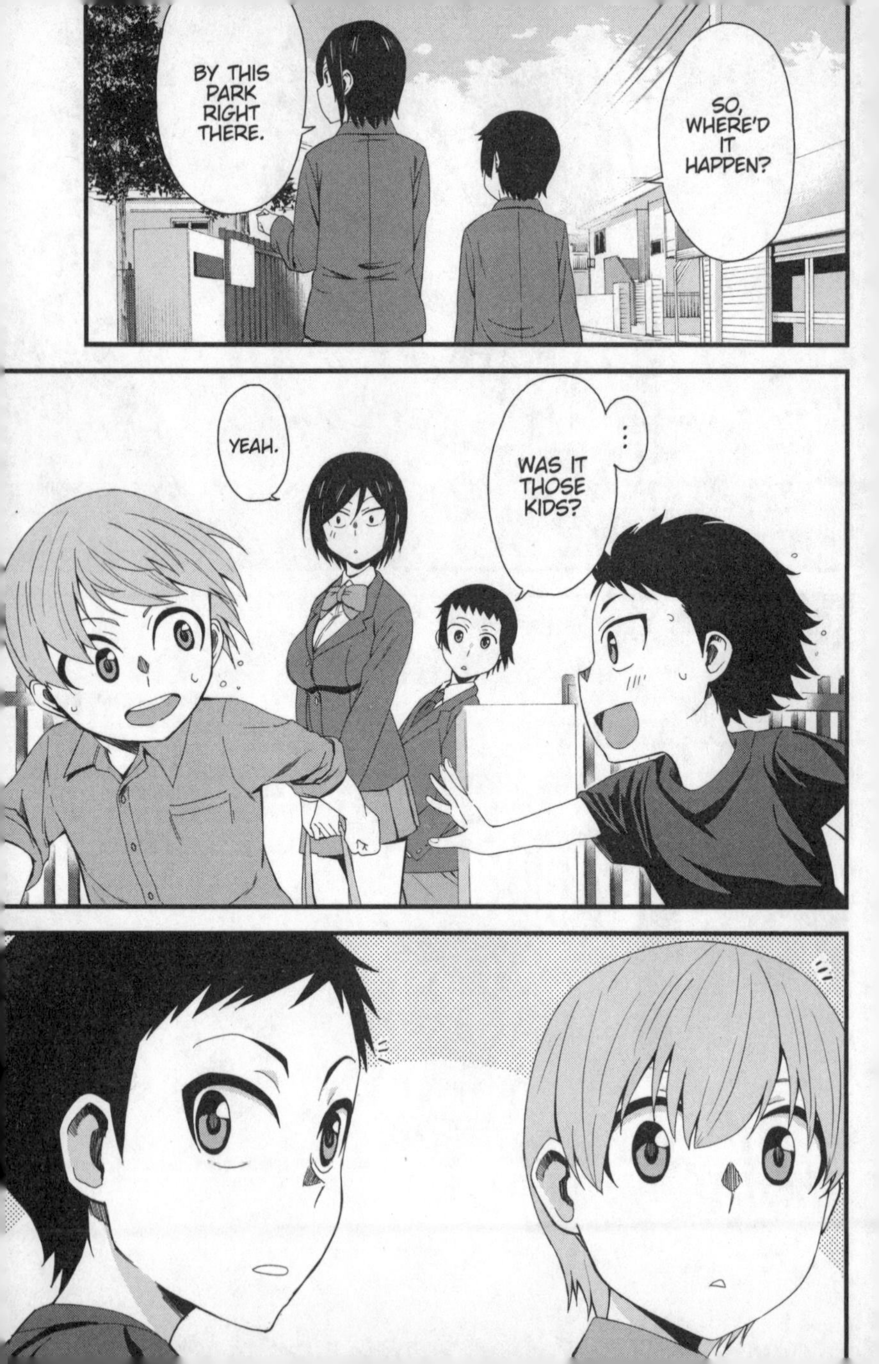

SO, WHERE'D IT HAPPEN?
BY THIS PARK RIGHT THERE.
... WAS IT THOSE KIDS?
YEAH.

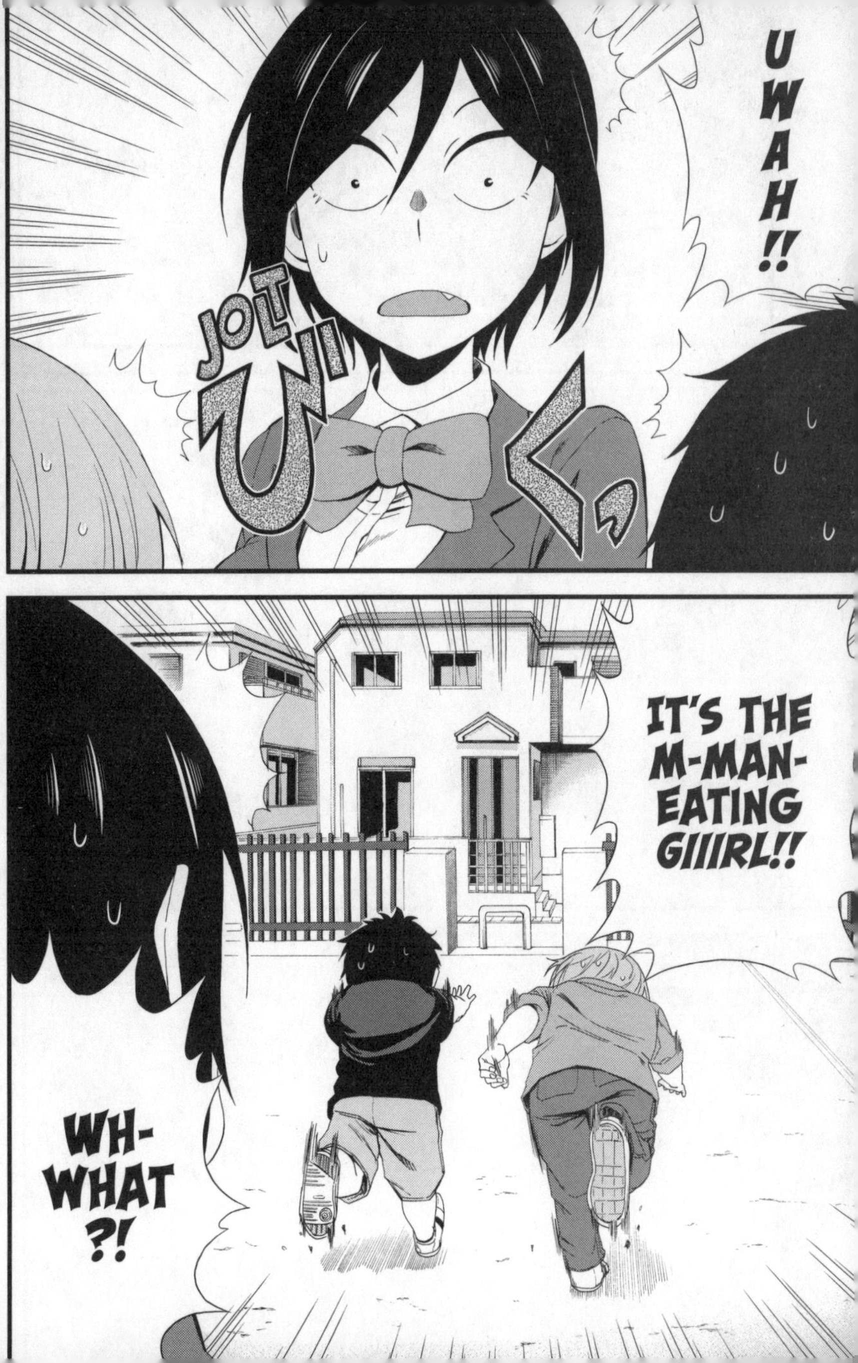
UWAH!!
JOLT
IT'S THE M-MAN-EATING GIIIRL!!
WH-WHAT?!

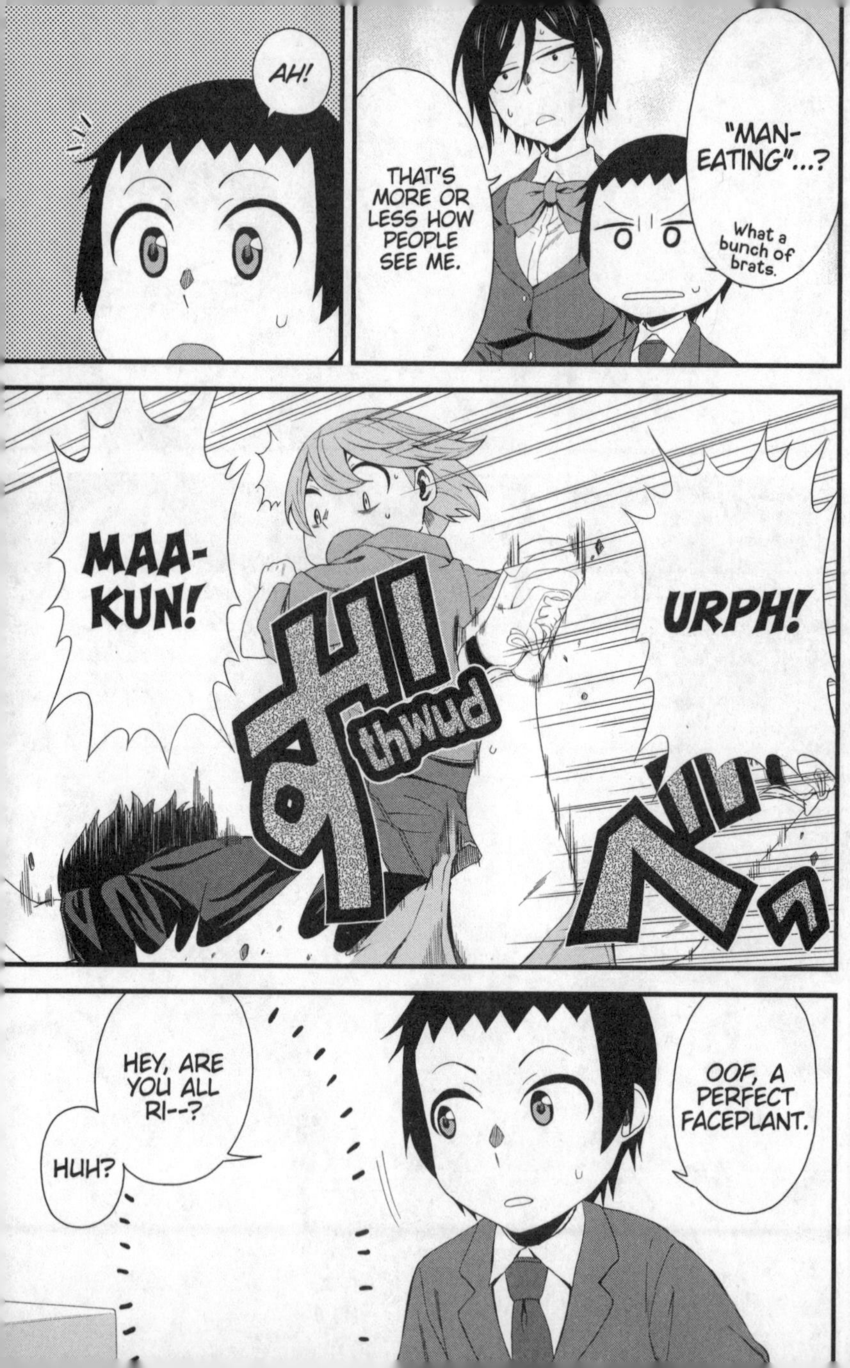
"MAN-EATING"...?
What a bunch of brats.
THAT'S MORE OR LESS HOW PEOPLE SEE ME.
AH!
URPH!
thwud
MAA-KUN!
OOF, A PERFECT FACEPLANT.
HEY, ARE YOU ALL RI--?
HUH?

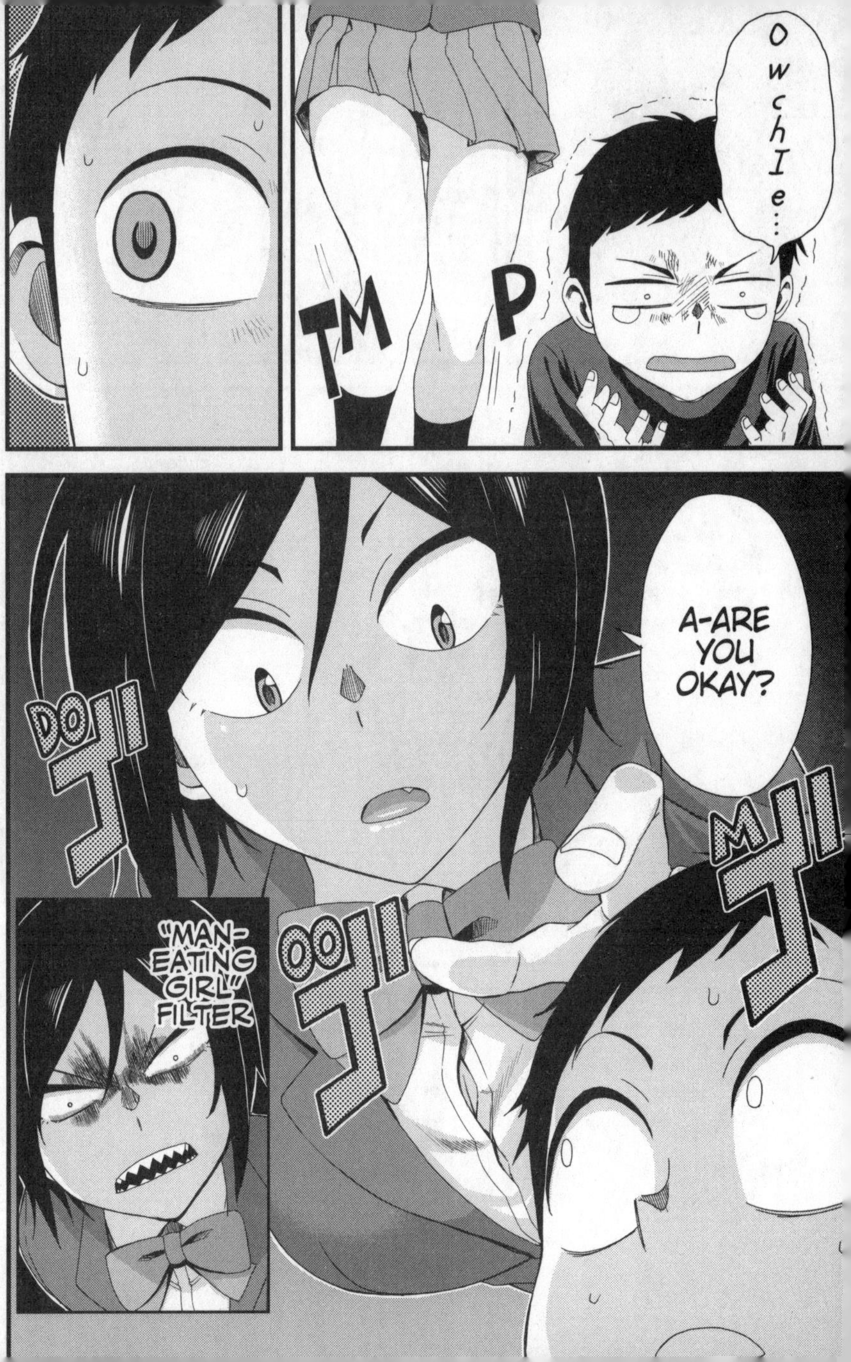
OwchIe...
TMP
A-ARE YOU OKAY?
M
DO
OO
"MAN-EATING GIRL" FILTER

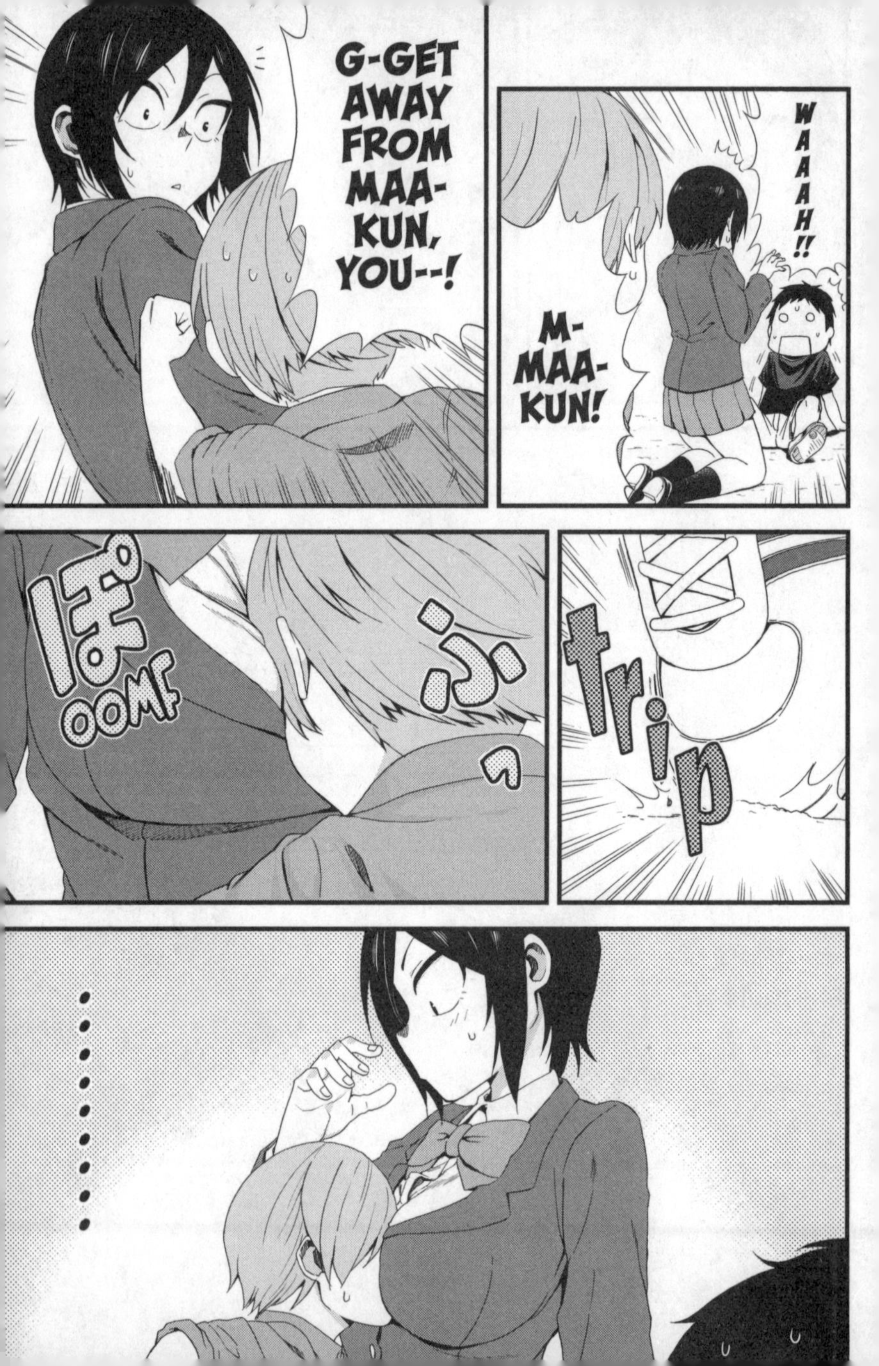
WAAAAH!!
M-MAA-KUN!
G-GET AWAY FROM MAA-KUN, YOU--!
trip
ふっ
ぽOOMF

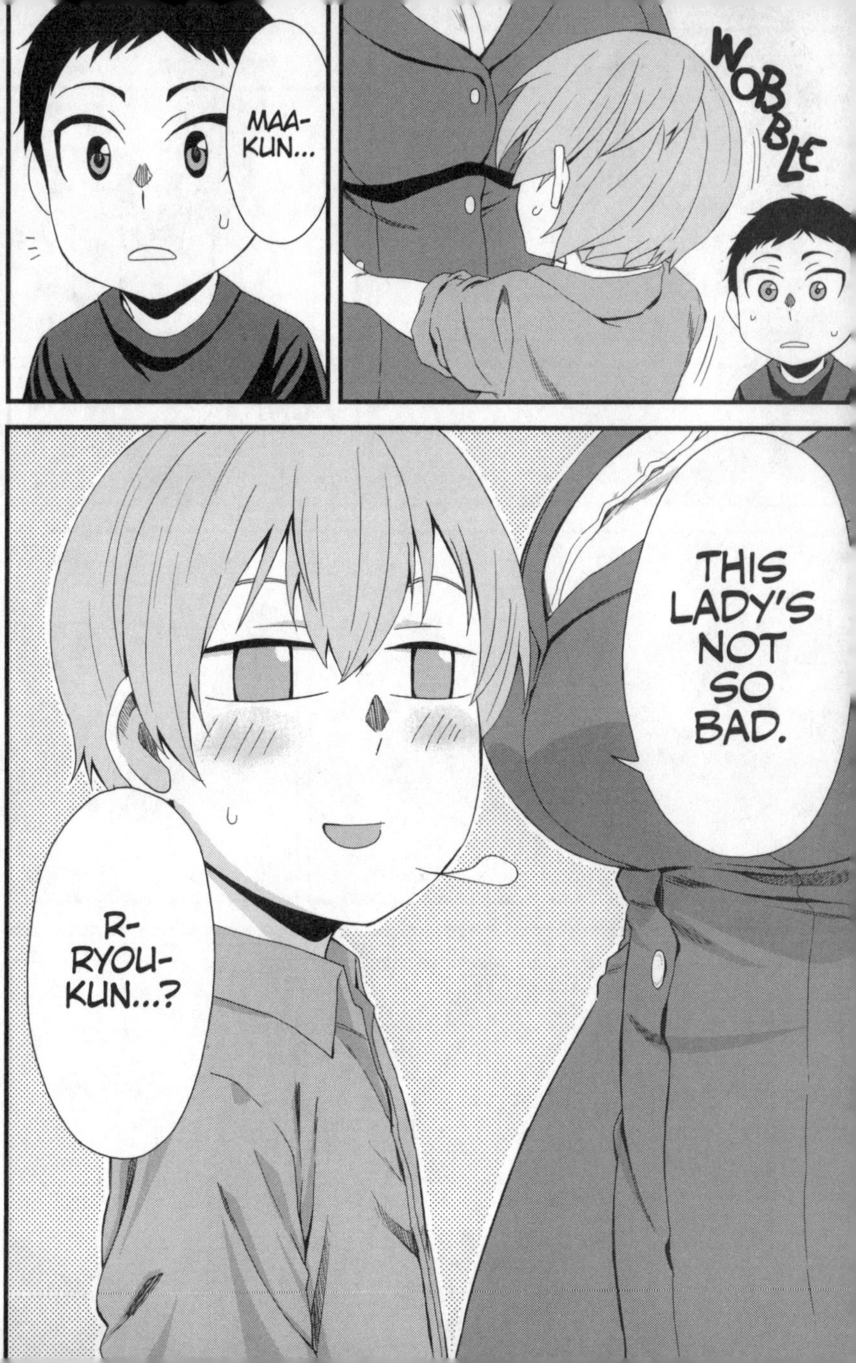
WOBBLE
MAA-KUN...
THIS LADY'S NOT SO BAD.
R-RYOU-KUN...?

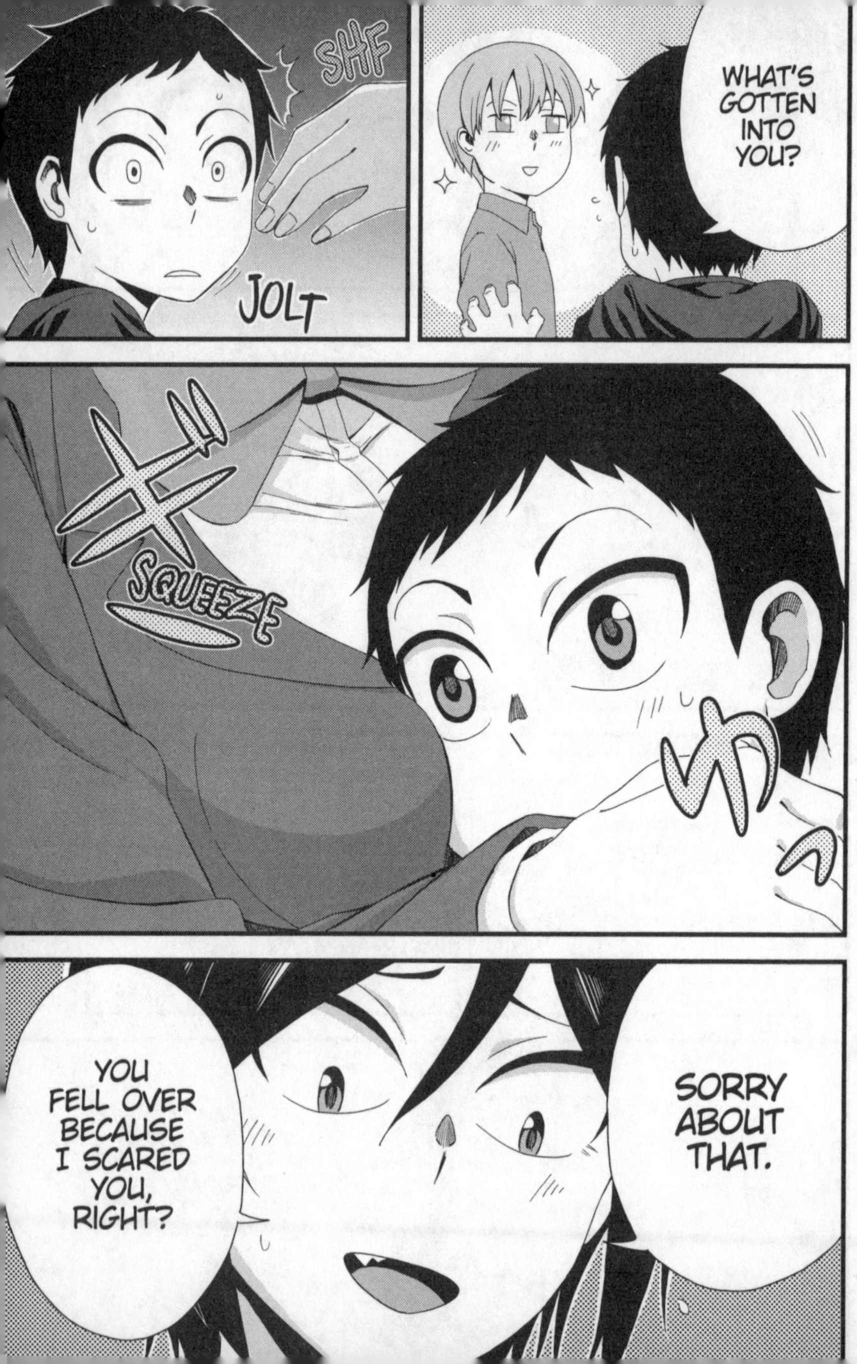
WHAT'S GOTTEN INTO YOU?
SHF
JOLT
SQUEEZE
SORRY ABOUT THAT.
YOU FELL OVER BECAUSE I SCARED YOU, RIGHT?

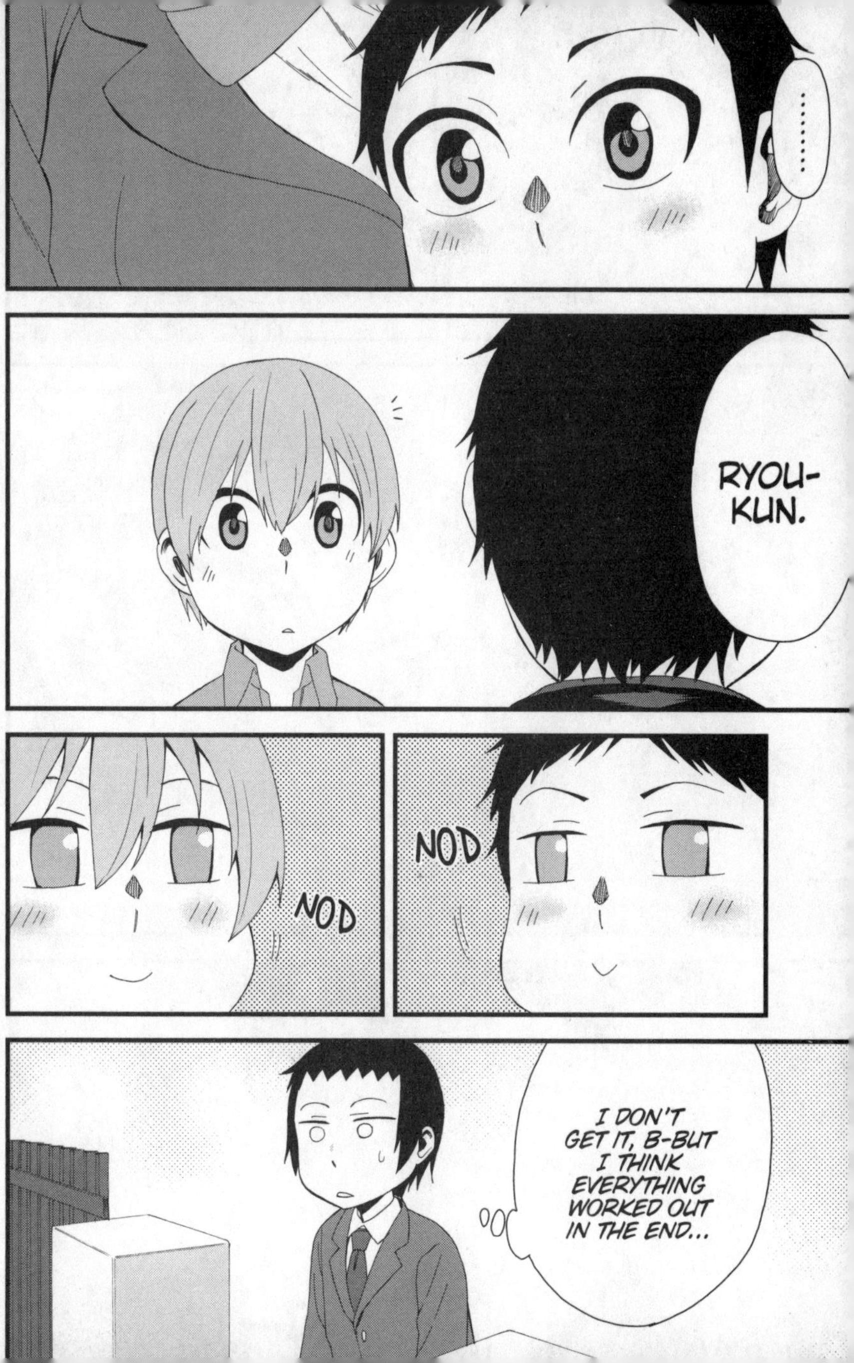
......
RYOU-KUN.
NOD
NOD
I DON'T GET IT, B-BUT I THINK EVERYTHING WORKED OUT IN THE END...

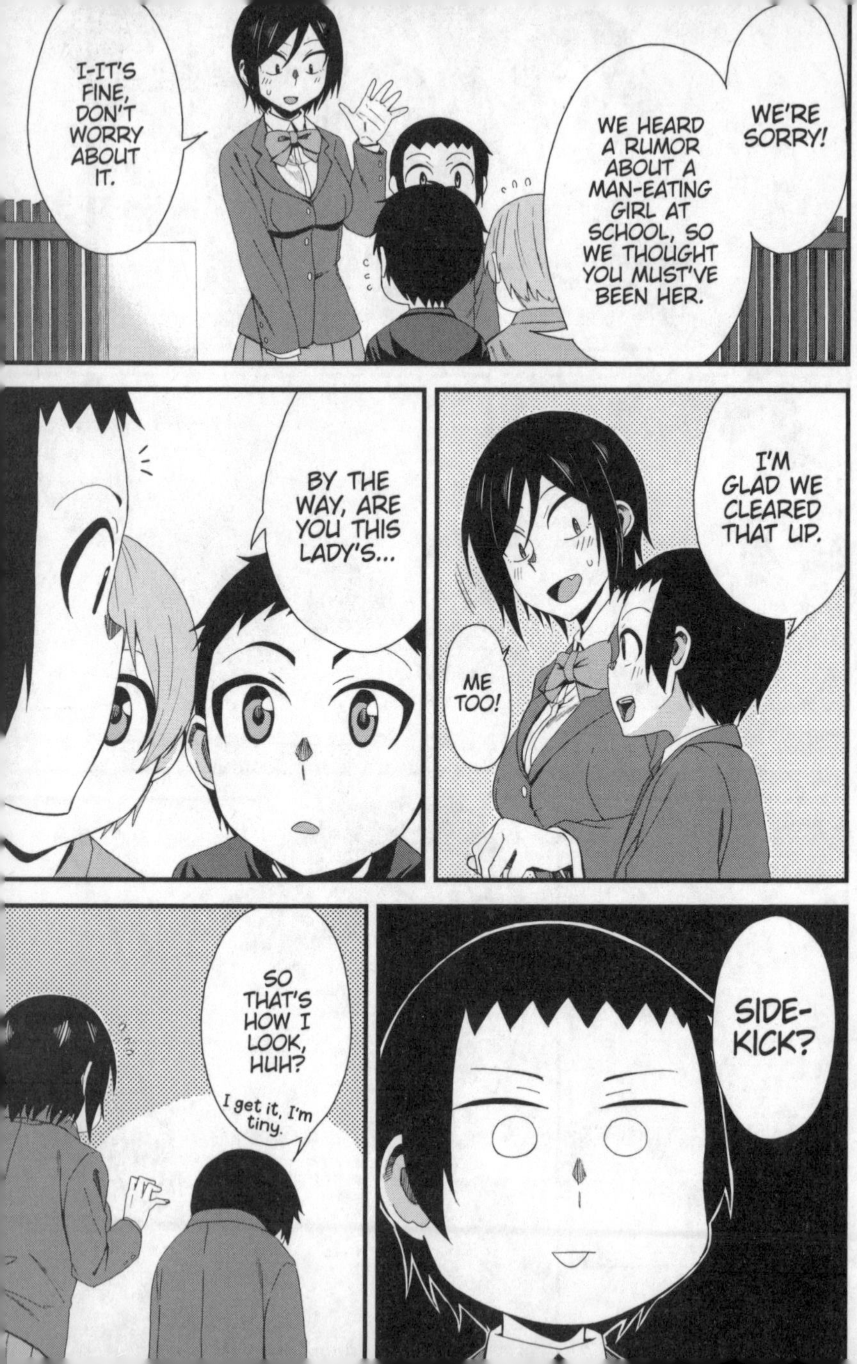
WE'RE SORRY!
WE HEARD A RUMOR ABOUT A MAN-EATING GIRL AT SCHOOL, SO WE THOUGHT YOU MUST'VE BEEN HER.
I-IT'S FINE, DON'T WORRY ABOUT IT.
I'M GLAD WE CLEARED THAT UP.
ME TOO!
BY THE WAY, ARE YOU THIS LADY'S...
SIDE-KICK?
SO THAT'S HOW I LOOK, HUH?
I get it, I'm tiny.

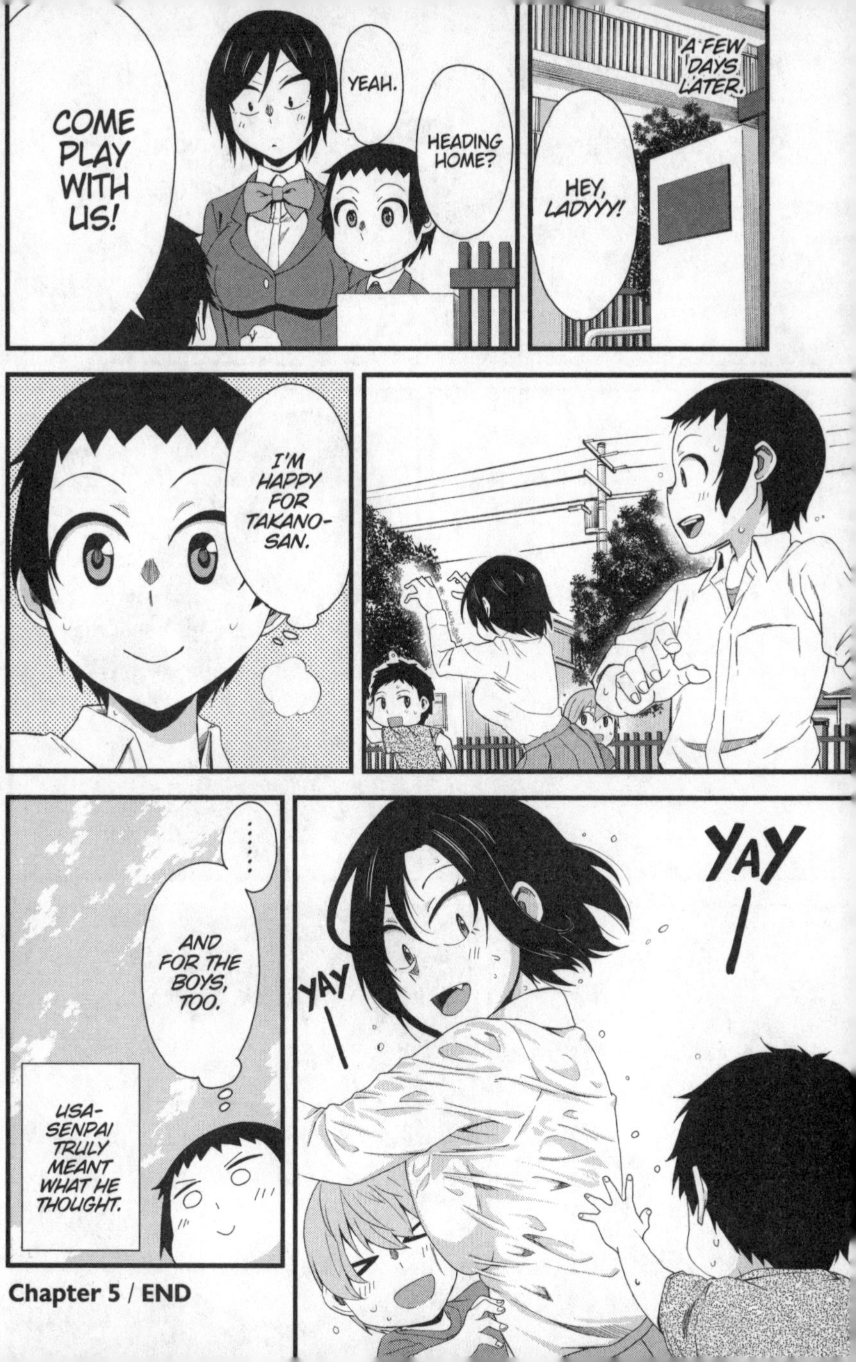
A FEW DAYS LATER.
HEY, LADYYY!
HEADING HOME?
YEAH.
COME PLAY WITH US!
I'M HAPPY FOR TAKANO-SAN.
YAY
YAY
......
AND FOR THE BOYS, TOO.
USA-SENPAI TRULY MEANT WHAT HE THOUGHT.

Chapter 5 / END

Hitomi-chan is Shy With Strangers

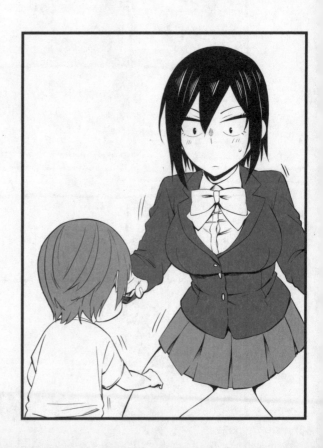

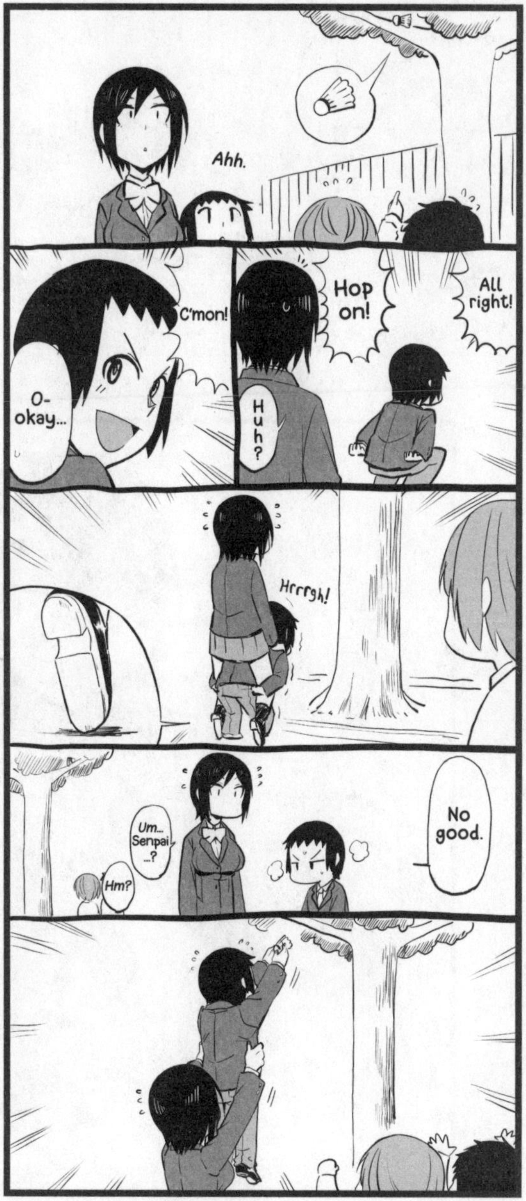
Ahh.
All right!
Hop on!
Huh?
C'mon!
O-okay...
Hrrrgh!
No good.
Um... Senpai ...?
Hm?

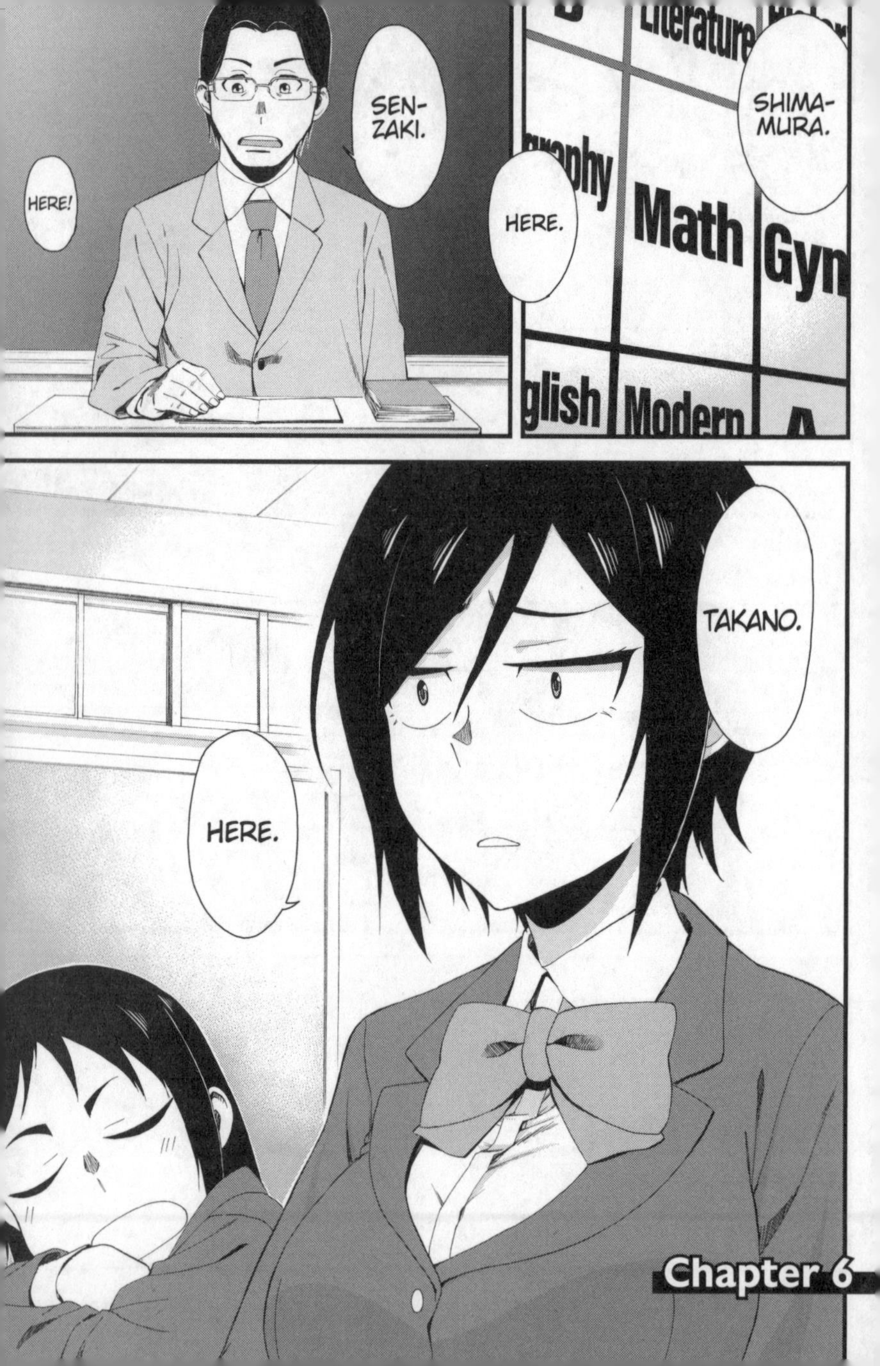
Literature
Math
SHIMA-MURA.
HERE.
SEN-ZAKI.
HERE!
TAKANO.
HERE.
Chapter 6

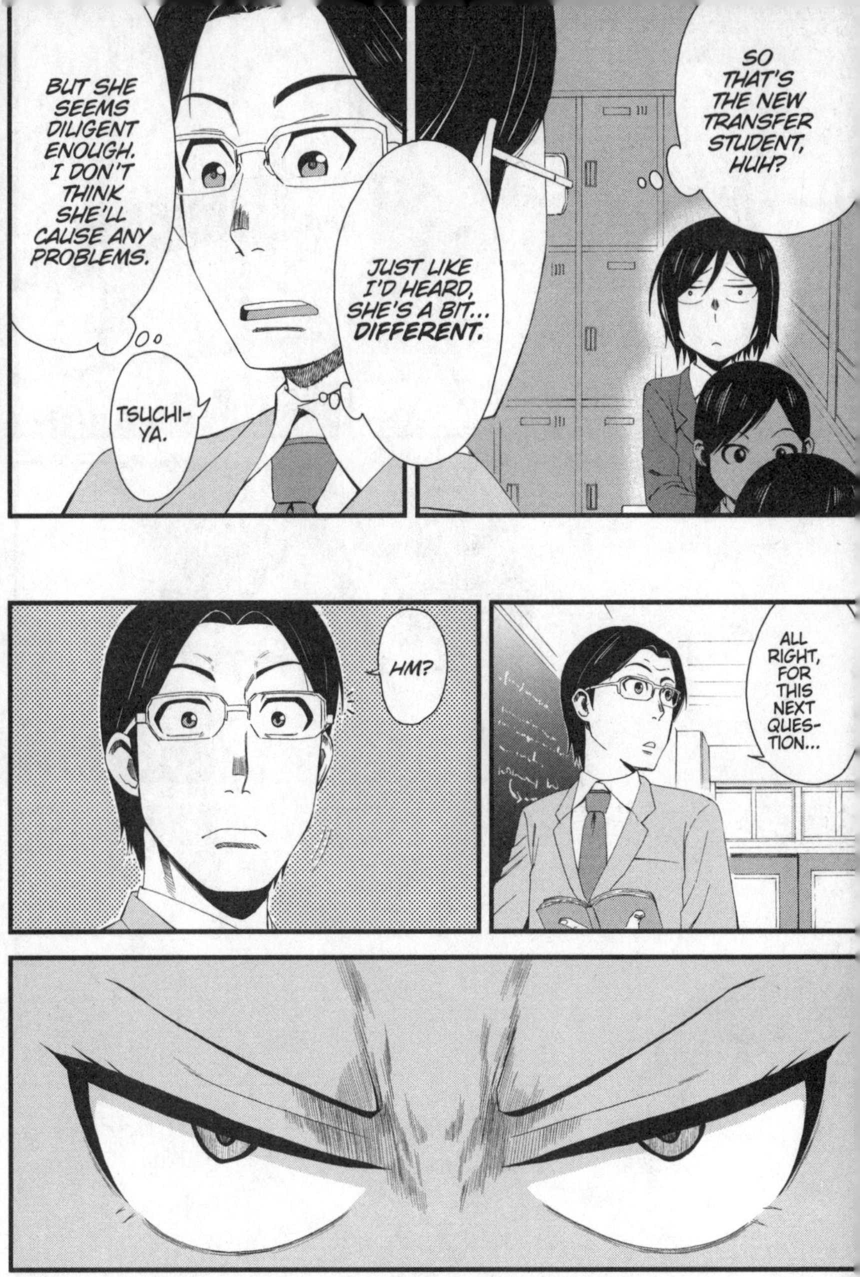
SO THAT'S THE NEW TRANSFER STUDENT, HUH?
JUST LIKE I'D HEARD, SHE'S A BIT... DIFFERENT.
BUT SHE SEEMS DILIGENT ENOUGH. I DON'T THINK SHE'LL CAUSE ANY PROBLEMS.
TSUCHI-YA.
ALL RIGHT, FOR THIS NEXT QUES-TION...
HM?

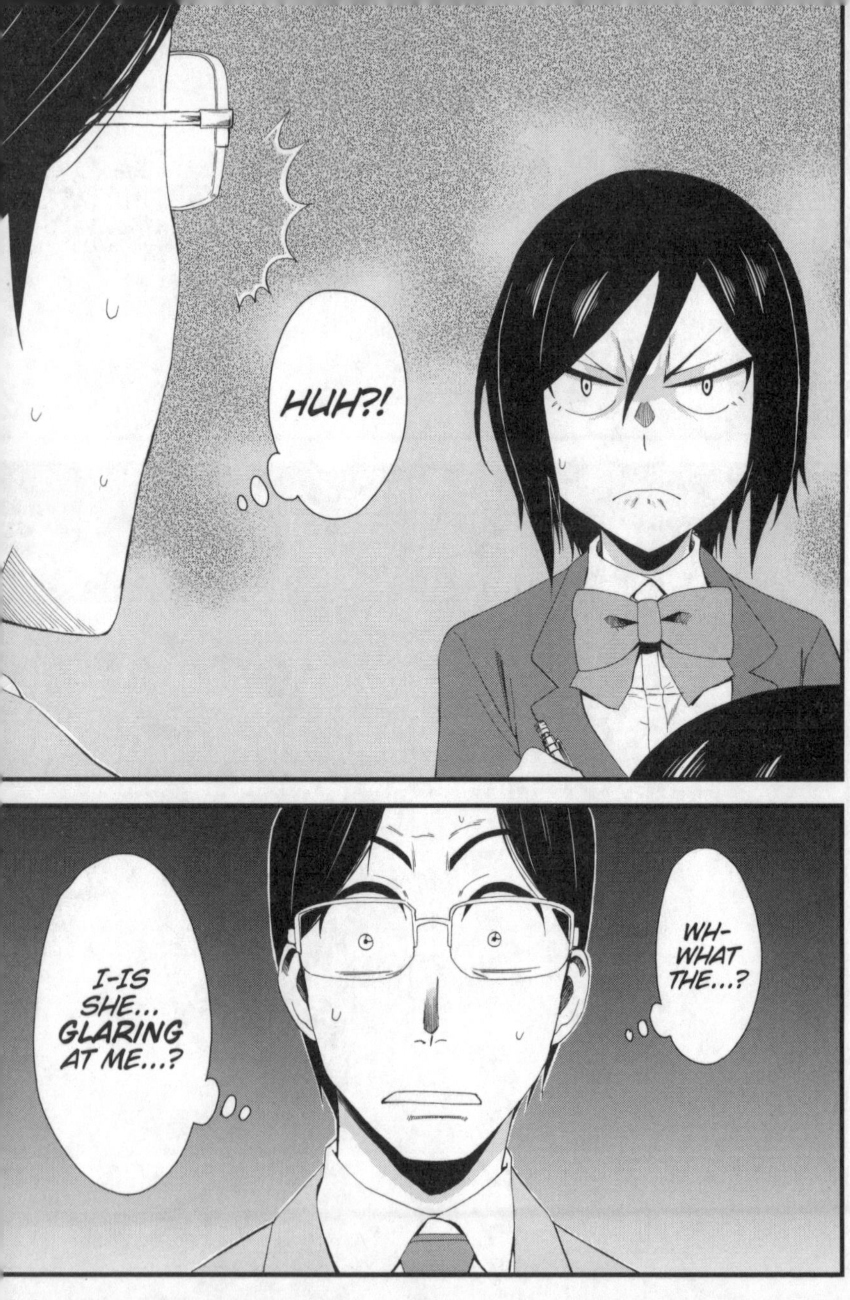
HUH?!
WH-WHAT THE...?
I-IS SHE... GLARING AT ME...?

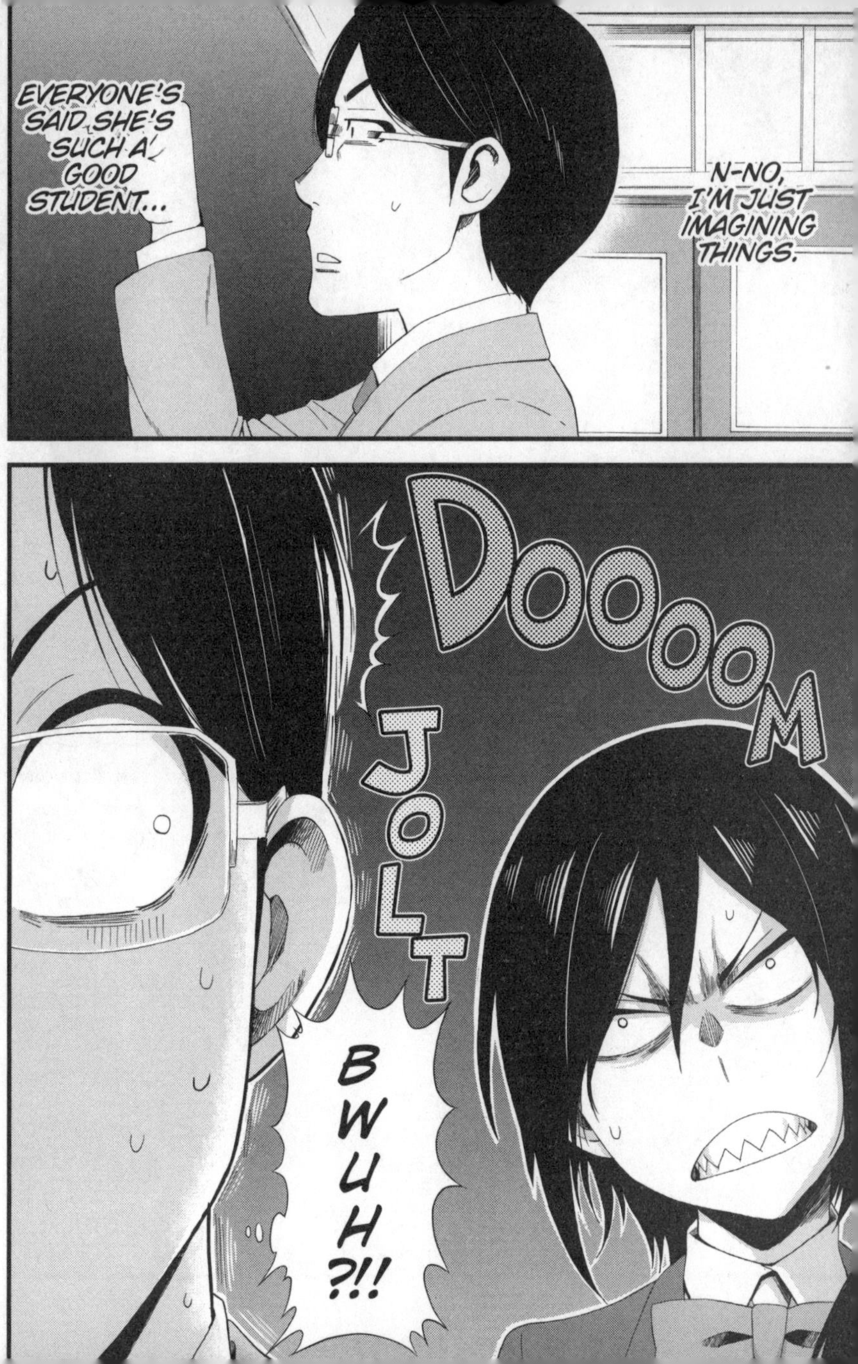
N-NO, I'M JUST IMAGINING THINGS.
EVERYONE'S SAID SHE'S SUCH A GOOD STUDENT...
DOOOOOOM
JOLT
BWUH?!!

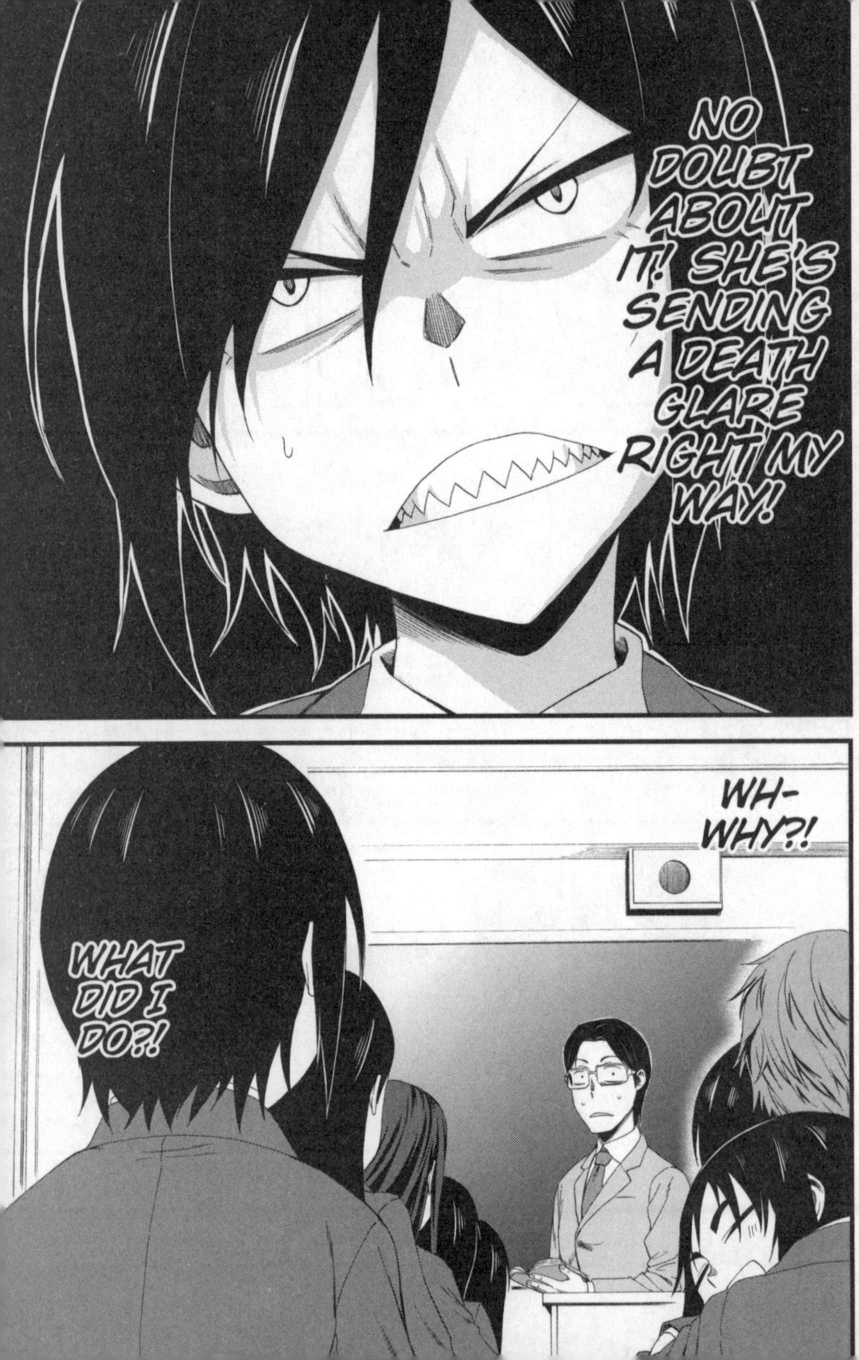
NO DOUBT ABOUT IT! SHE'S SENDING A DEATH GLARE RIGHT MY WAY!
WH- WHY?!
WHAT DID I DO?!

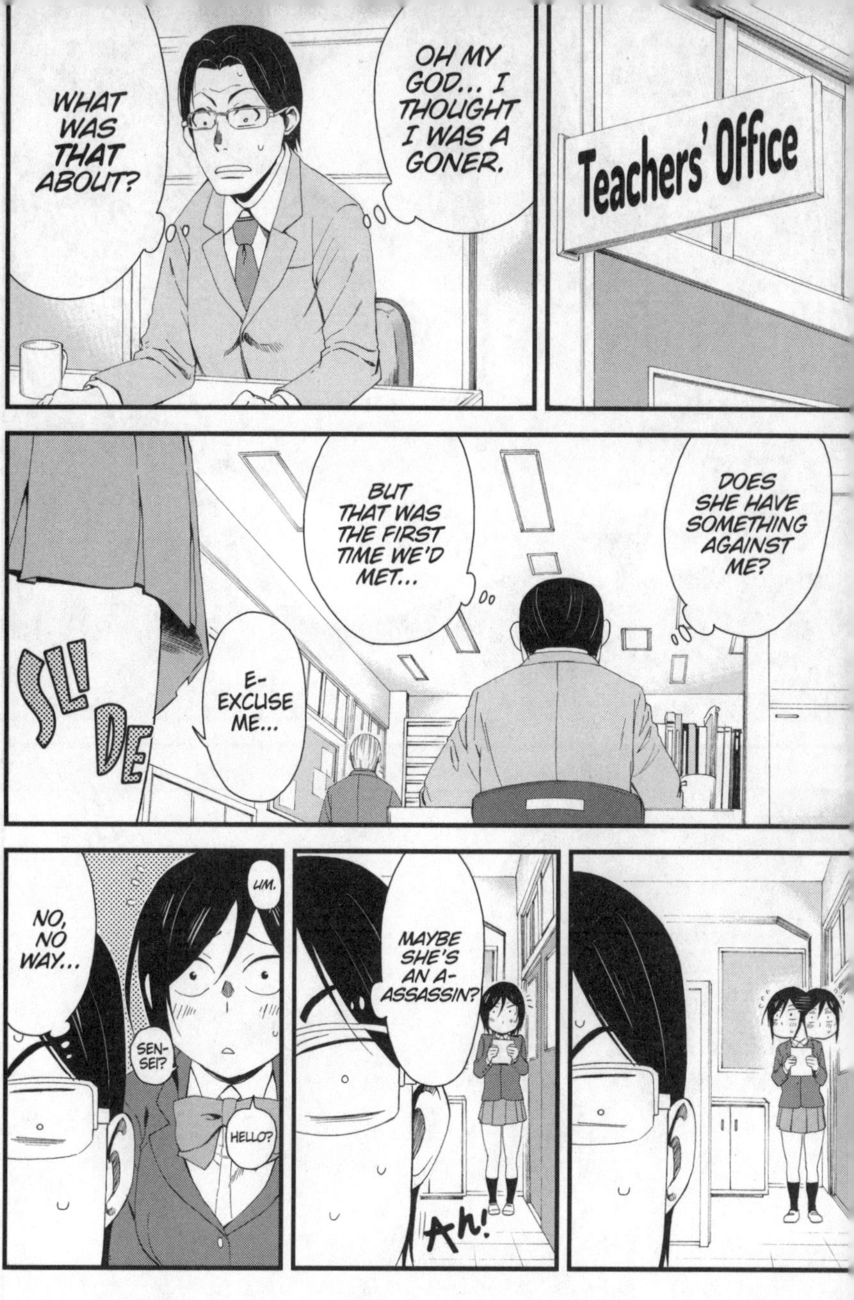
Teachers' Office
OH MY GOD... I THOUGHT I WAS A GONER.
WHAT WAS THAT ABOUT?
DOES SHE HAVE SOMETHING AGAINST ME?
BUT THAT WAS THE FIRST TIME WE'D MET...
E-EXCUSE ME...
SLIDE
MAYBE SHE'S AN A-ASSASSIN?
Ah!
UM.
NO, NO WAY...
SEN-SEI?
HELLO?

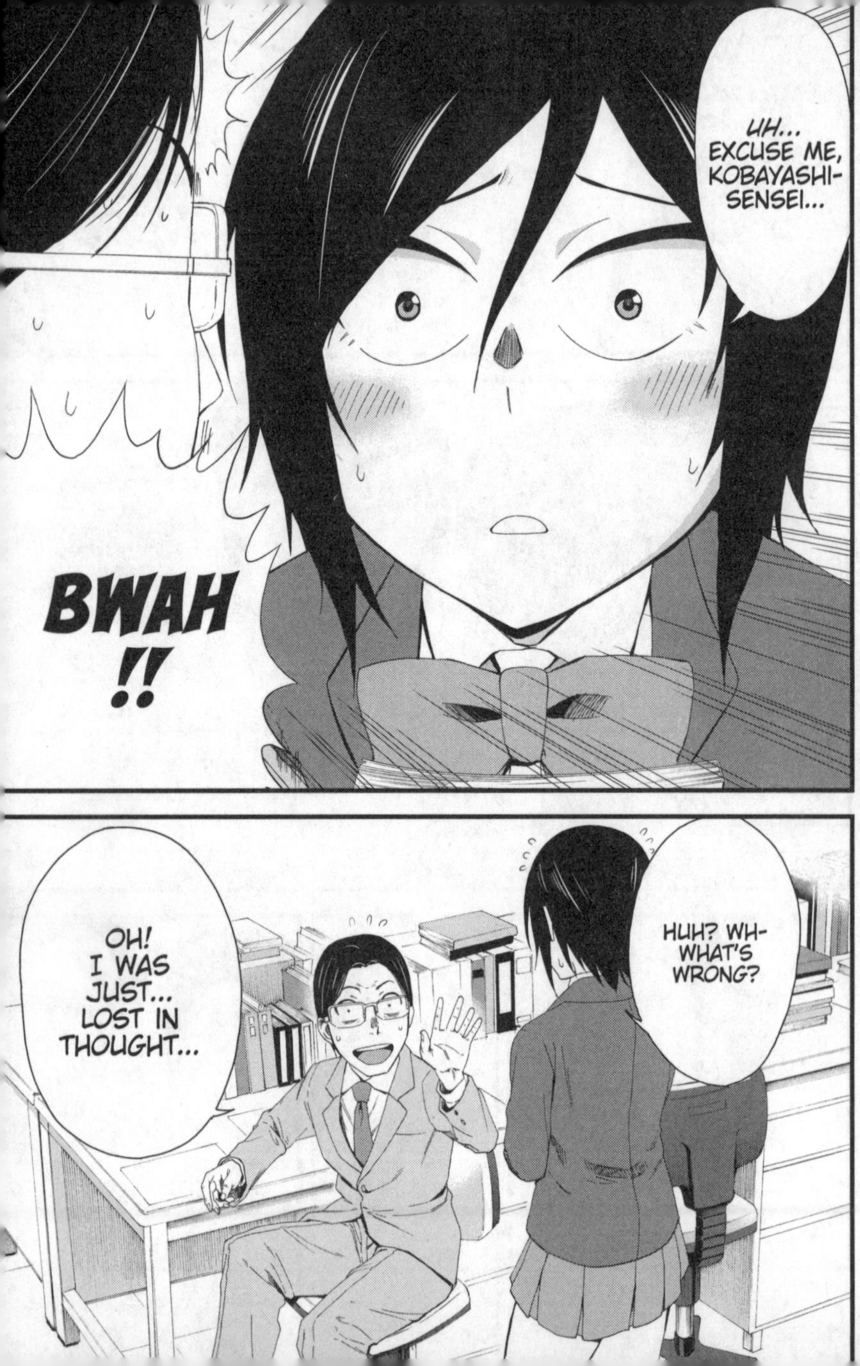
UH... EXCUSE ME, KOBAYASHI-SENSEI...
BWAH !!
HUH? WH-WHAT'S WRONG?
OH! I WAS JUST... LOST IN THOUGHT...

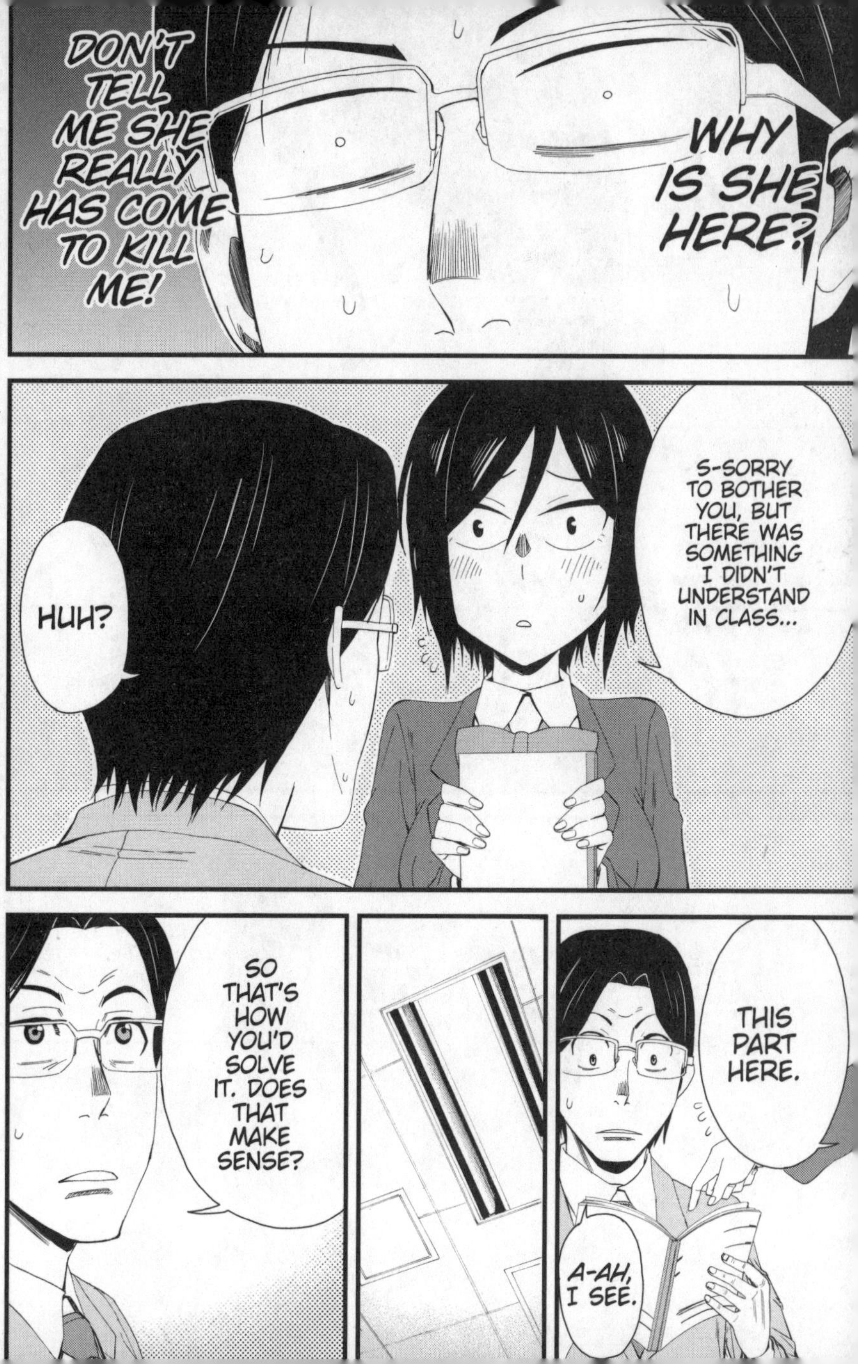
WHY IS SHE HERE?
DON'T TELL ME SHE REALLY HAS COME TO KILL ME!
S-SORRY TO BOTHER YOU, BUT THERE WAS SOMETHING I DIDN'T UNDERSTAND IN CLASS...
HUH?
THIS PART HERE.
A-AH, I SEE.
SO THAT'S HOW YOU'D SOLVE IT. DOES THAT MAKE SENSE?

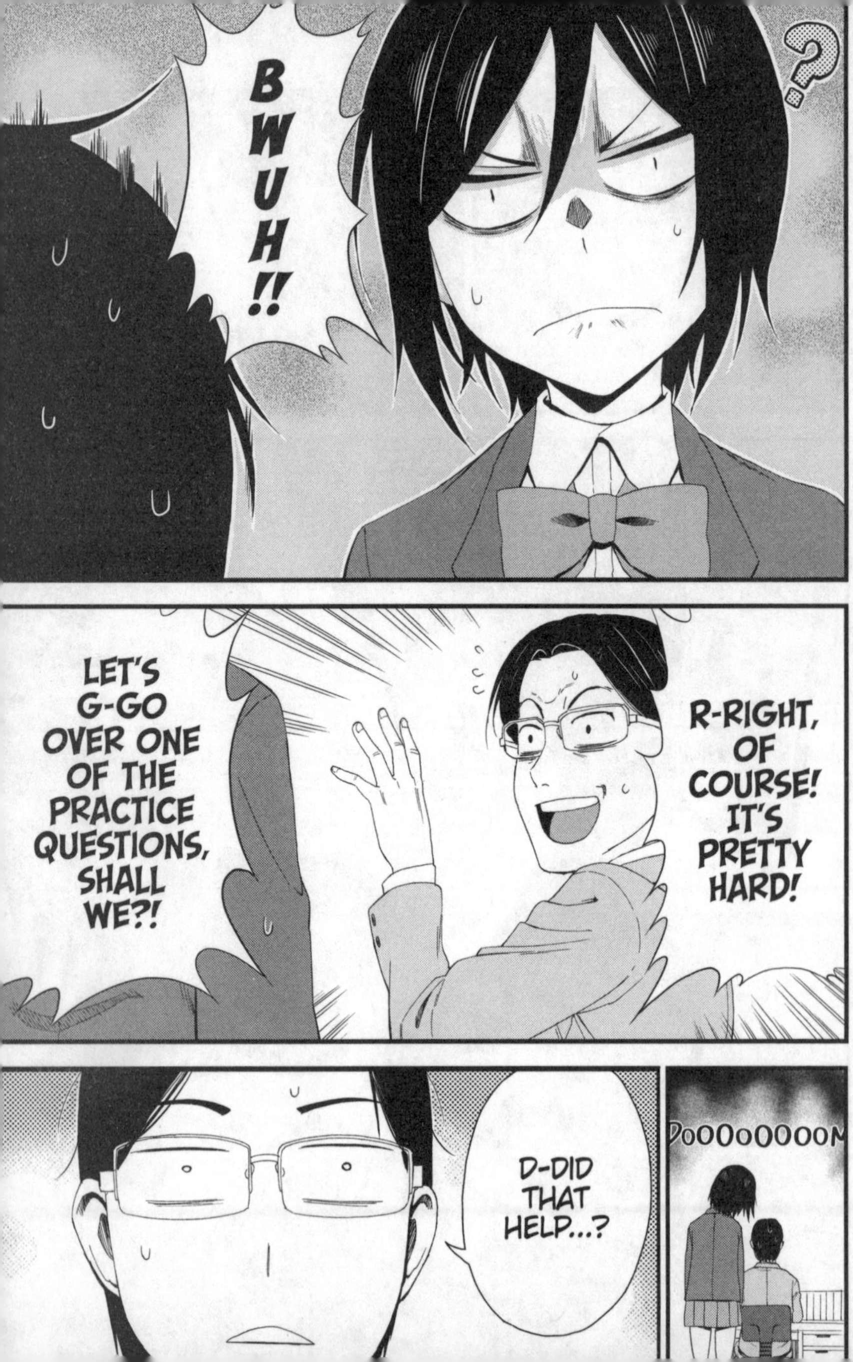
?
BWUH!!
R-RIGHT, OF COURSE! IT'S PRETTY HARD!
LET'S G-GO OVER ONE OF THE PRACTICE QUESTIONS, SHALL WE?!
DOOOOOOOOM
D-DID THAT HELP...?

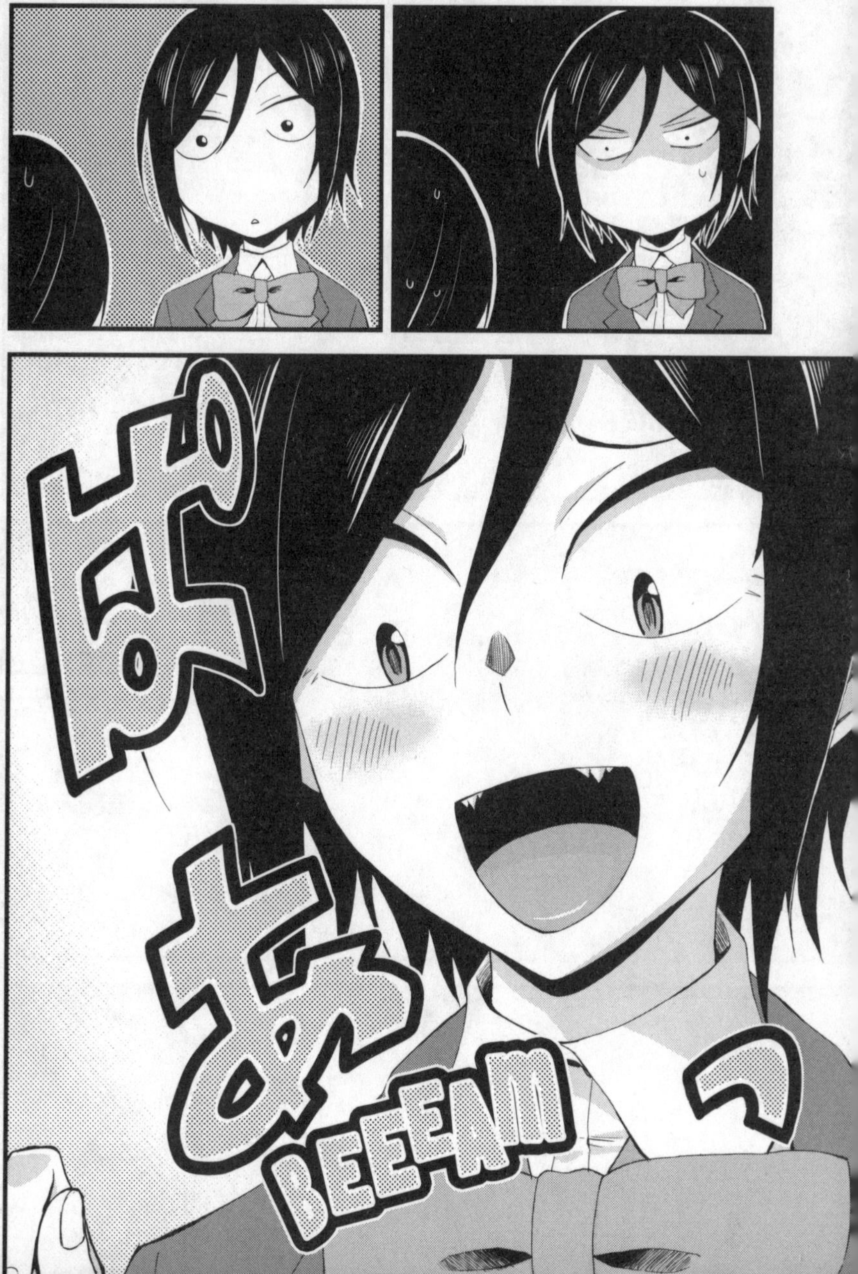
BEEEAM

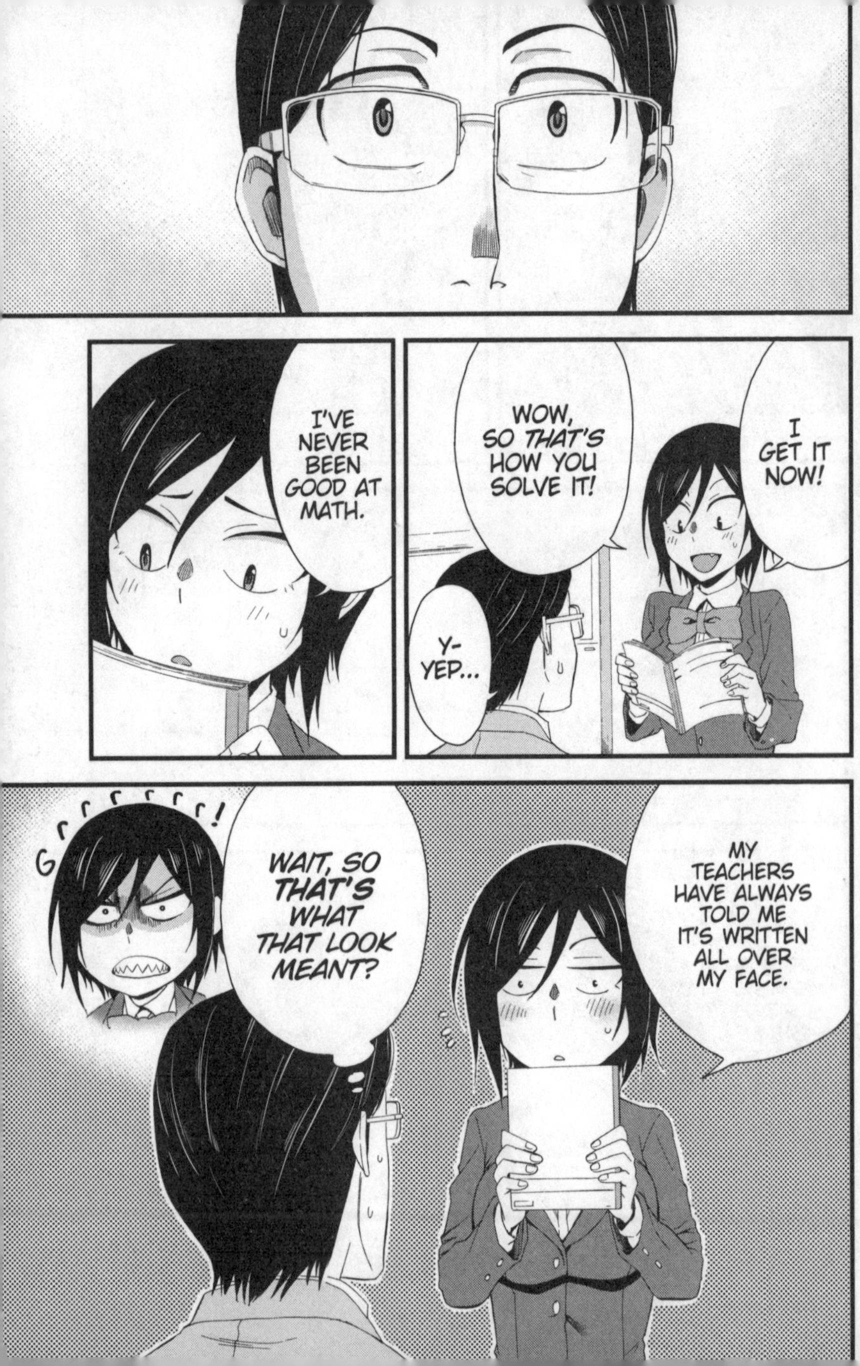
I GET IT NOW!
WOW, SO THAT'S HOW YOU SOLVE IT!
Y-YEP...
I'VE NEVER BEEN GOOD AT MATH.
MY TEACHERS HAVE ALWAYS TOLD ME IT'S WRITTEN ALL OVER MY FACE.
WAIT, SO THAT'S WHAT THAT LOOK MEANT?
Grrrrrrr!

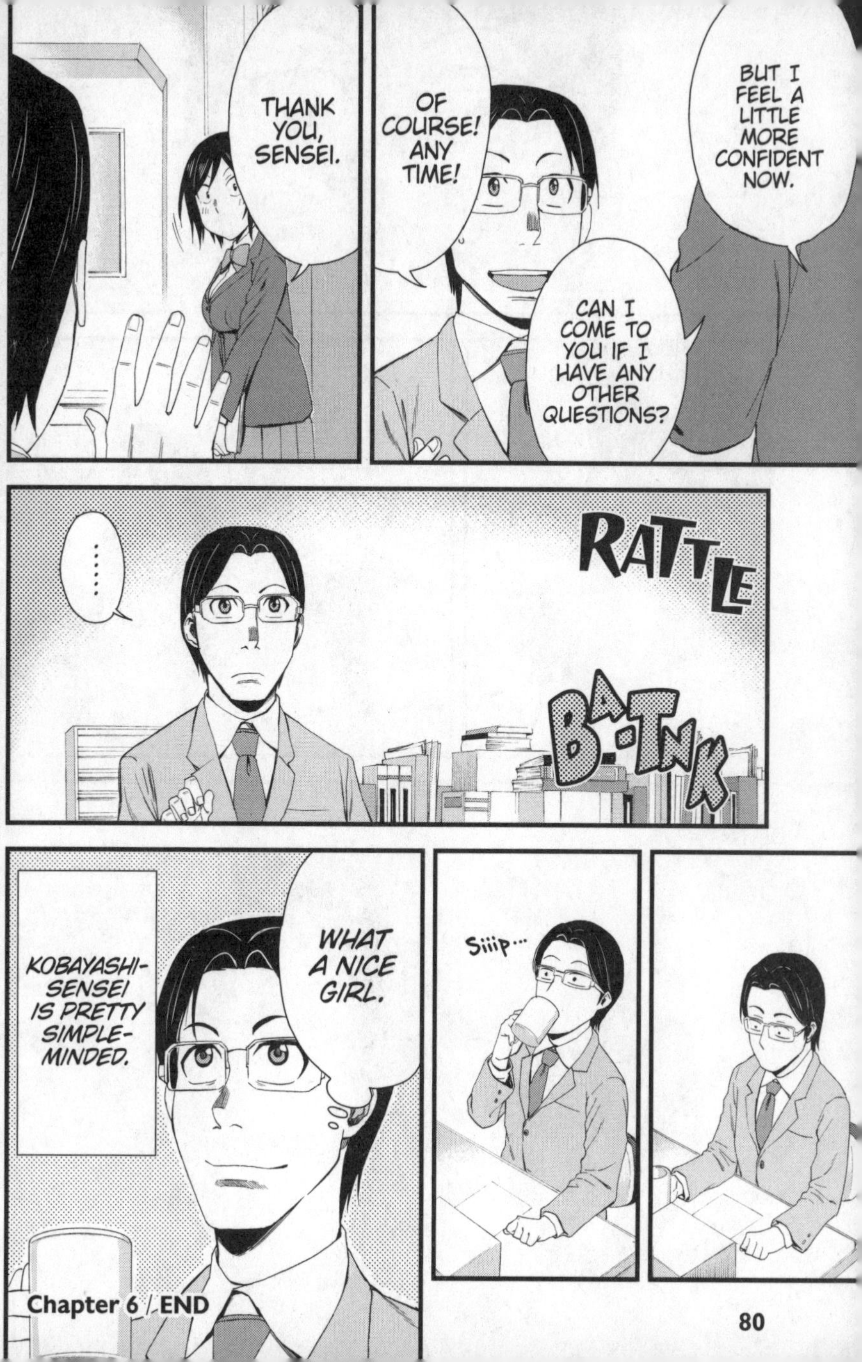
BUT I FEEL A LITTLE MORE CONFIDENT NOW.
CAN I COME TO YOU IF I HAVE ANY OTHER QUESTIONS?
OF COURSE! ANY TIME!
THANK YOU, SENSEI.
RATTLE
BA-TNK
......
Siiip...
WHAT A NICE GIRL.
KOBAYASHI-SENSEI IS PRETTY SIMPLE-MINDED.
Chapter 6 / END

Chapter 7

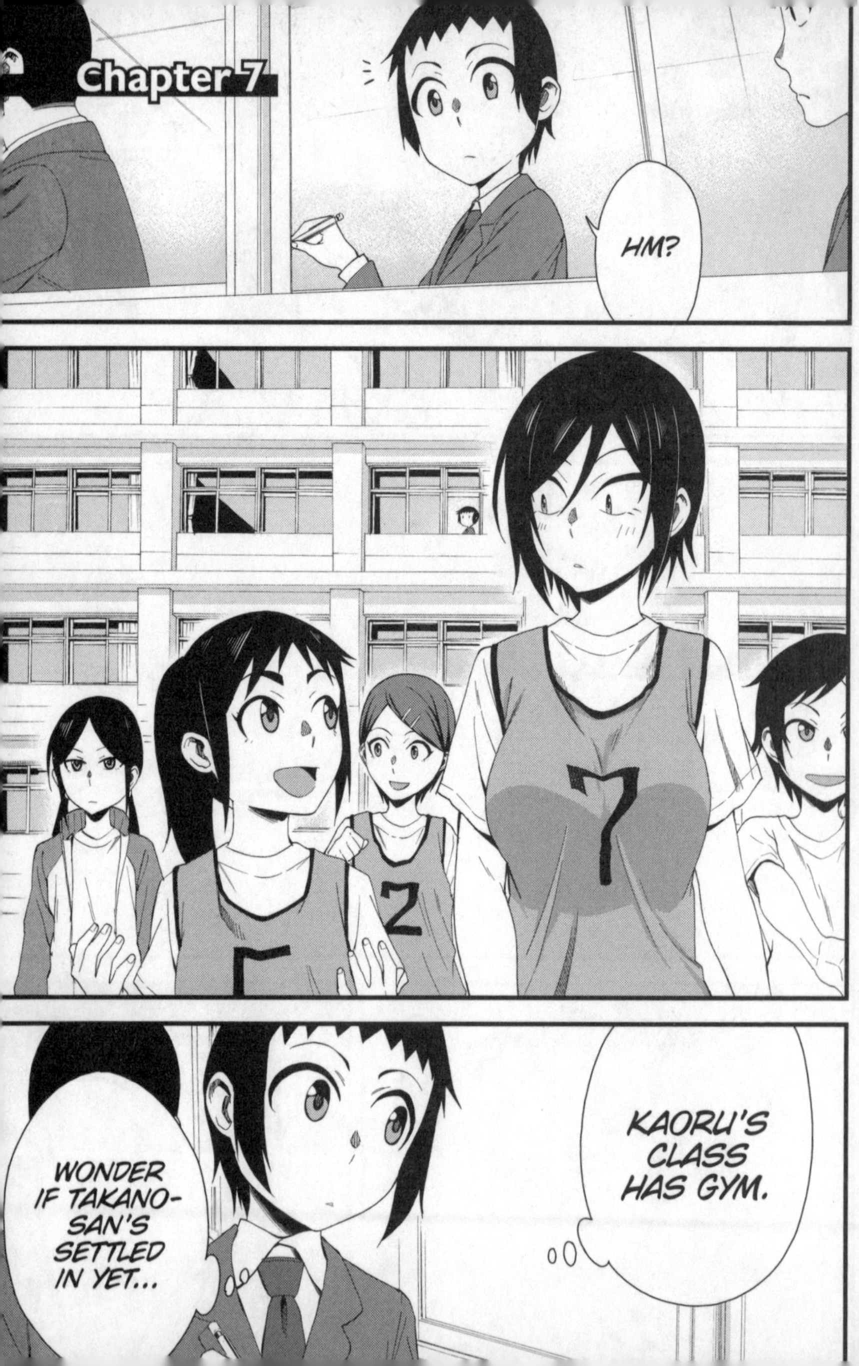
HM?
KAORU'S CLASS HAS GYM.
WONDER IF TAKANO-SAN'S SETTLED IN YET...

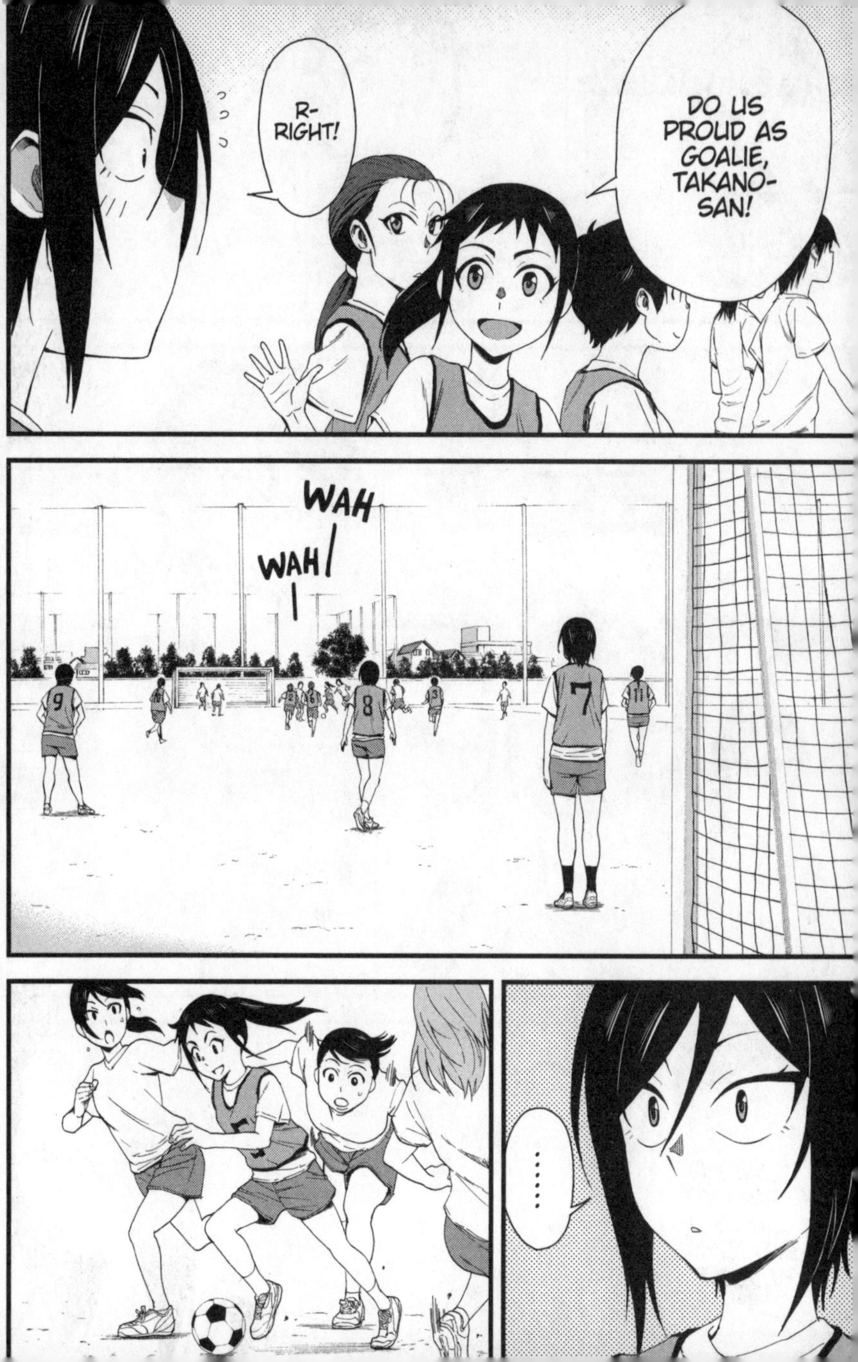
DO US PROUD AS GOALIE, TAKANO-SAN!
R- RIGHT!
WAH WAH
......

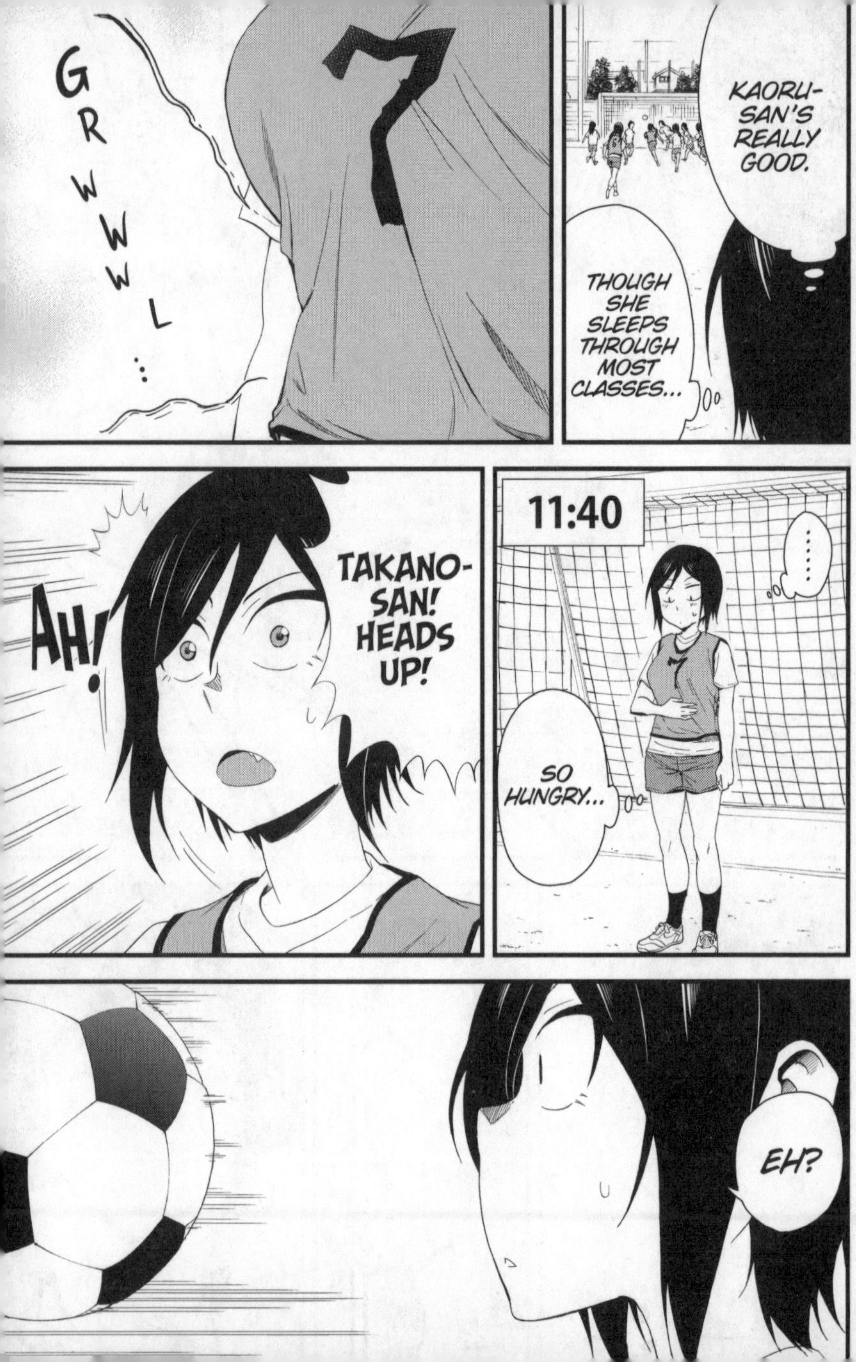
KAORU-SAN'S REALLY GOOD.
THOUGH SHE SLEEPS THROUGH MOST CLASSES...
GRWWWL...
11:40
......
SO HUNGRY...
TAKANO-SAN! HEADS UP!
AH!
EH?

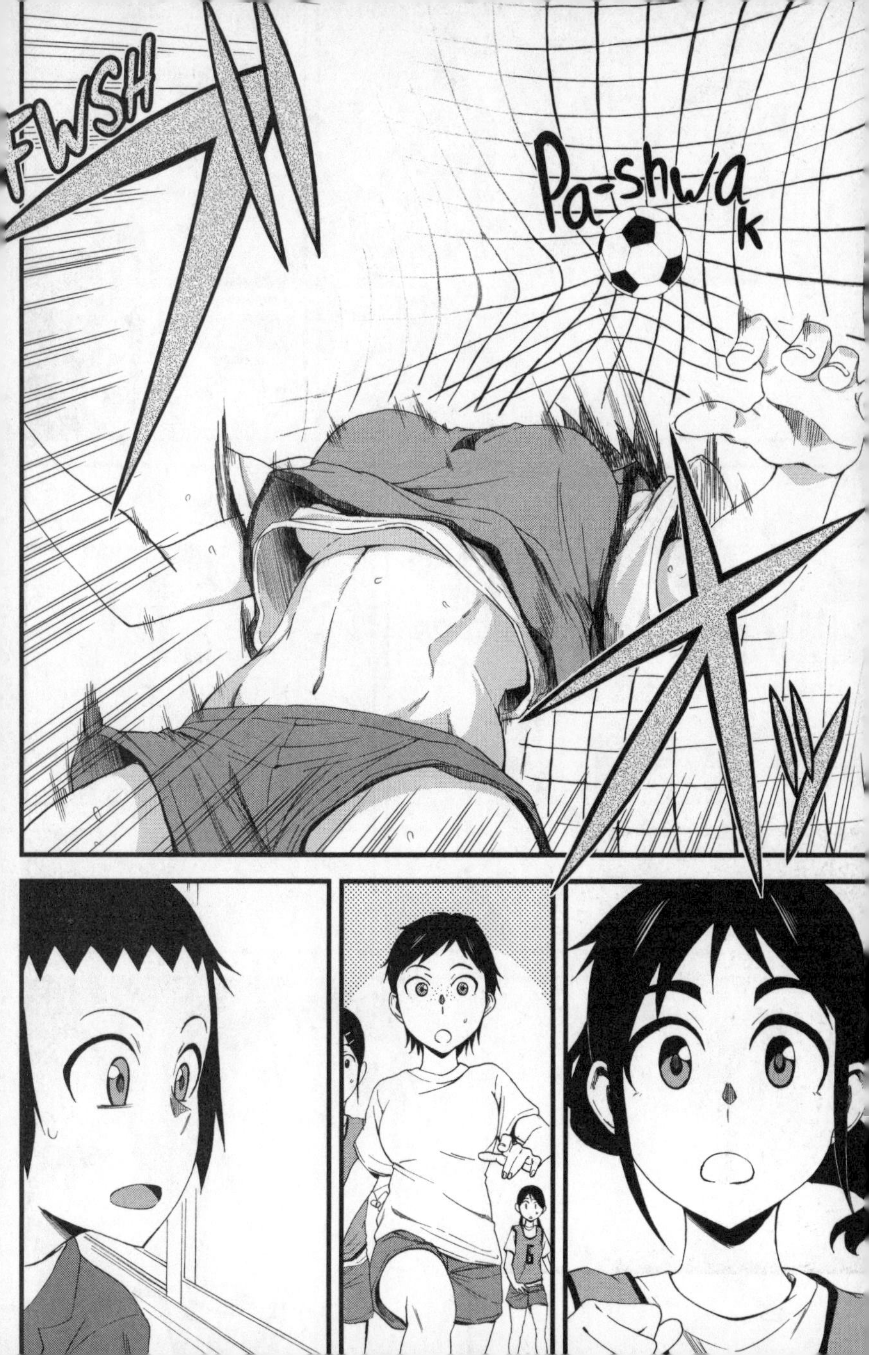
FWSH
Pa-shwak

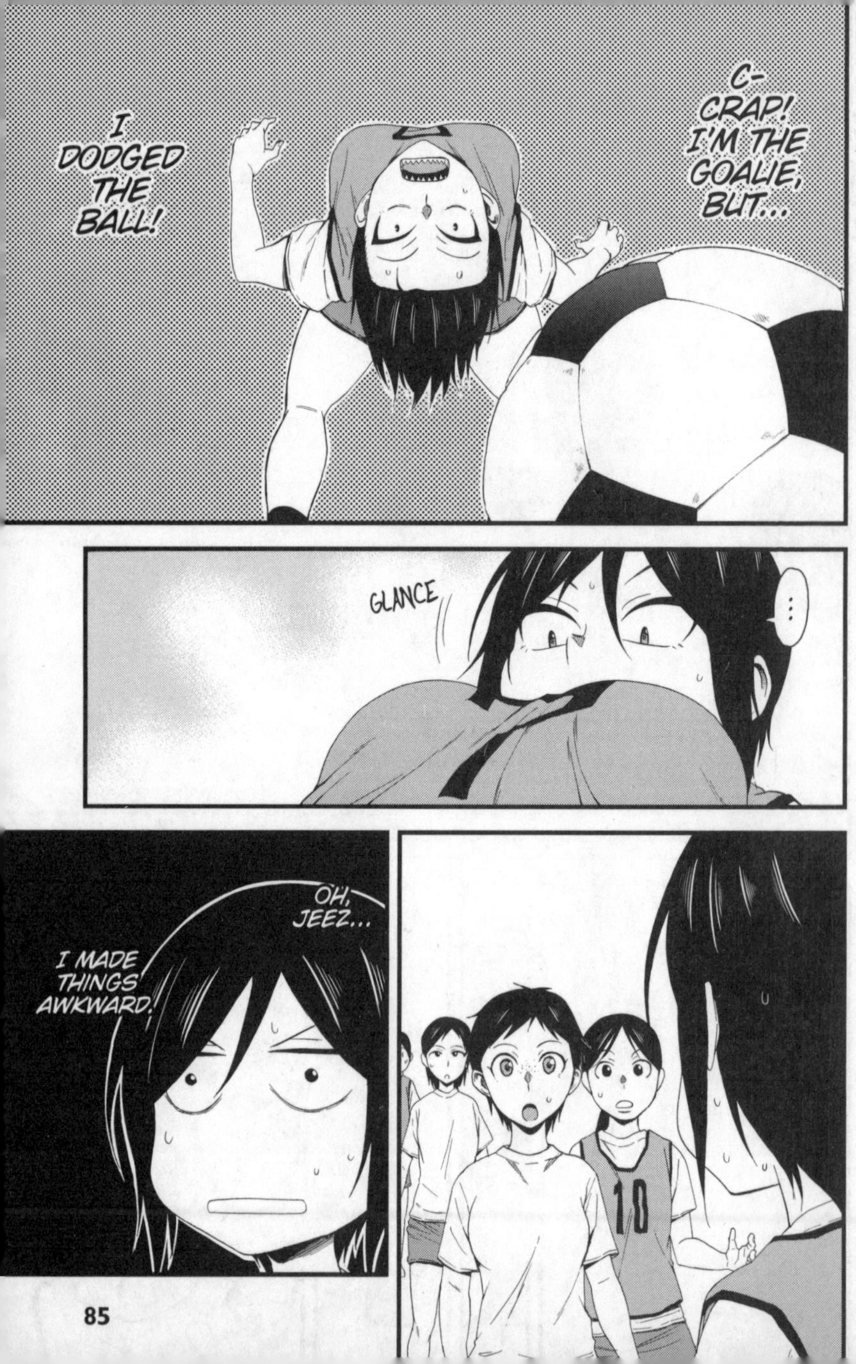
C-CRAP! I'M THE GOALIE, BUT...
I DODGED THE BALL!
GLANCE
...
OH, JEEZ...
I MADE THINGS AWKWARD!

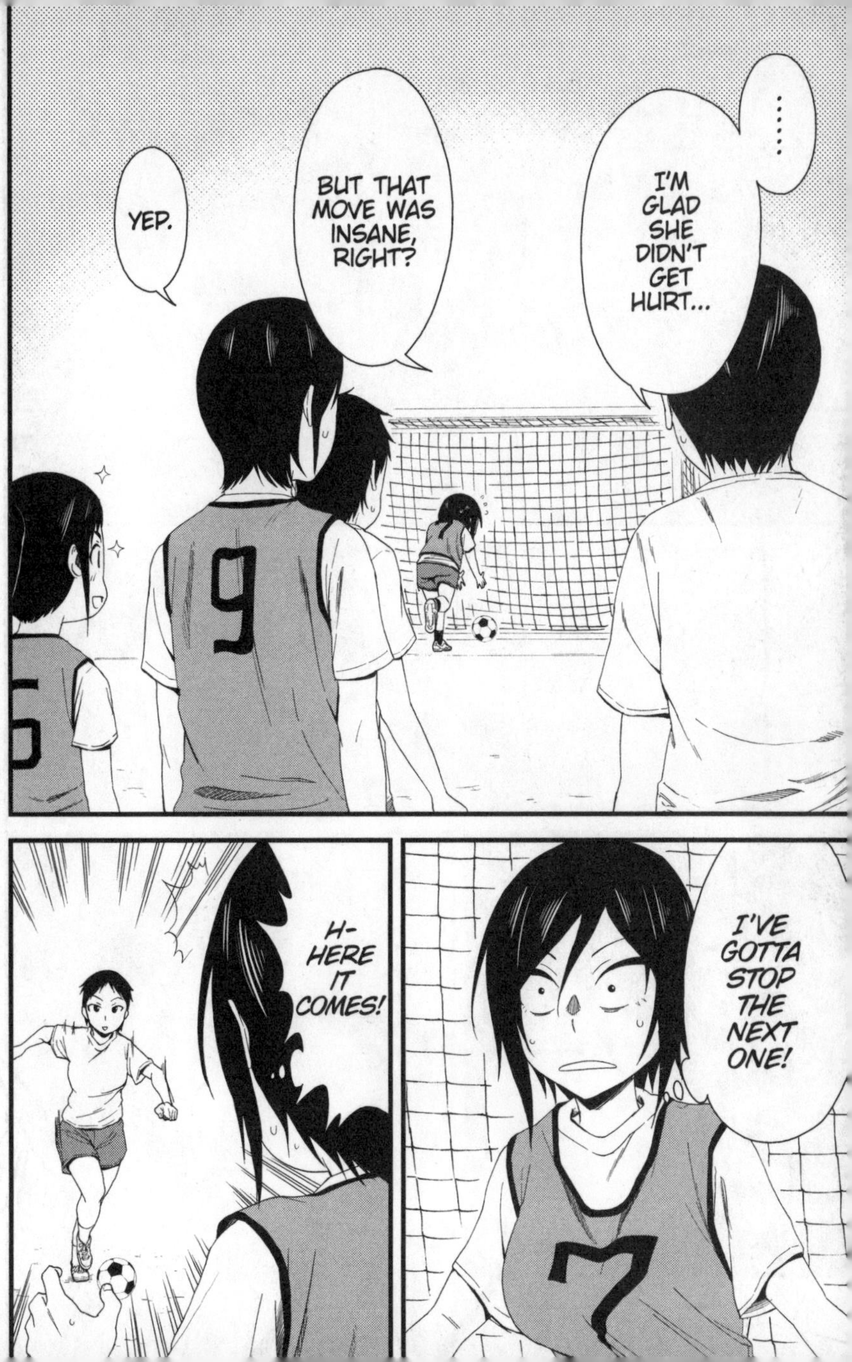
……
I'M GLAD SHE DIDN'T GET HURT...
BUT THAT MOVE WAS INSANE, RIGHT?
YEP.
I'VE GOTTA STOP THE NEXT ONE!
H-HERE IT COMES!

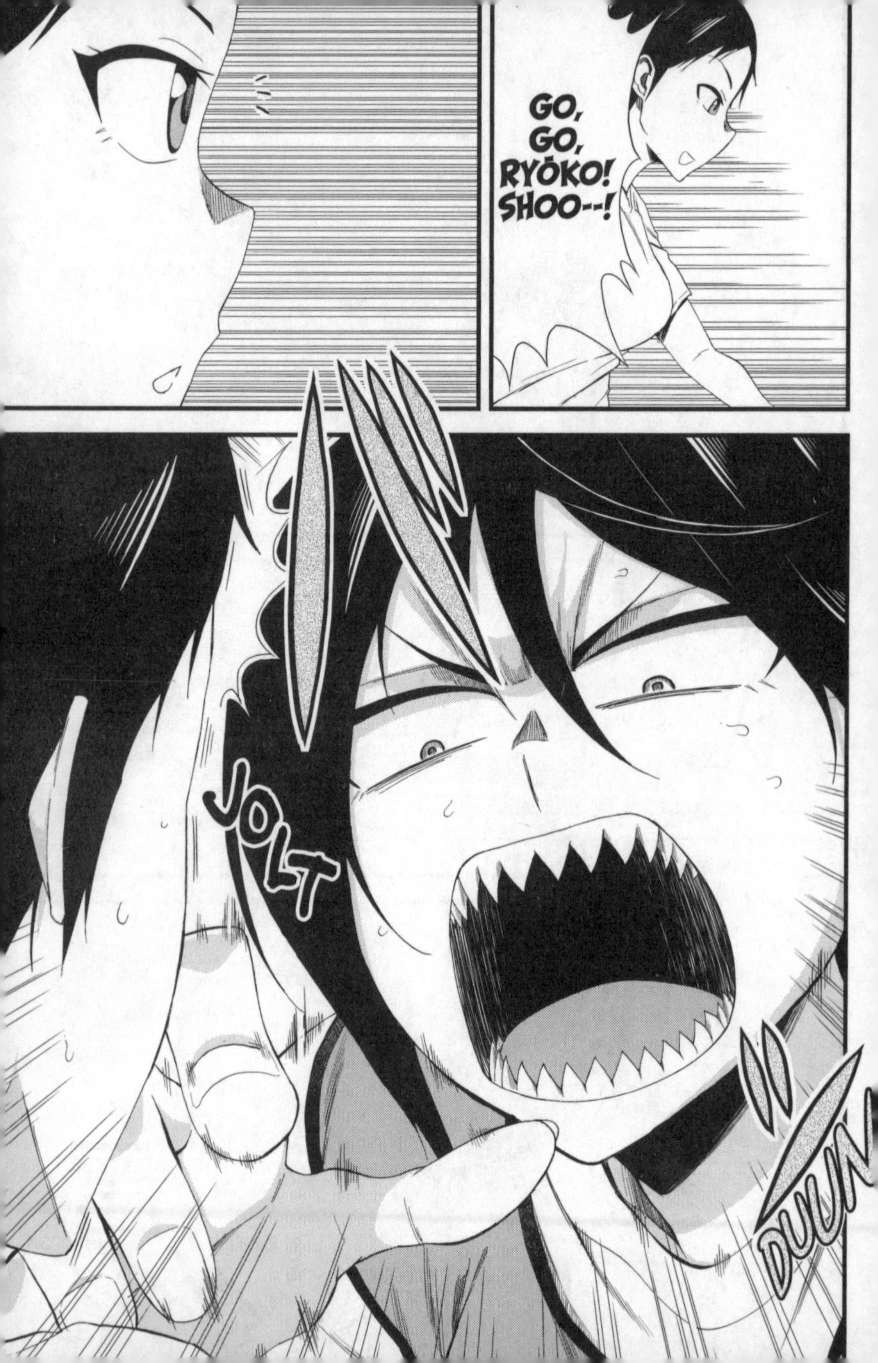
GO, GO, RYŌKO! SHOO--!
JOLT
DUUN

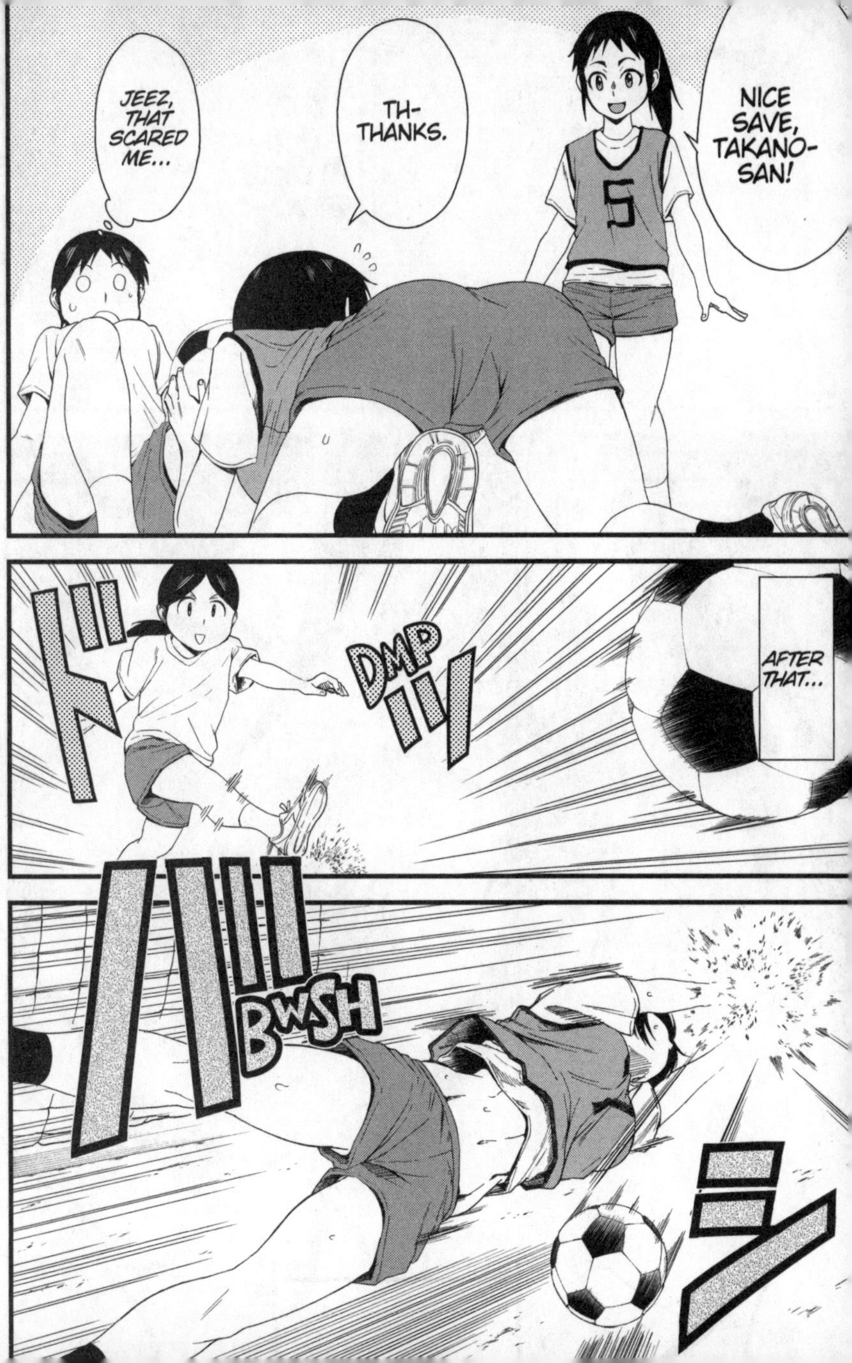
NICE SAVE, TAKANO-SAN!
TH- THANKS.
JEEZ, THAT SCARED ME...
AFTER THAT...
DMP
BWSH

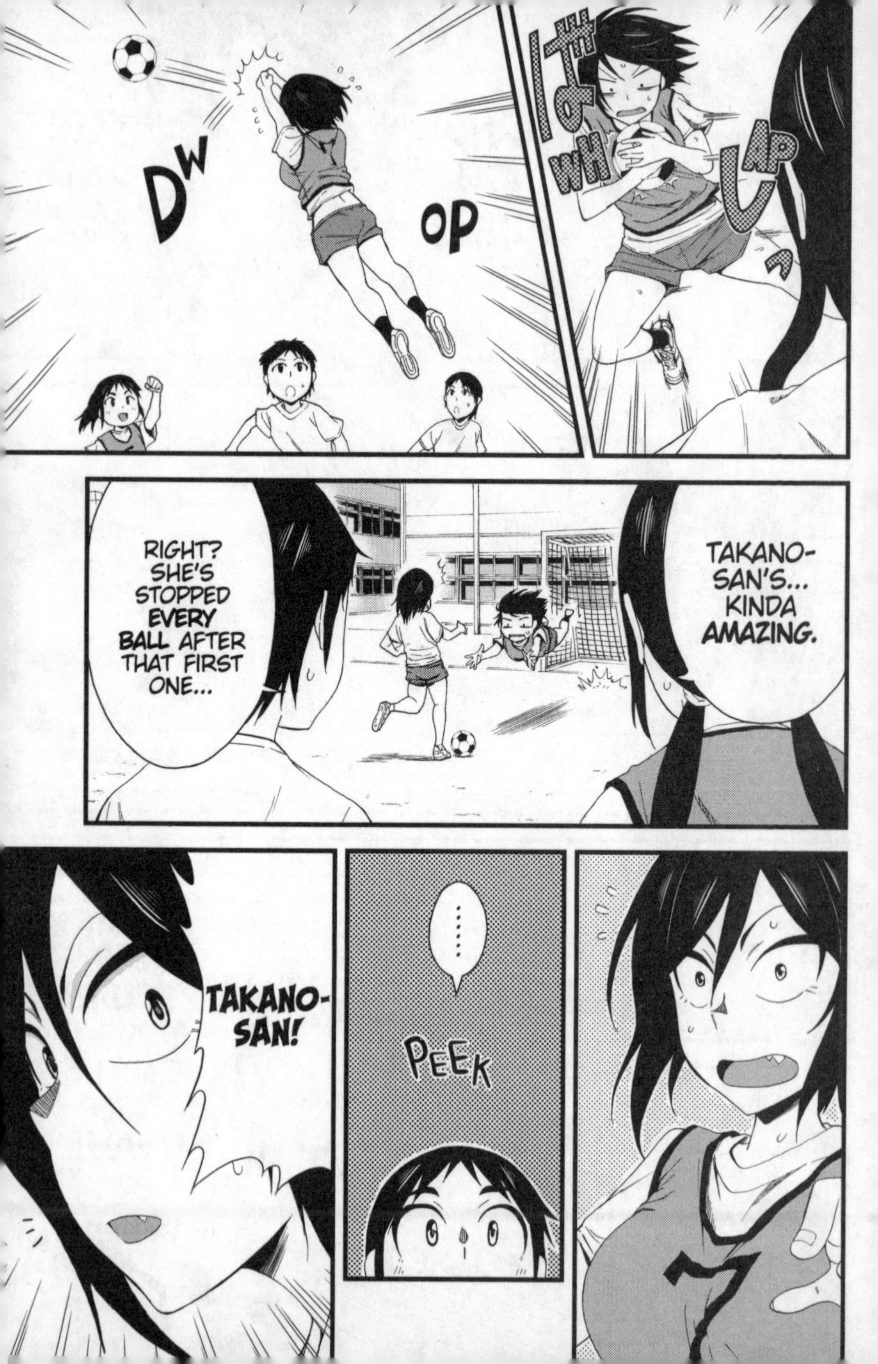
WHAP
DWOP
TAKANO-SAN'S... KINDA **AMAZING.**
RIGHT? SHE'S STOPPED **EVERY BALL** AFTER THAT FIRST ONE...
......
PEEK
TAKANO-SAN!

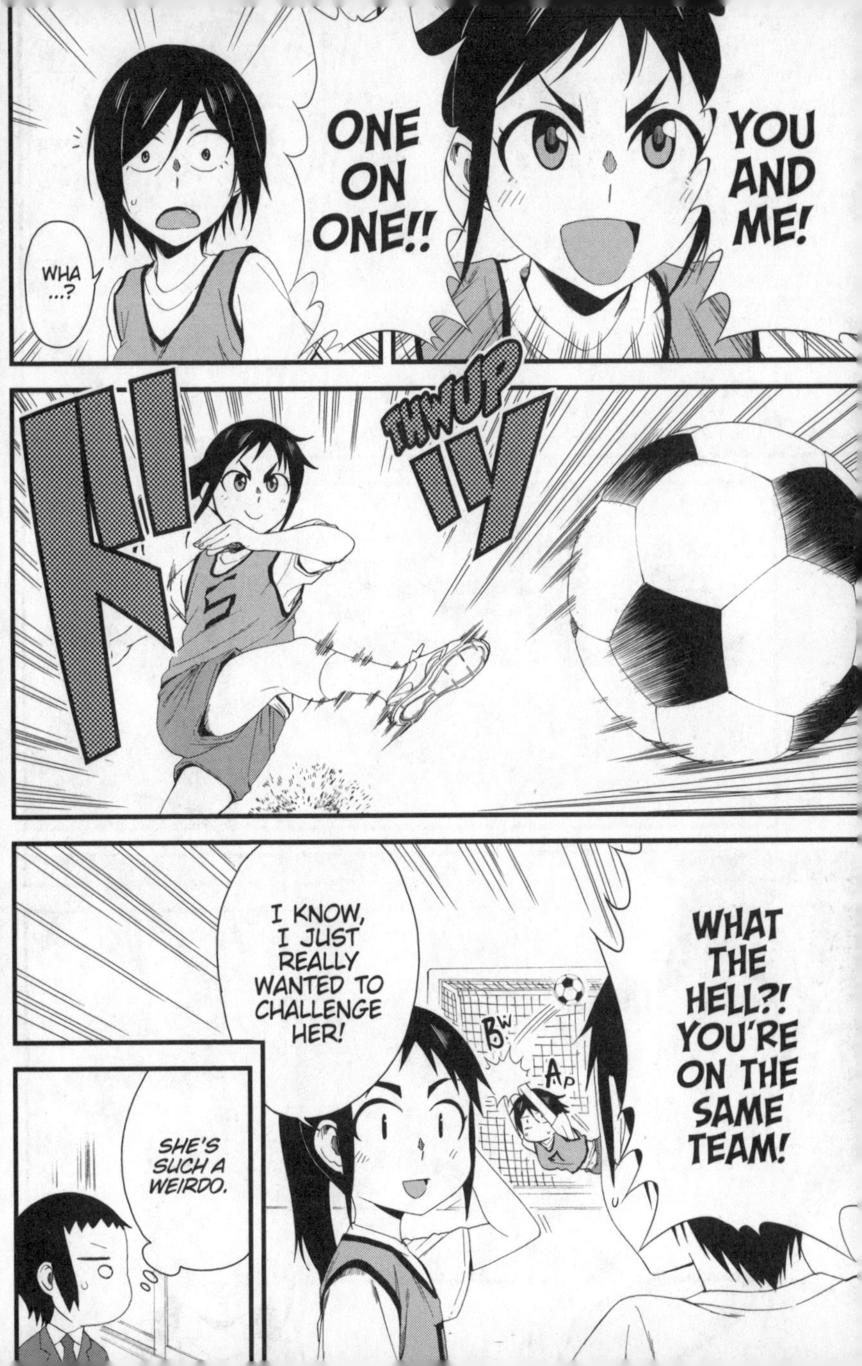
YOU AND ME!
ONE ON ONE!!
WHA ...?
THWUP
ドッ
WHAT THE HELL?! YOU'RE ON THE SAME TEAM!
I KNOW, I JUST REALLY WANTED TO CHALLENGE HER!
BW
AP
SHE'S SUCH A WEIRDO.

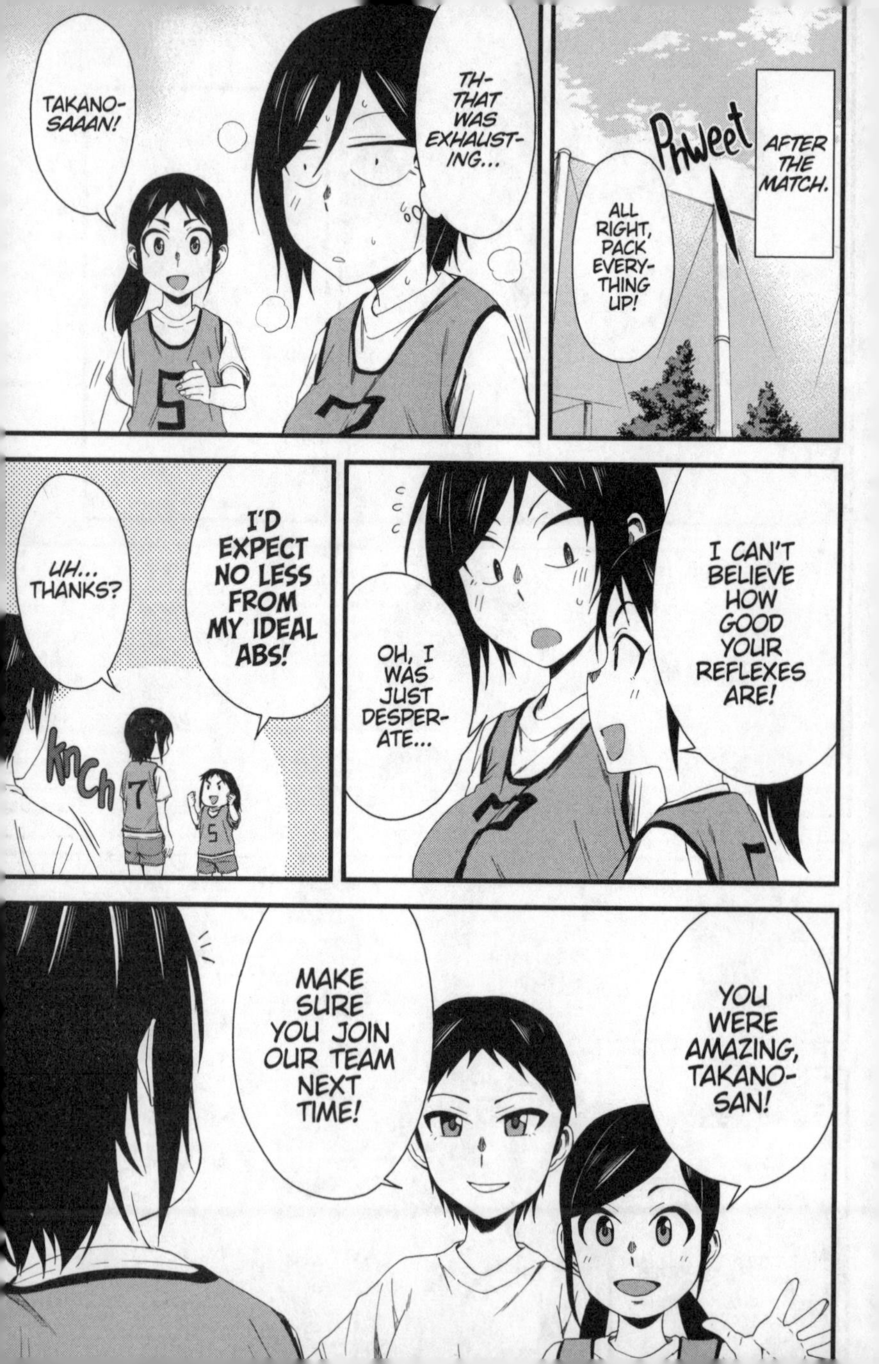
AFTER THE MATCH.
Phweet
ALL RIGHT, PACK EVERYTHING UP!
TH-THAT WAS EXHAUSTING...
TAKANO-SAAAN!
I CAN'T BELIEVE HOW GOOD YOUR REFLEXES ARE!
OH, I WAS JUST DESPERATE...
I'D EXPECT NO LESS FROM MY IDEAL ABS!
knch
UH... THANKS?
YOU WERE AMAZING, TAKANO-SAN!
MAKE SURE YOU JOIN OUR TEAM NEXT TIME!

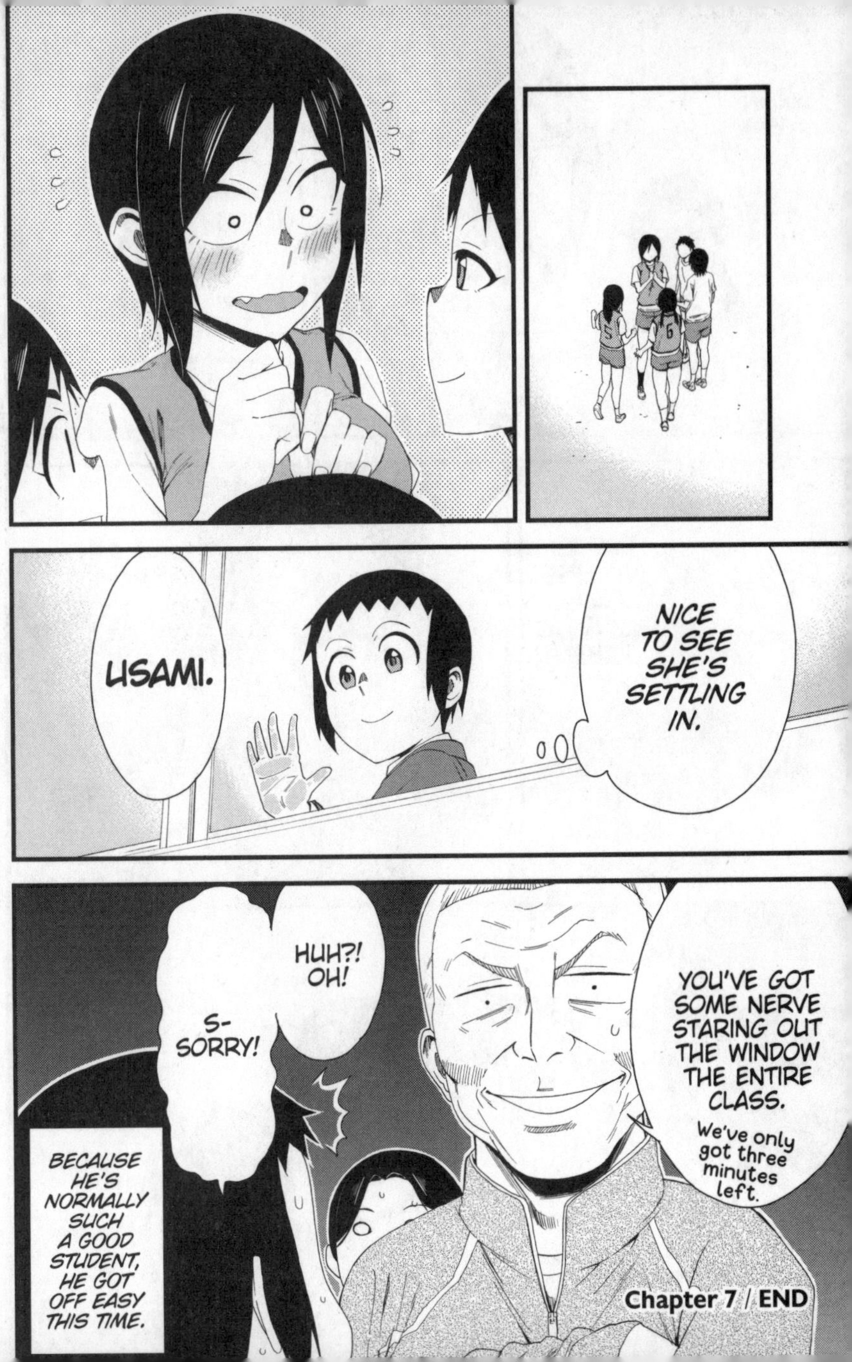
NICE TO SEE SHE'S SETTLING IN.
USAMI.
YOU'VE GOT SOME NERVE STARING OUT THE WINDOW THE ENTIRE CLASS.
We've only got three minutes left.
HUH?! OH!
S- SORRY!
BECAUSE HE'S NORMALLY SUCH A GOOD STUDENT, HE GOT OFF EASY THIS TIME.
Chapter 7 / END

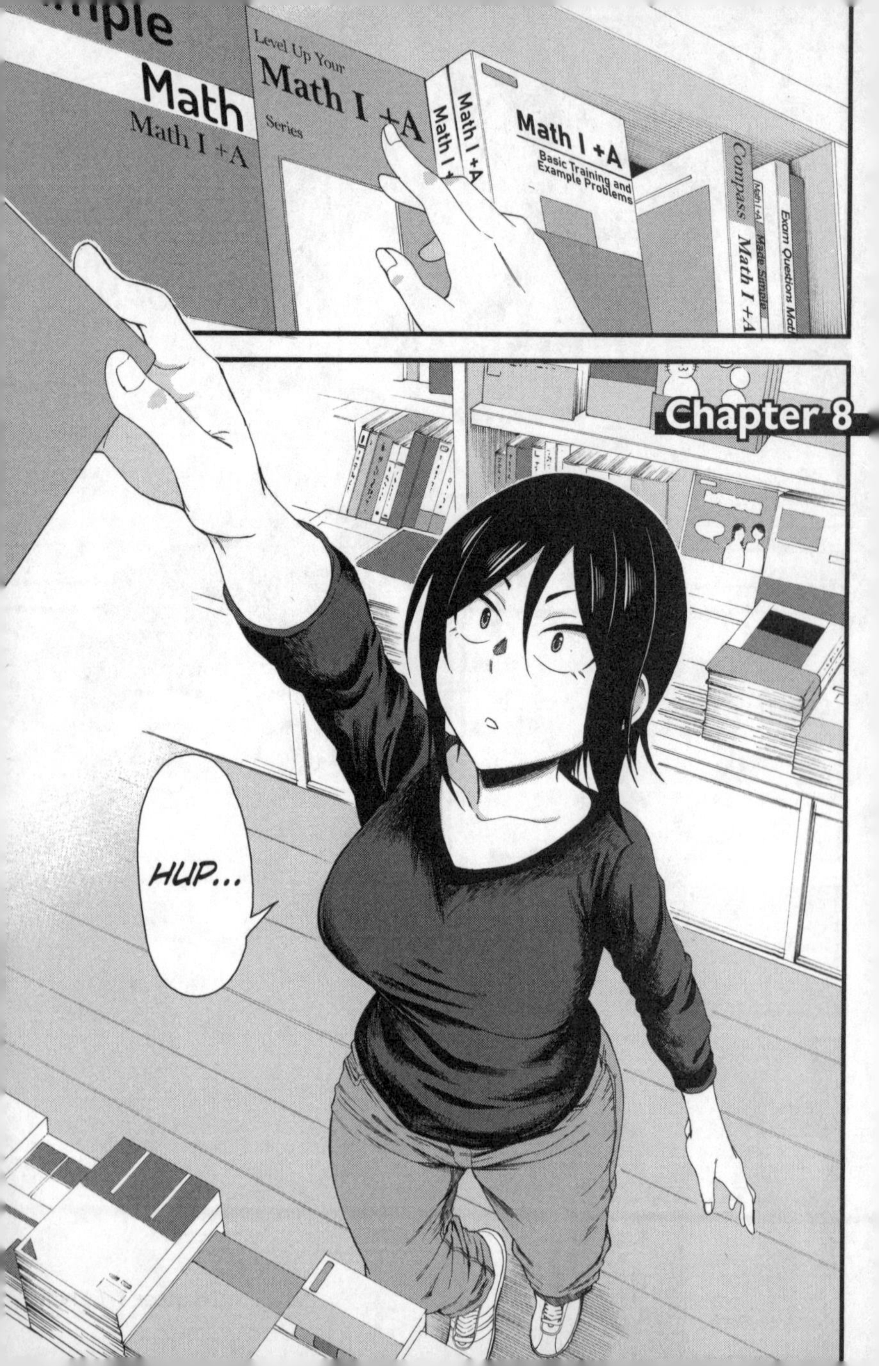
Math
Math I +A
Level Up Your
Math I +A
Series
Math I +A
Basic Training and Example Problems
Compass
Math I +A
Math I +A Made Simple
Exam Questions Math
Chapter 8
HUP...

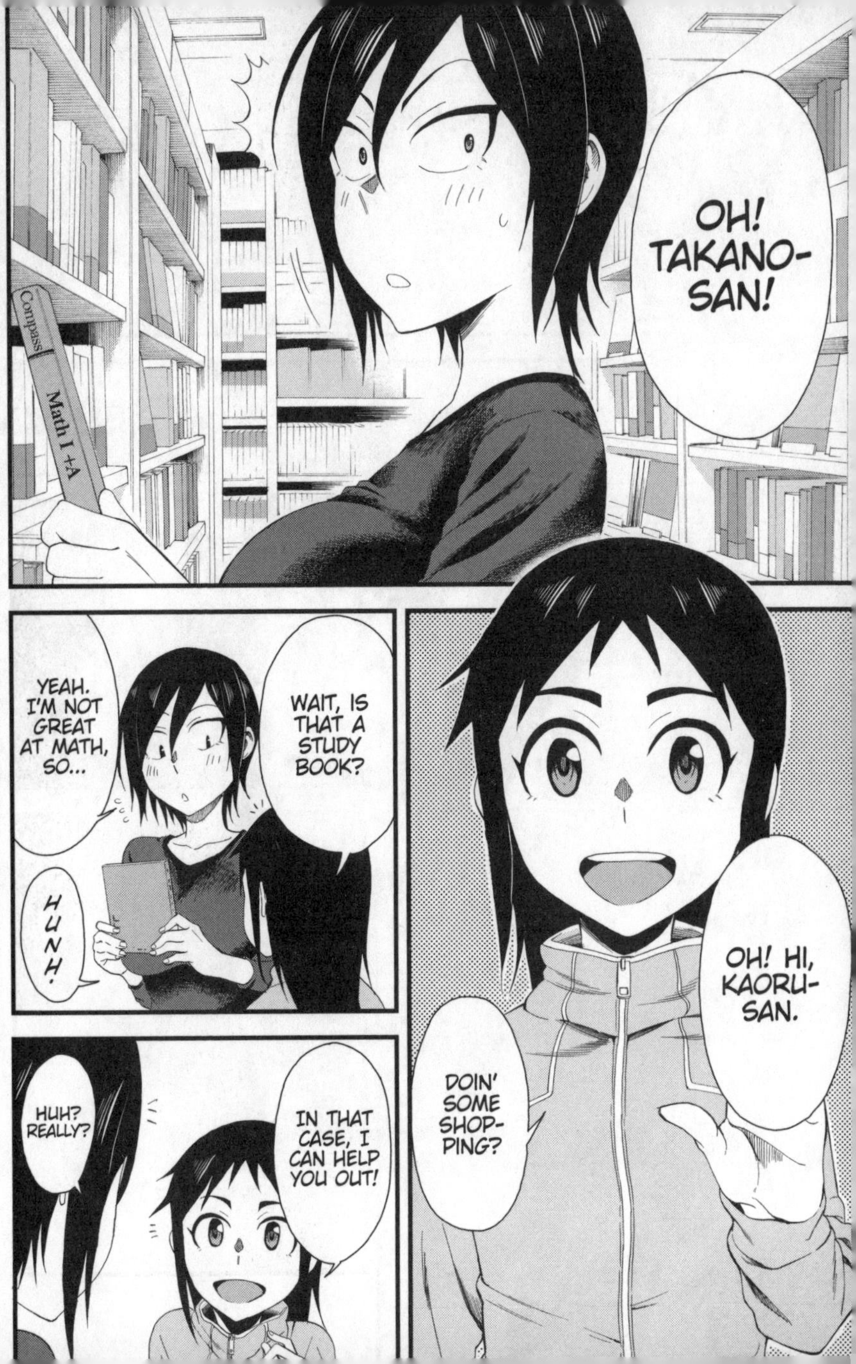
OH! TAKANO-SAN!
Compass
Math I +A
OH! HI, KAORU-SAN.
DOIN' SOME SHOP-PING?
WAIT, IS THAT A STUDY BOOK?
YEAH. I'M NOT GREAT AT MATH, SO...
HUNH!
IN THAT CASE, I CAN HELP YOU OUT!
HUH? REALLY?

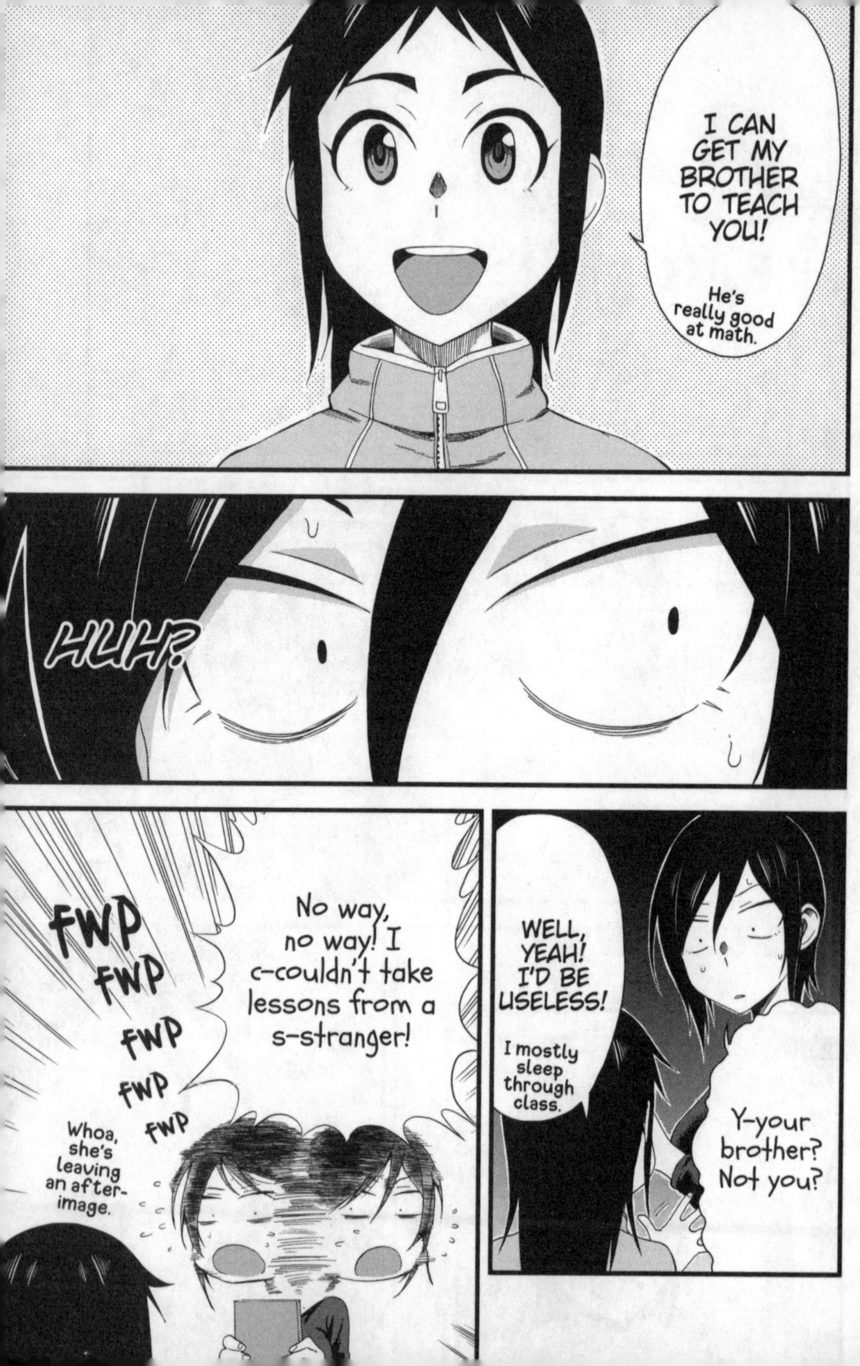
I CAN GET MY BROTHER TO TEACH YOU!
He's really good at math.
HUH?
Y-your brother? Not you?
WELL, YEAH! I'D BE USELESS!
I mostly sleep through class.
No way, no way! I c-couldn't take lessons from a s-stranger!
FWP FWP FWP FWP FWP
Whoa, she's leaving an after-image.

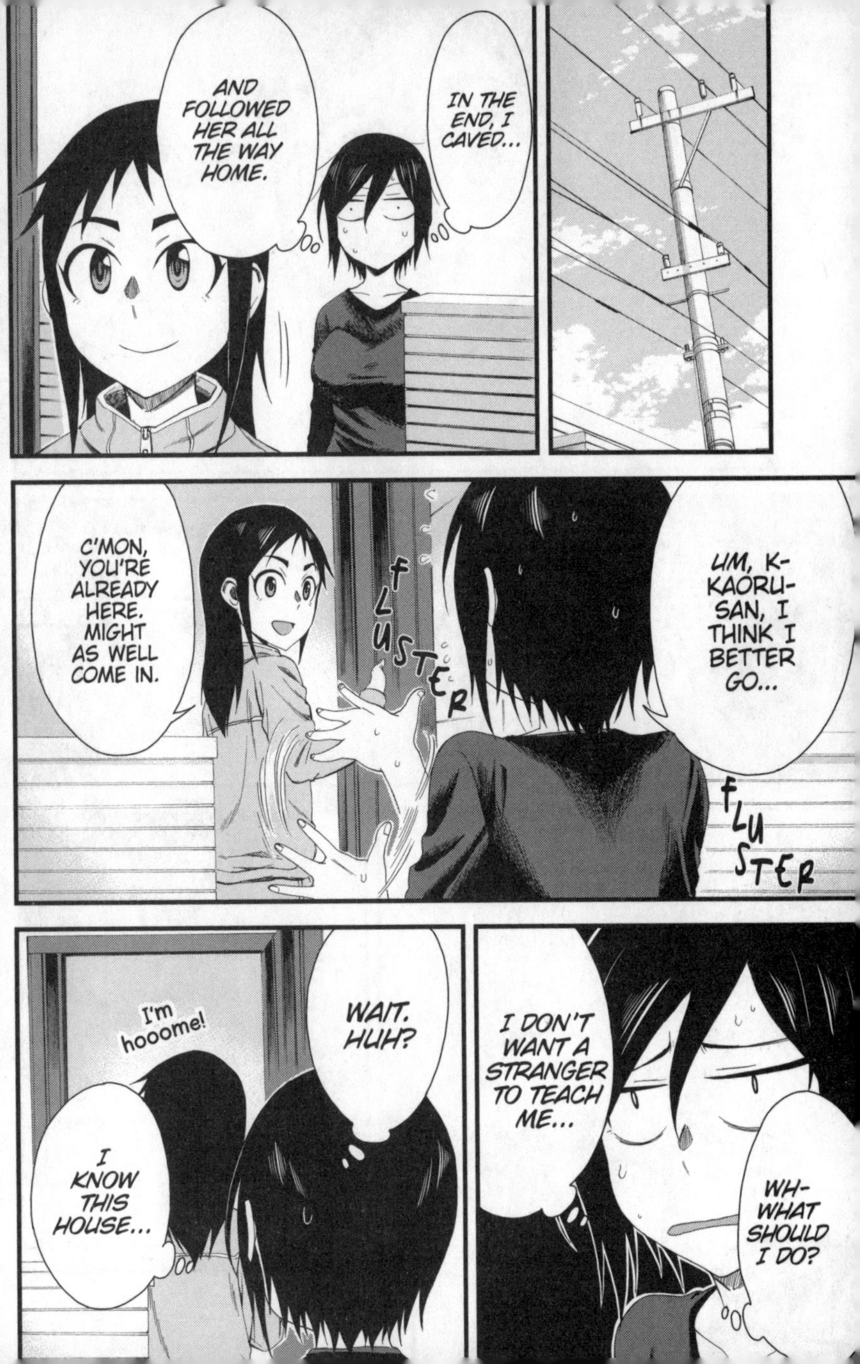
IN THE END, I CAVED...
AND FOLLOWED HER ALL THE WAY HOME.
UM, K-KAORU-SAN, I THINK I BETTER GO...
FLUSTER
FLUSTER
C'MON, YOU'RE ALREADY HERE. MIGHT AS WELL COME IN.
I DON'T WANT A STRANGER TO TEACH ME...
WH-WHAT SHOULD I DO?
WAIT. HUH?
I'm hooome!
I KNOW THIS HOUSE...

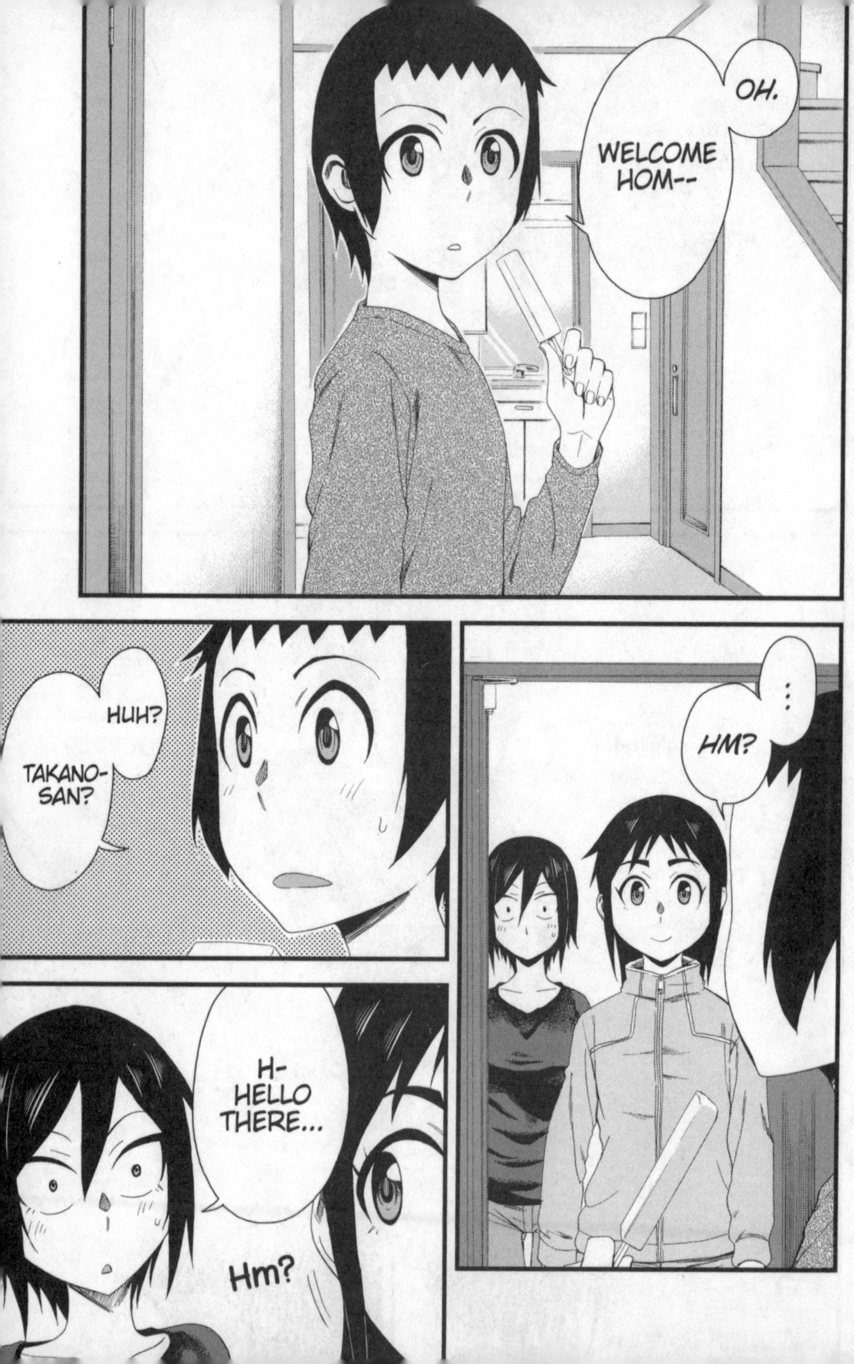

OH.
WELCOME HOM--
...
HM?
HUH?
TAKANO-SAN?
H- HELLO THERE...
Hm?

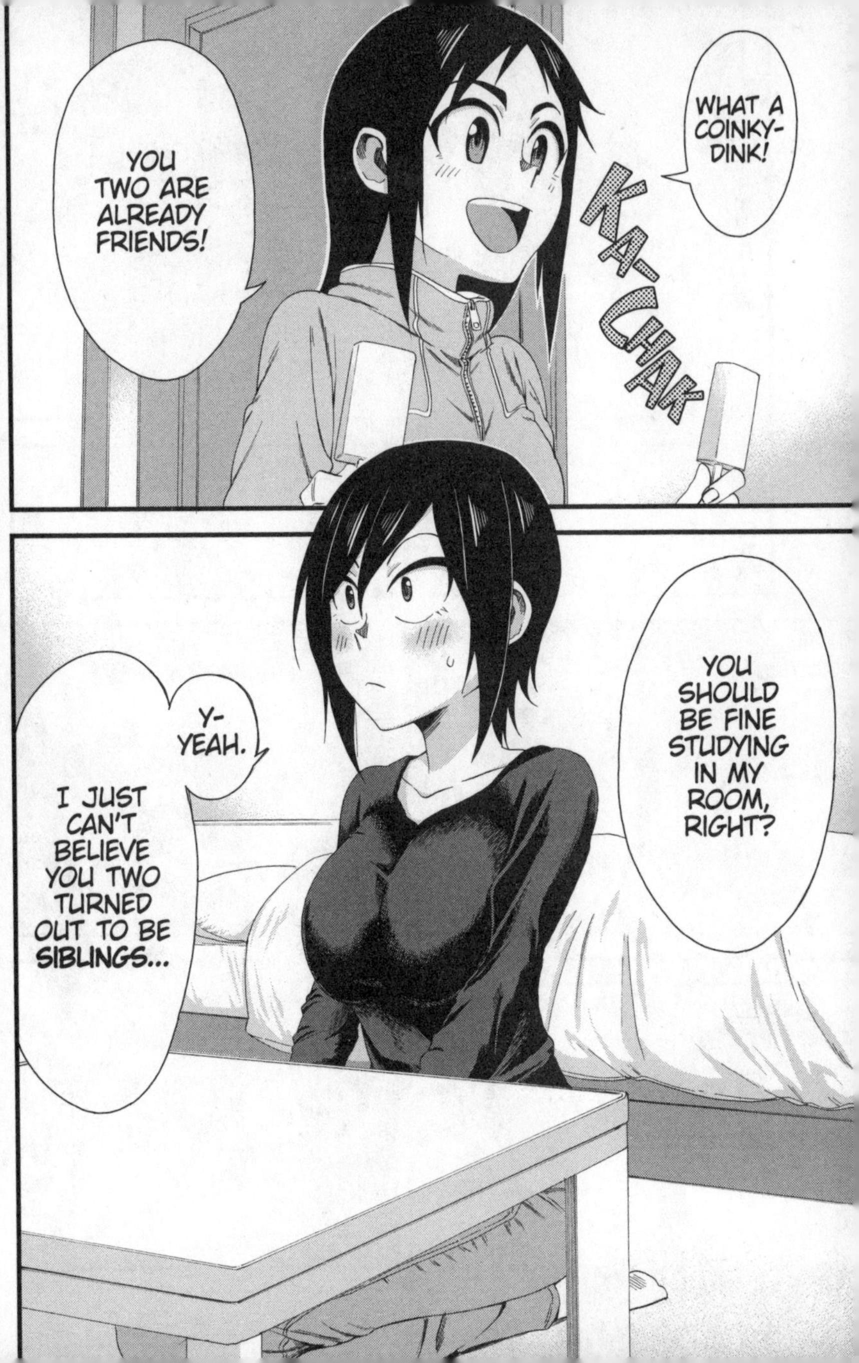
WHAT A COINKY-DINK!
KA-CHAK
YOU TWO ARE ALREADY FRIENDS!
YOU SHOULD BE FINE STUDYING IN MY ROOM, RIGHT?
Y-YEAH.
I JUST CAN'T BELIEVE YOU TWO TURNED OUT TO BE SIBLINGS...

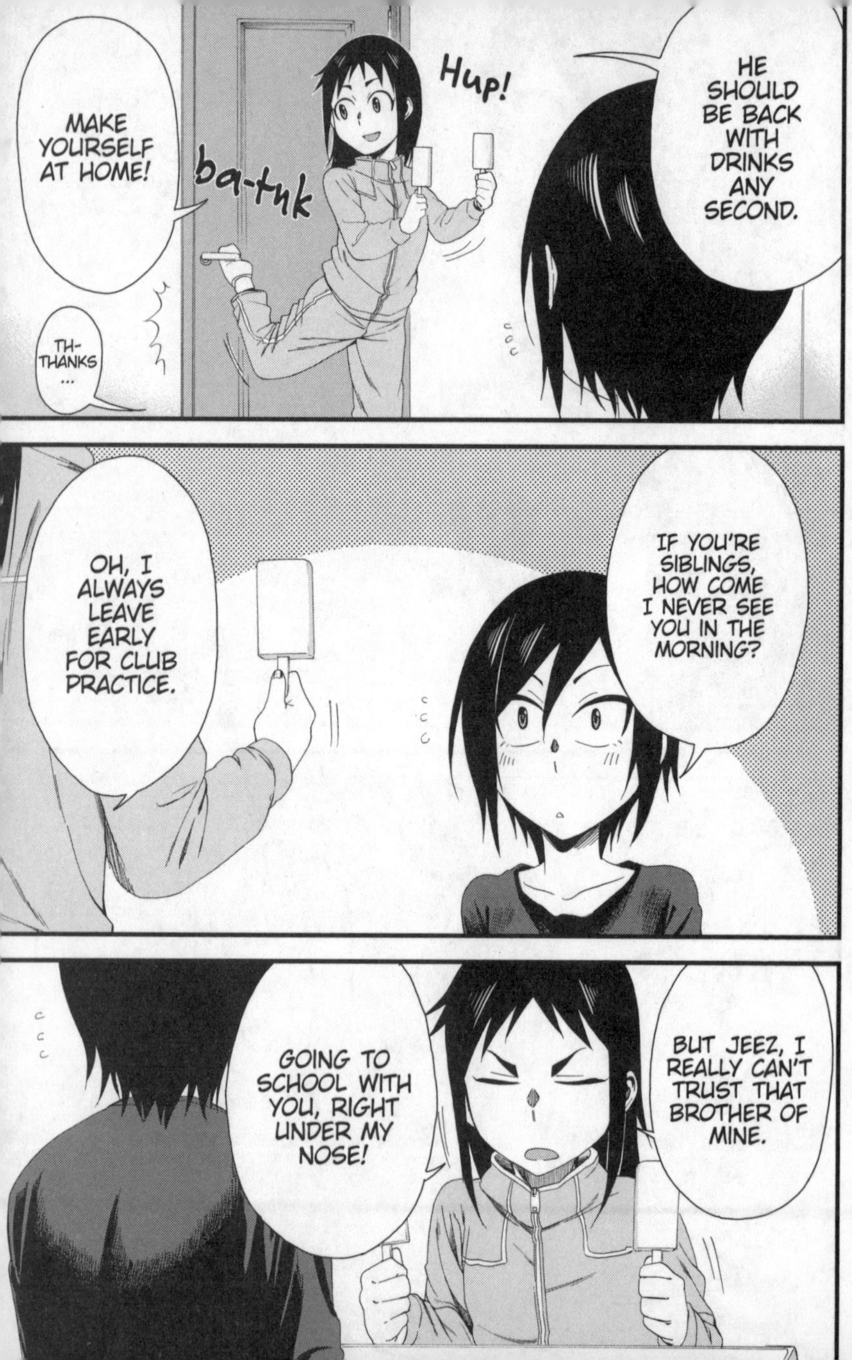
HE SHOULD BE BACK WITH DRINKS ANY SECOND.
Hup!
ba-tnk
MAKE YOURSELF AT HOME!
TH- THANKS ...
IF YOU'RE SIBLINGS, HOW COME I NEVER SEE YOU IN THE MORNING?
OH, I ALWAYS LEAVE EARLY FOR CLUB PRACTICE.
BUT JEEZ, I REALLY CAN'T TRUST THAT BROTHER OF MINE.
GOING TO SCHOOL WITH YOU, RIGHT UNDER MY NOSE!

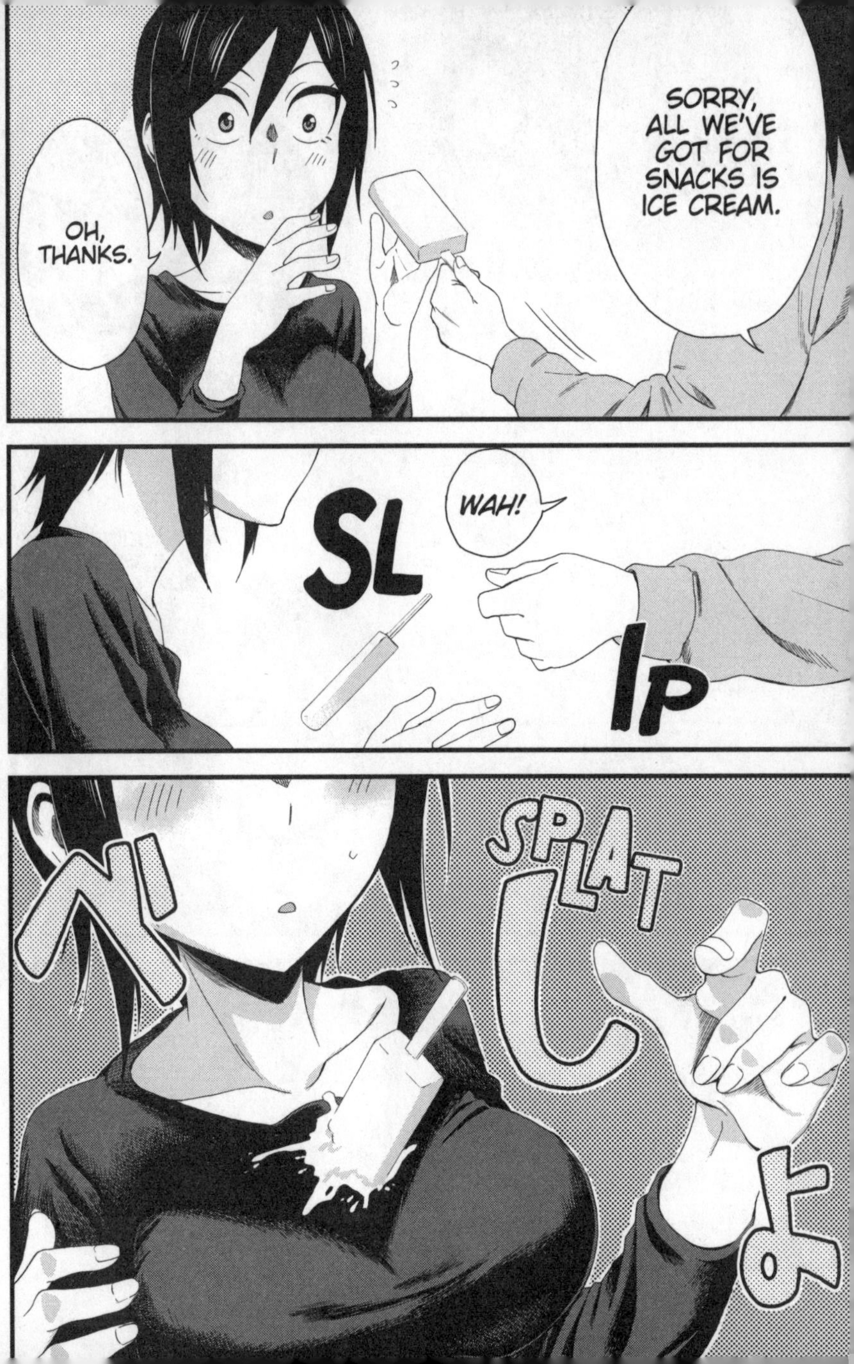
SORRY, ALL WE'VE GOT FOR SNACKS IS ICE CREAM.
OH, THANKS.
WAH!
SLIP
SPLAT

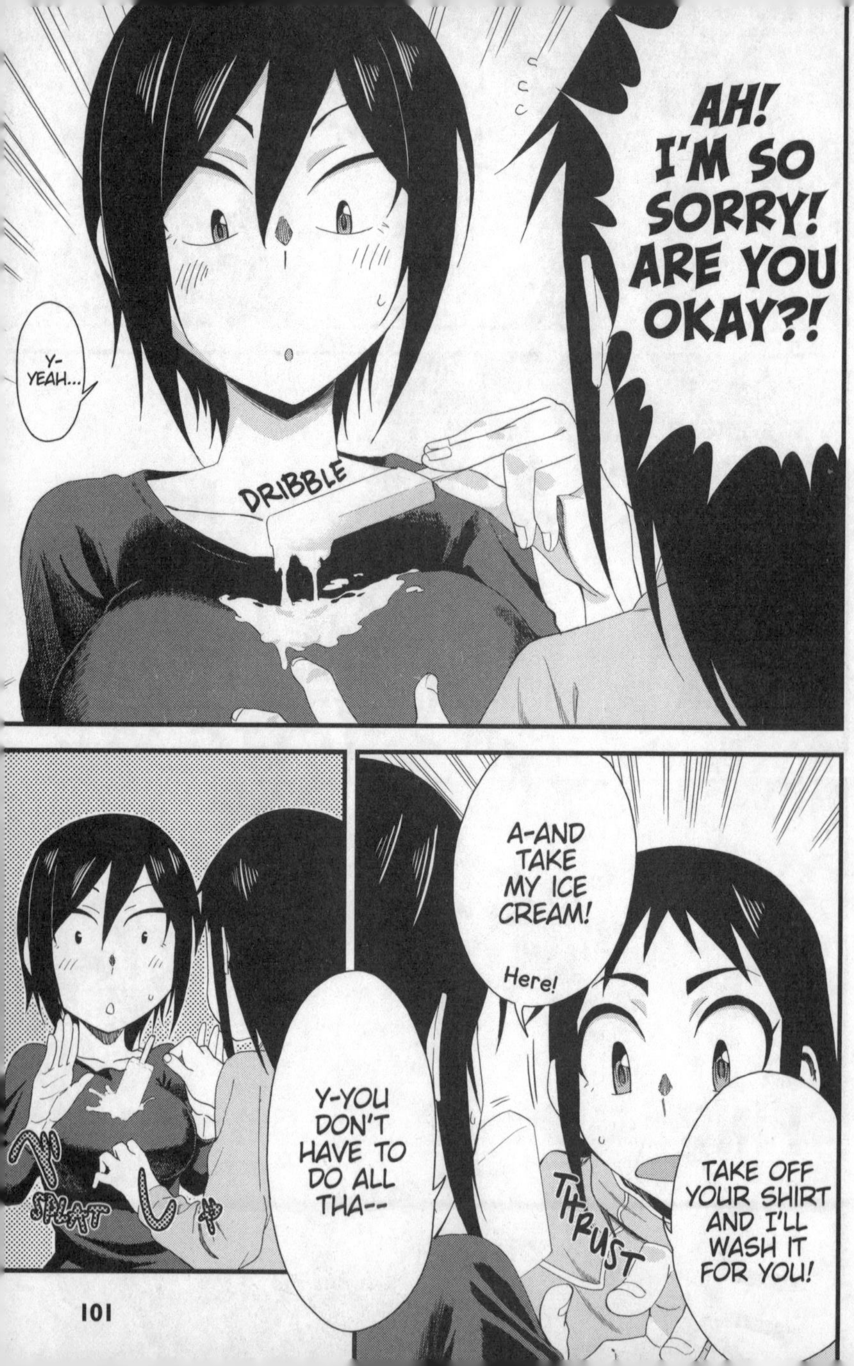
AH! I'M SO SORRY! ARE YOU OKAY?!
Y-YEAH...
DRIBBLE
A-AND TAKE MY ICE CREAM!
Here!
TAKE OFF YOUR SHIRT AND I'LL WASH IT FOR YOU!
THRUST
Y-YOU DON'T HAVE TO DO ALL THA--
SPLAT

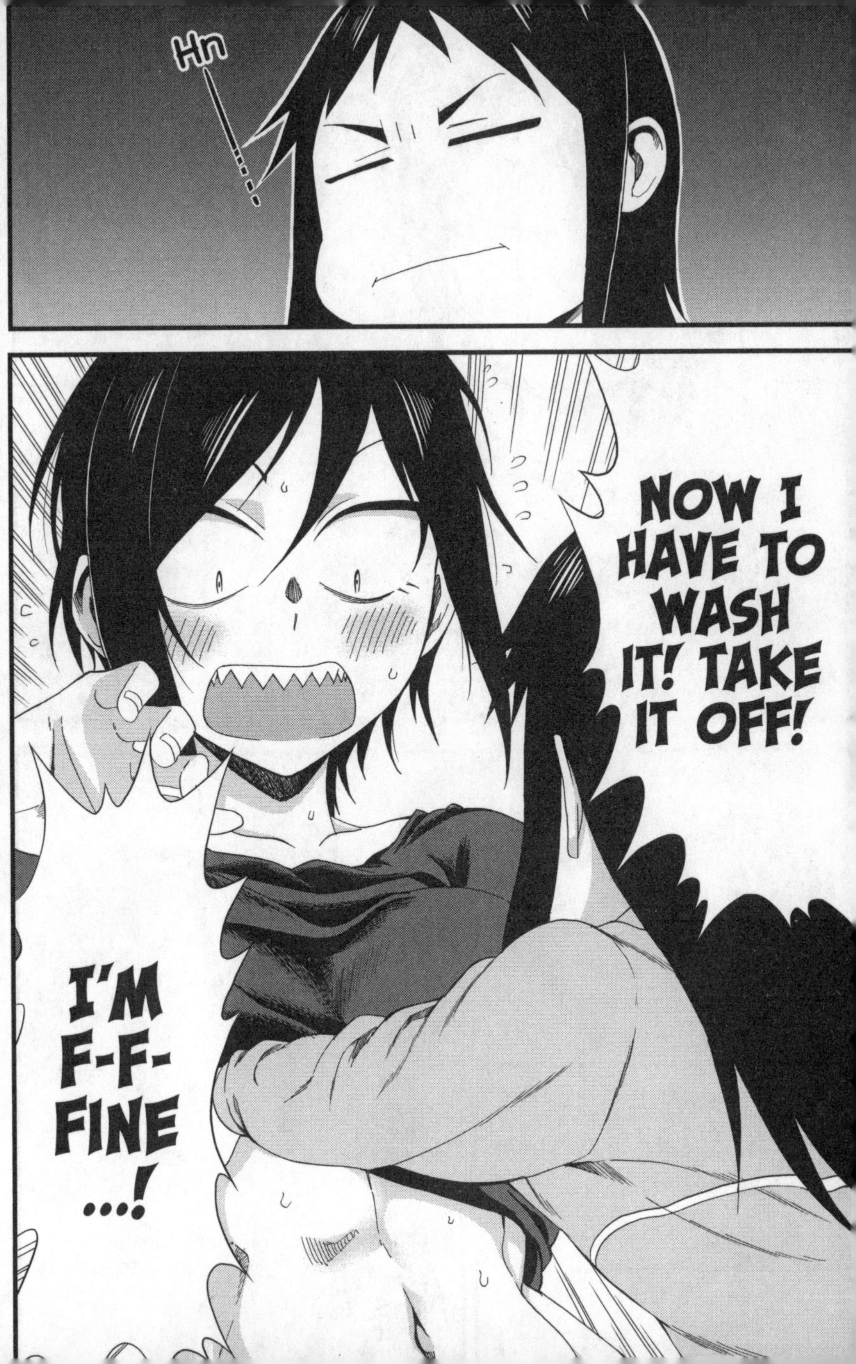
Hn
NOW I HAVE TO WASH IT! TAKE IT OFF!
I'M F-F-FINE ...!

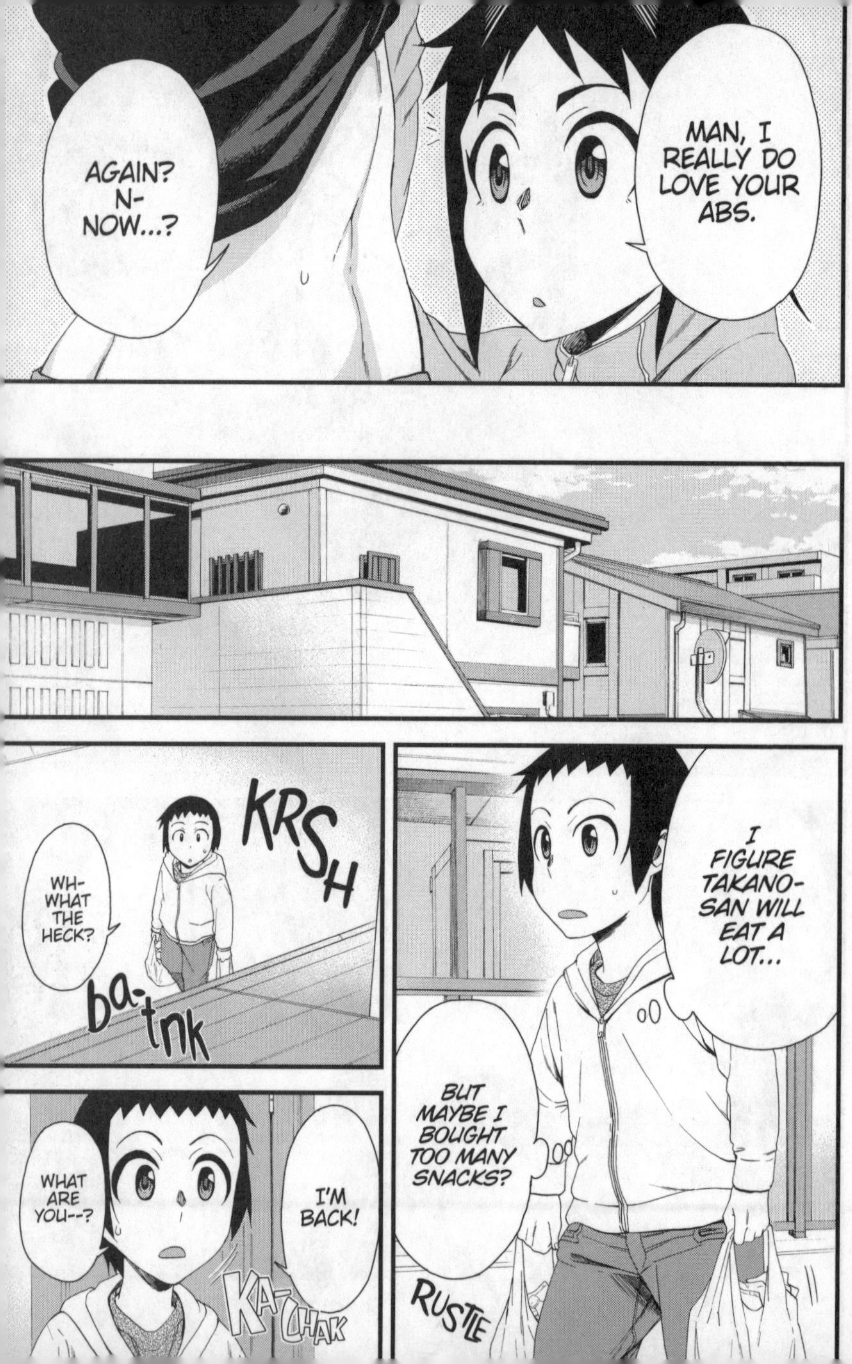
MAN, I REALLY DO LOVE YOUR ABS.
AGAIN? N-NOW...?
I FIGURE TAKANO-SAN WILL EAT A LOT...
BUT MAYBE I BOUGHT TOO MANY SNACKS?
RUSTLE
KRSH
WH-WHAT THE HECK?
ba-tnk
I'M BACK!
KA-CHAK
WHAT ARE YOU--?

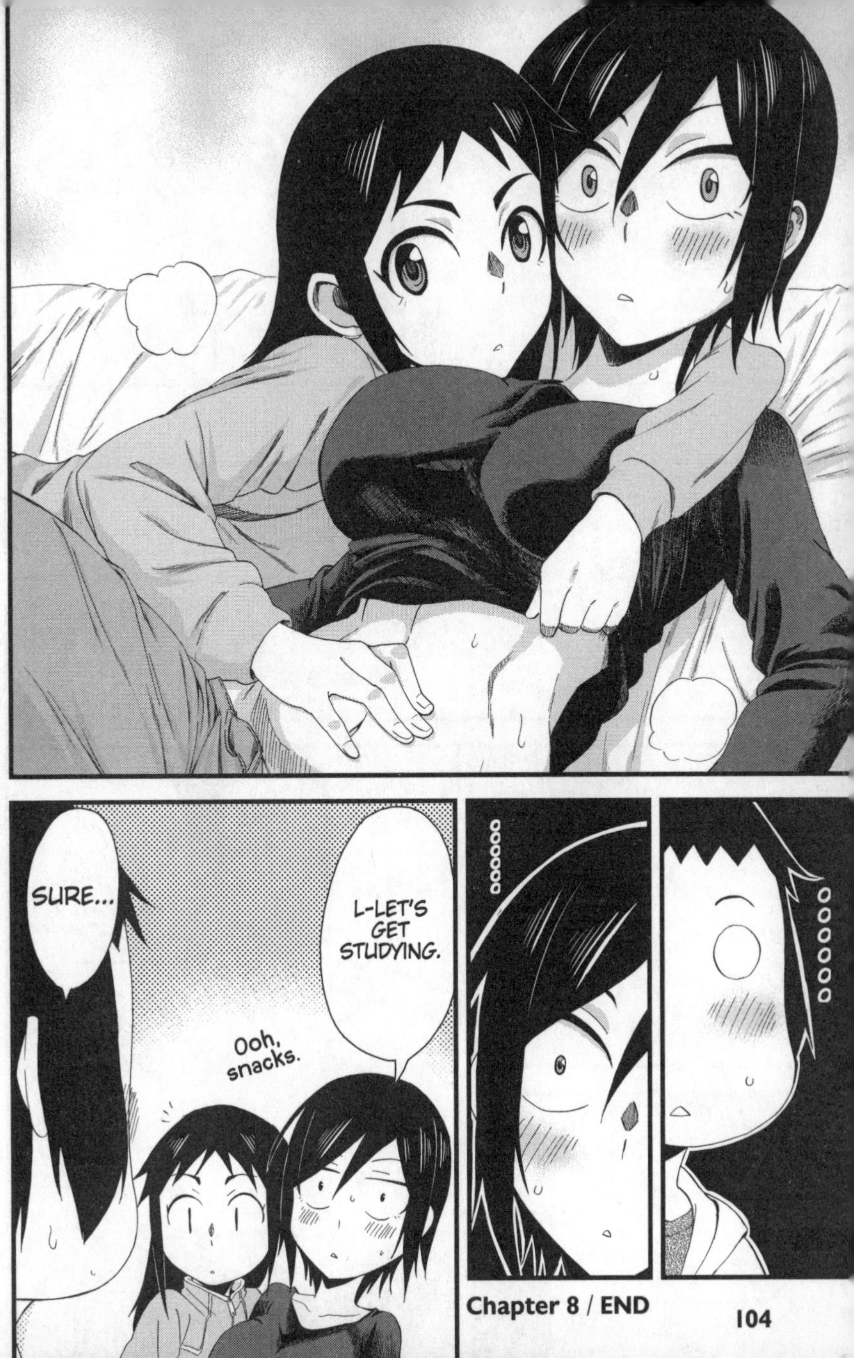
OOOOOOO
OOOOOO
L-LET'S GET STUDYING.
SURE...
Ooh, snacks.

Chapter 8 / END

Chapter 9

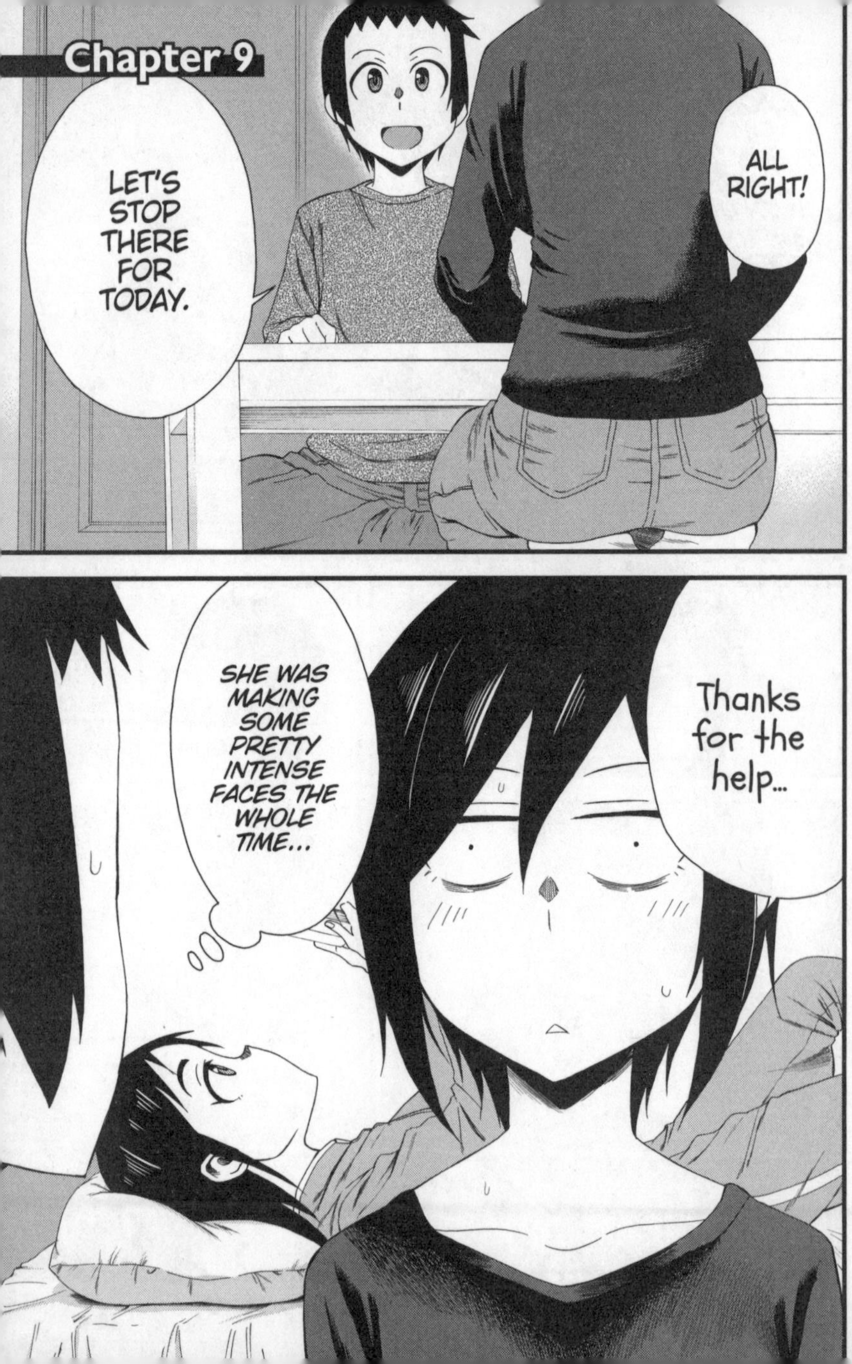
ALL RIGHT!
LET'S STOP THERE FOR TODAY.
Thanks for the help...
SHE WAS MAKING SOME PRETTY INTENSE FACES THE WHOLE TIME...

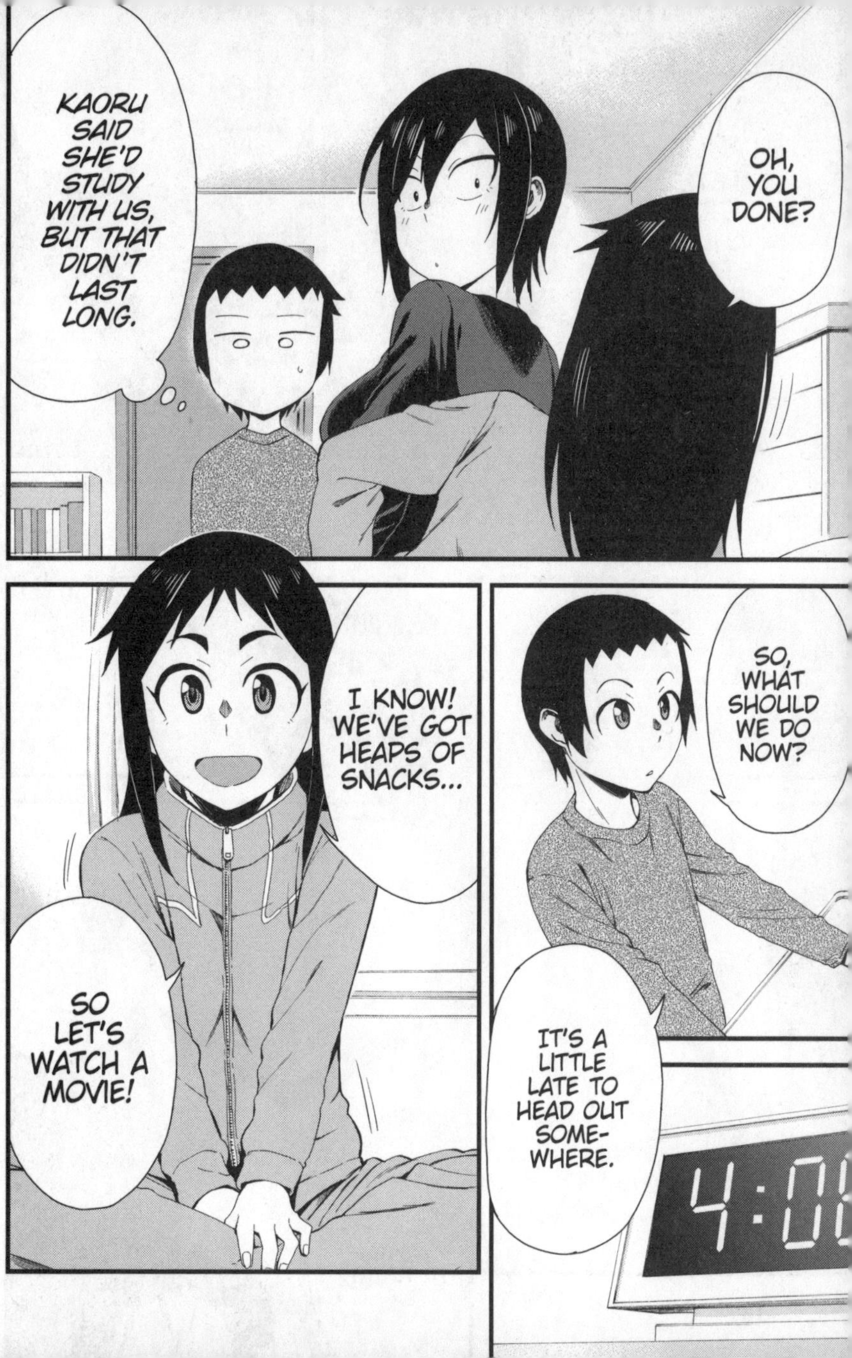
OH, YOU DONE?
KAORU SAID SHE'D STUDY WITH US, BUT THAT DIDN'T LAST LONG.
SO, WHAT SHOULD WE DO NOW?
IT'S A LITTLE LATE TO HEAD OUT SOME-WHERE.
I KNOW! WE'VE GOT HEAPS OF SNACKS...
SO LET'S WATCH A MOVIE!

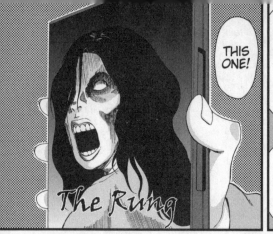

THIS ONE!

The Ring

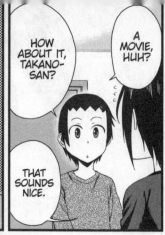

HOW ABOUT IT, TAKANO-SAN?

A MOVIE, HUH?

THAT SOUNDS NICE.

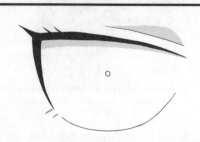

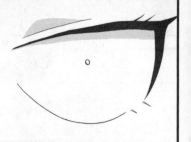

U-UM...

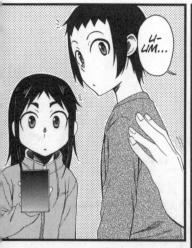

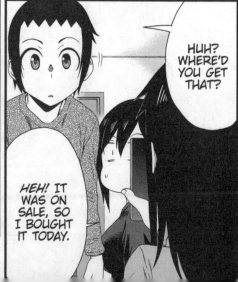

HUH? WHERE'D YOU GET THAT?

HEH! IT WAS ON SALE, SO I BOUGHT IT TODAY.

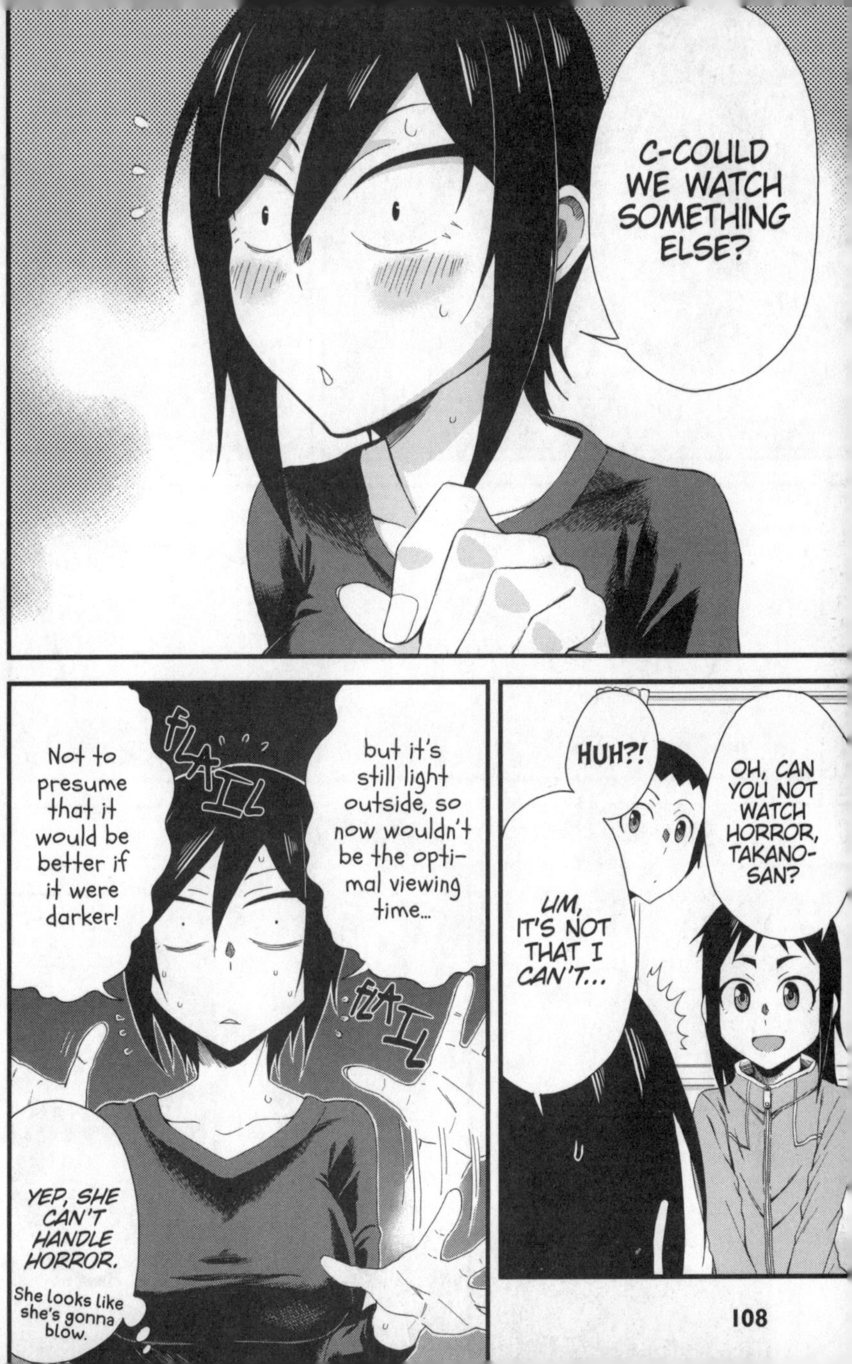
C-COULD WE WATCH SOMETHING ELSE?
OH, CAN YOU NOT WATCH HORROR, TAKANO-SAN?
HUH?!
UM, IT'S NOT THAT I CAN'T...
but it's still light outside, so now wouldn't be the optimal viewing time...
Not to presume that it would be better if it were darker!
FLAIL
FLAIL
YEP, SHE CAN'T HANDLE HORROR.
She looks like she's gonna blow.

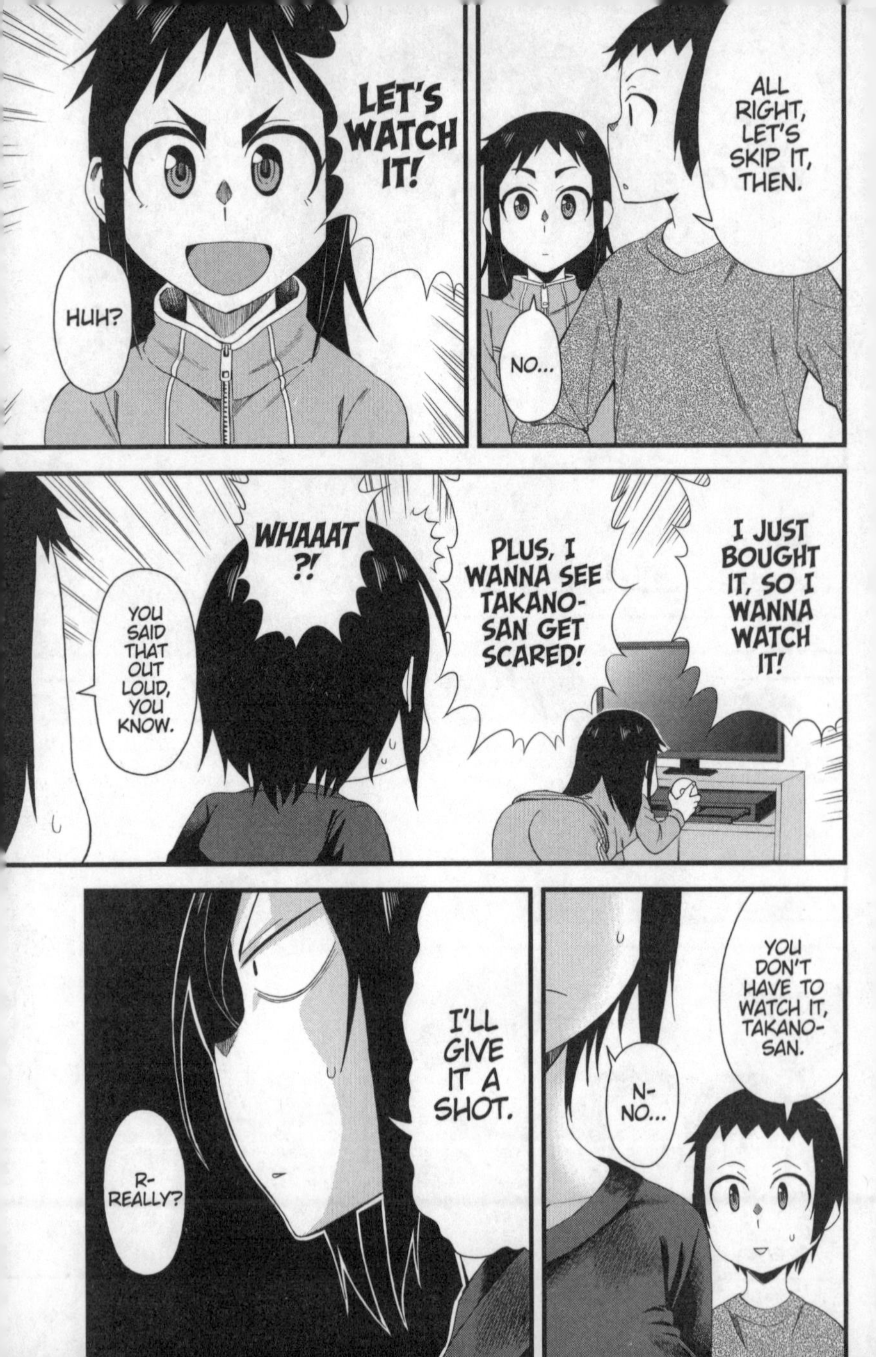
ALL RIGHT, LET'S SKIP IT, THEN.
NO...
LET'S WATCH IT!
HUH?
I JUST BOUGHT IT, SO I WANNA WATCH IT!
PLUS, I WANNA SEE TAKANO-SAN GET SCARED!
WHAAAT?!
YOU SAID THAT OUT LOUD, YOU KNOW.
YOU DON'T HAVE TO WATCH IT, TAKANO-SAN.
N-NO...
I'LL GIVE IT A SHOT.
R-REALLY?

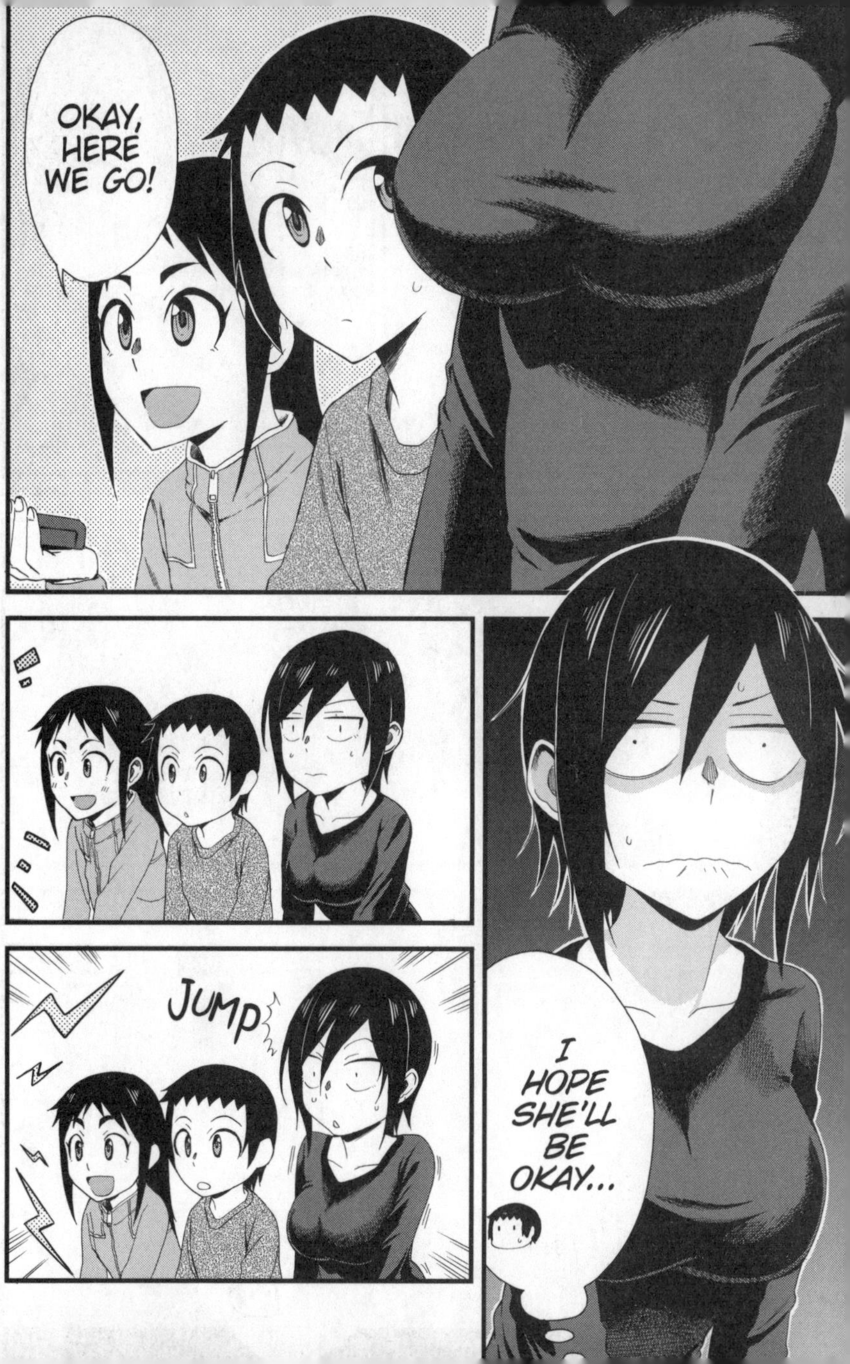
OKAY, HERE WE GO!
I HOPE SHE'LL BE OKAY...
JUMP

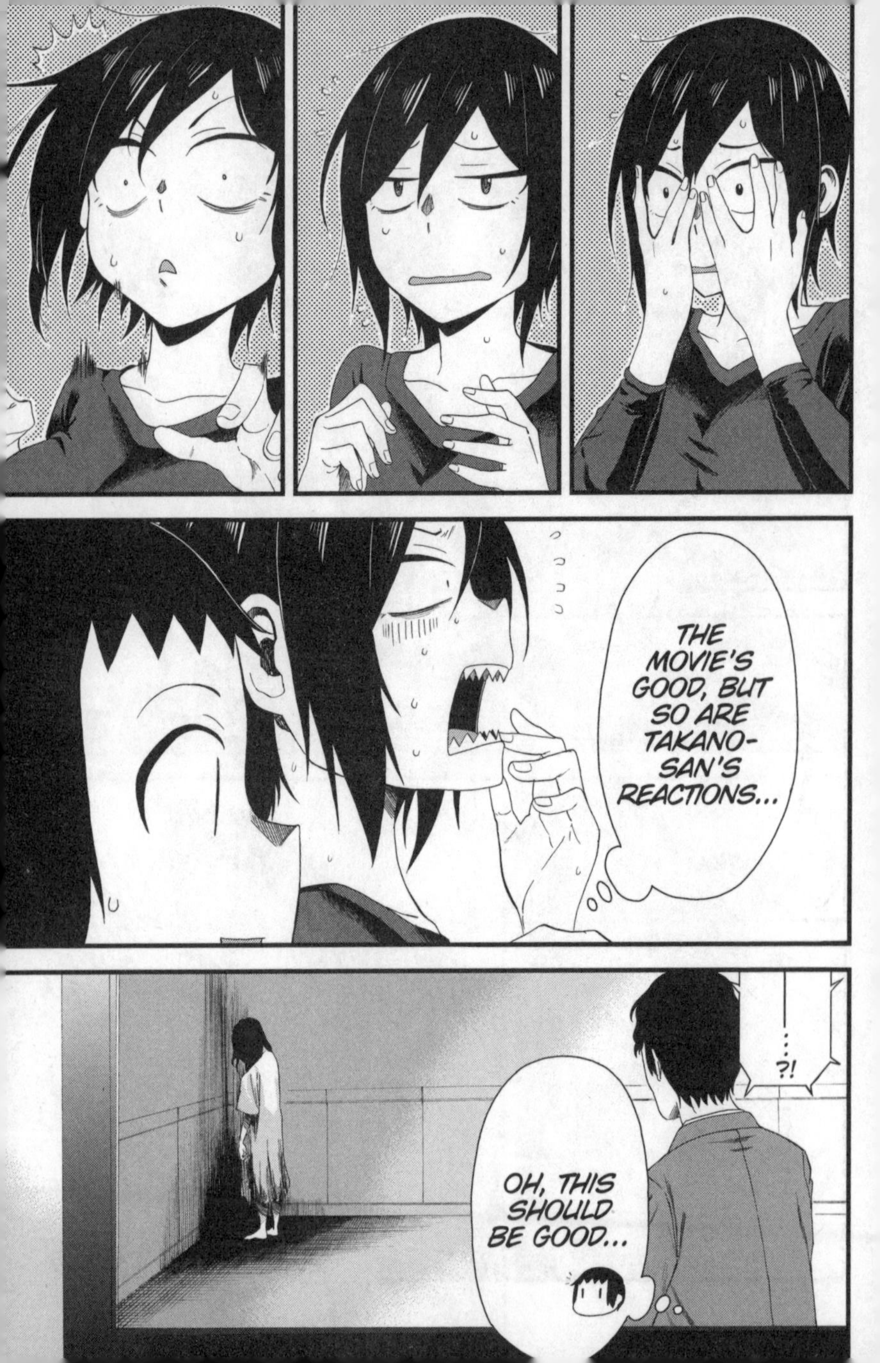
THE MOVIE'S GOOD, BUT SO ARE TAKANO-SAN'S REACTIONS...
...?!
OH, THIS SHOULD BE GOOD...

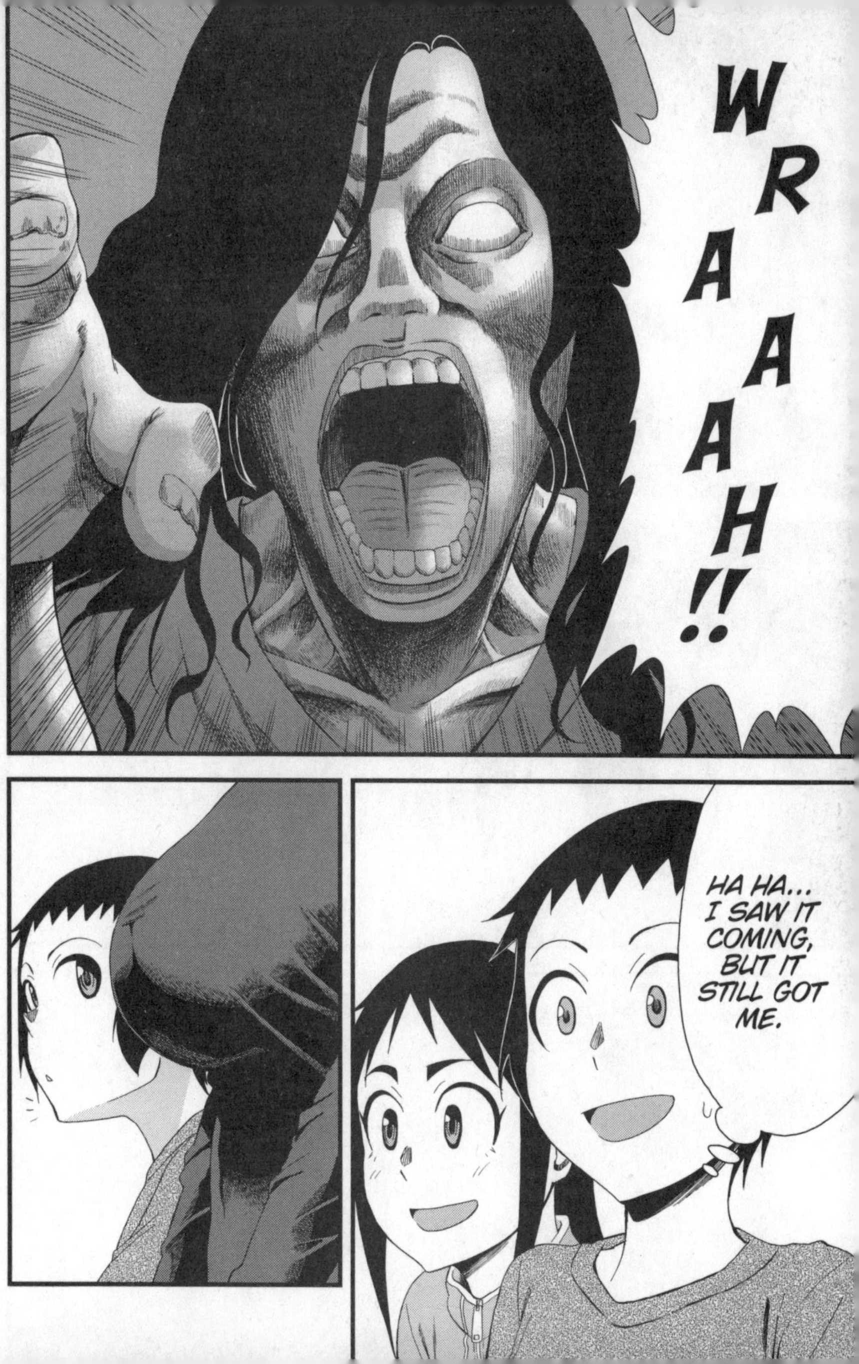
WRAAAH!!
HA HA... I SAW IT COMING, BUT IT STILL GOT ME.

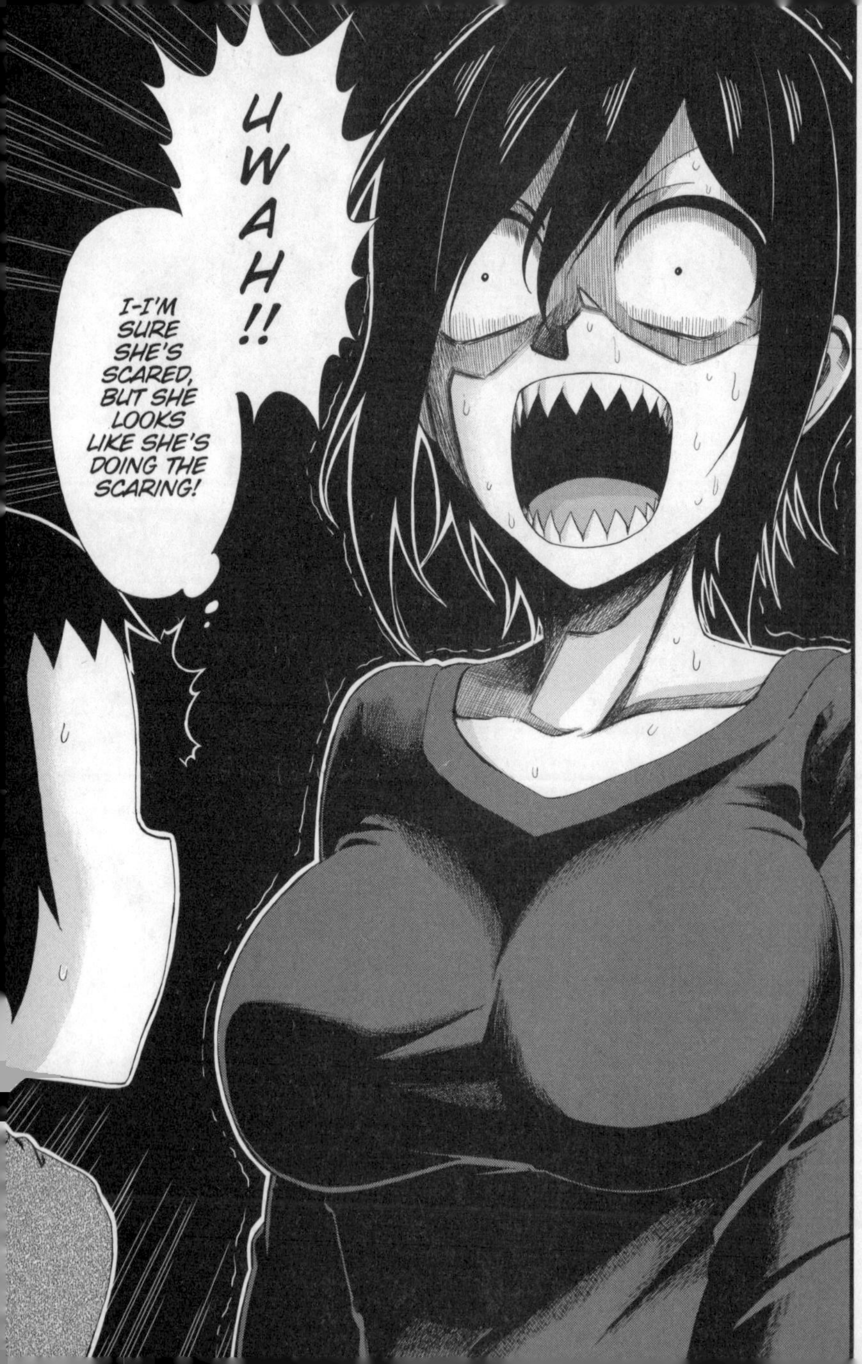
UWAH!!
I-I'M SURE SHE'S SCARED, BUT SHE LOOKS LIKE SHE'S DOING THE SCARING!

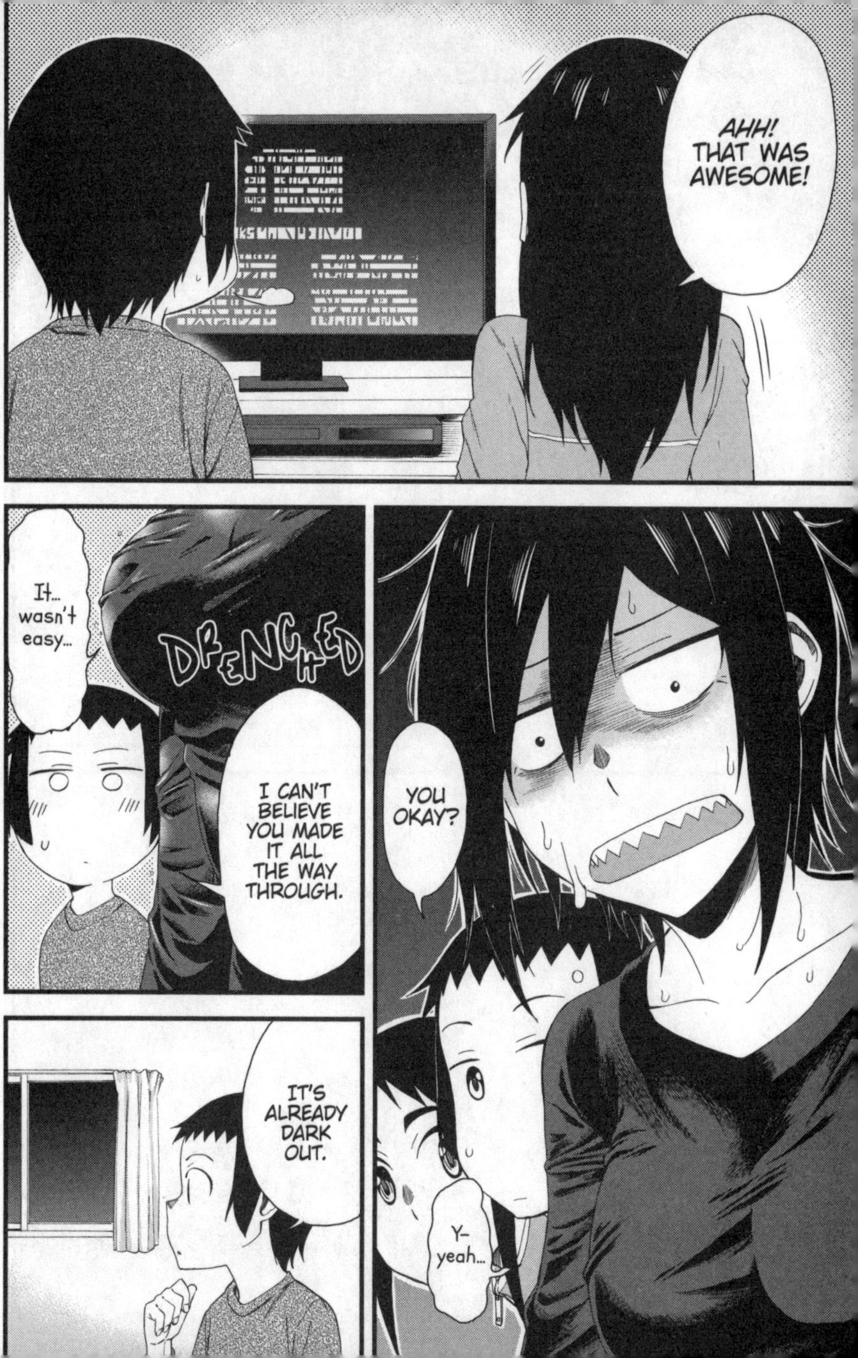
AHH! THAT WAS AWESOME!
YOU OKAY?
Y-yeah...
I CAN'T BELIEVE YOU MADE IT ALL THE WAY THROUGH.
DRENCHED
It... wasn't easy...
IT'S ALREADY DARK OUT.

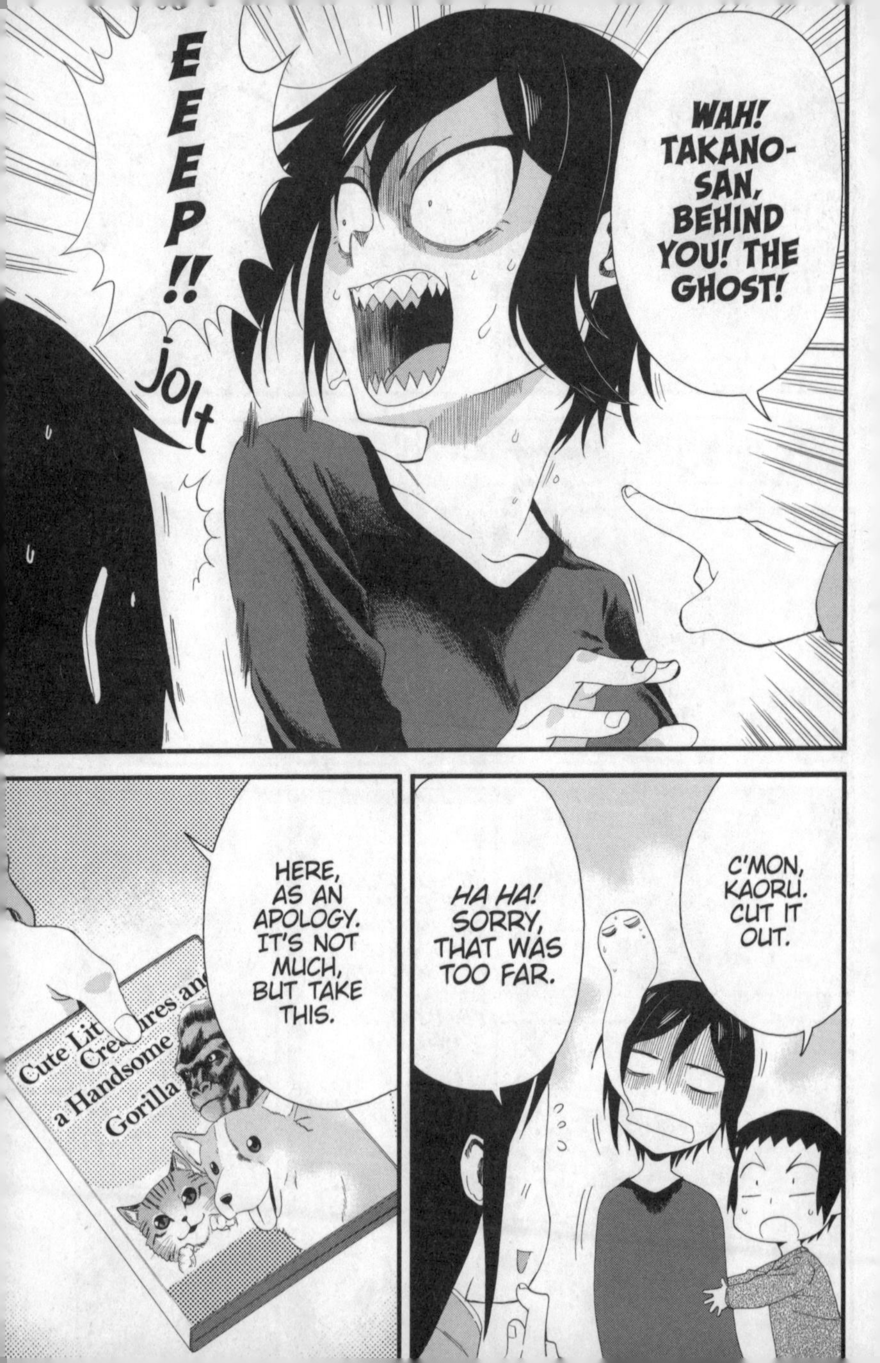
WAH! TAKANO-SAN, BEHIND YOU! THE GHOST!
EEEP!!
jolt
C'MON, KAORU. CUT IT OUT.
HA HA! SORRY, THAT WAS TOO FAR.
HERE, AS AN APOLOGY. IT'S NOT MUCH, BUT TAKE THIS.
a Handsome Gorilla

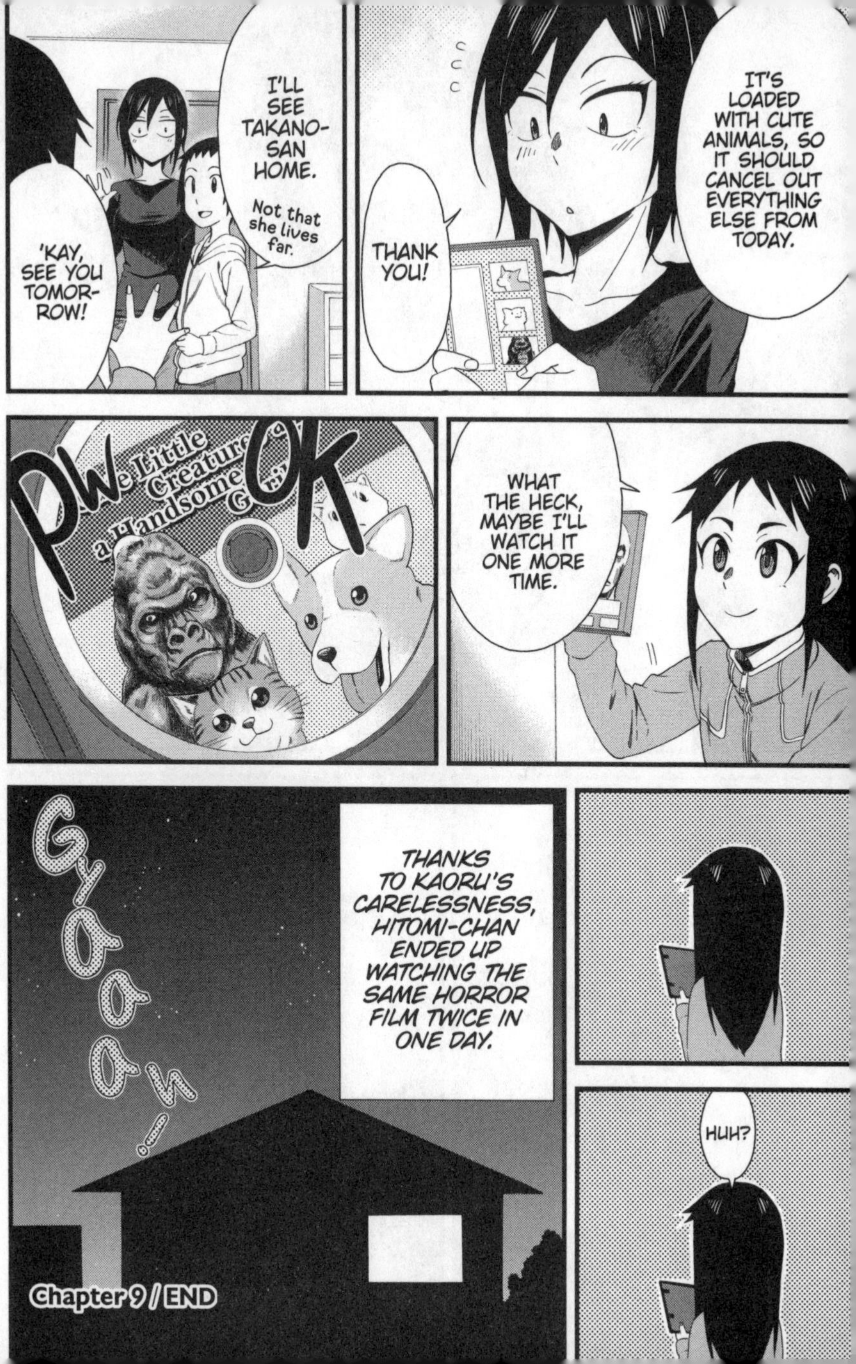
IT'S LOADED WITH CUTE ANIMALS, SO IT SHOULD CANCEL OUT EVERYTHING ELSE FROM TODAY.
THANK YOU!
I'LL SEE TAKANO-SAN HOME.
Not that she lives far.
'KAY, SEE YOU TOMORROW!
WHAT THE HECK, MAYBE I'LL WATCH IT ONE MORE TIME.
PWOK
HUH?
THANKS TO KAORU'S CARELESSNESS, HITOMI-CHAN ENDED UP WATCHING THE SAME HORROR FILM TWICE IN ONE DAY.
Gyaaaan...!
Chapter 9 / END

Hitomi-chan is Shy With Strangers

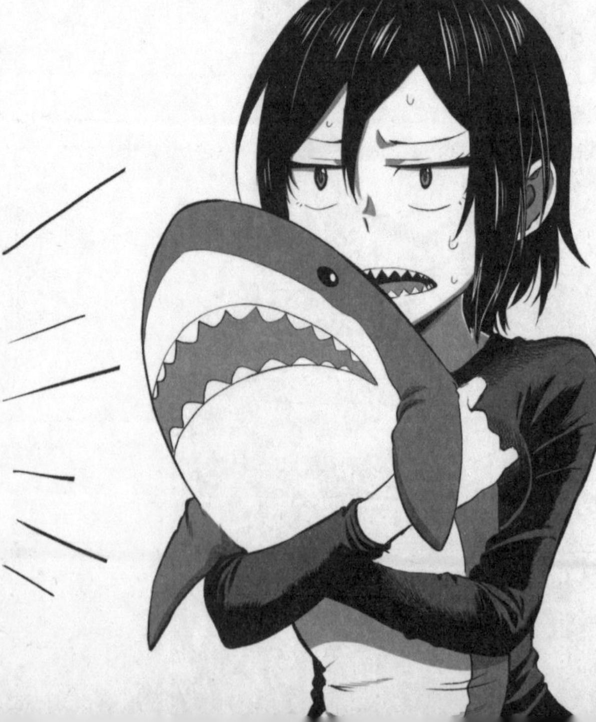

Hitomi-chan is Shy with Strangers

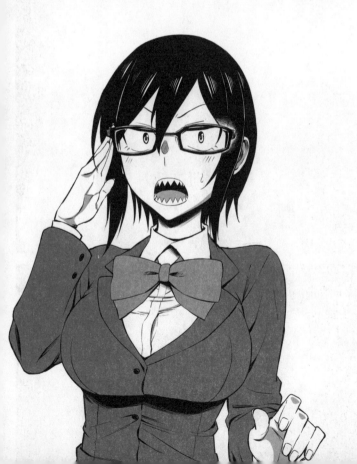

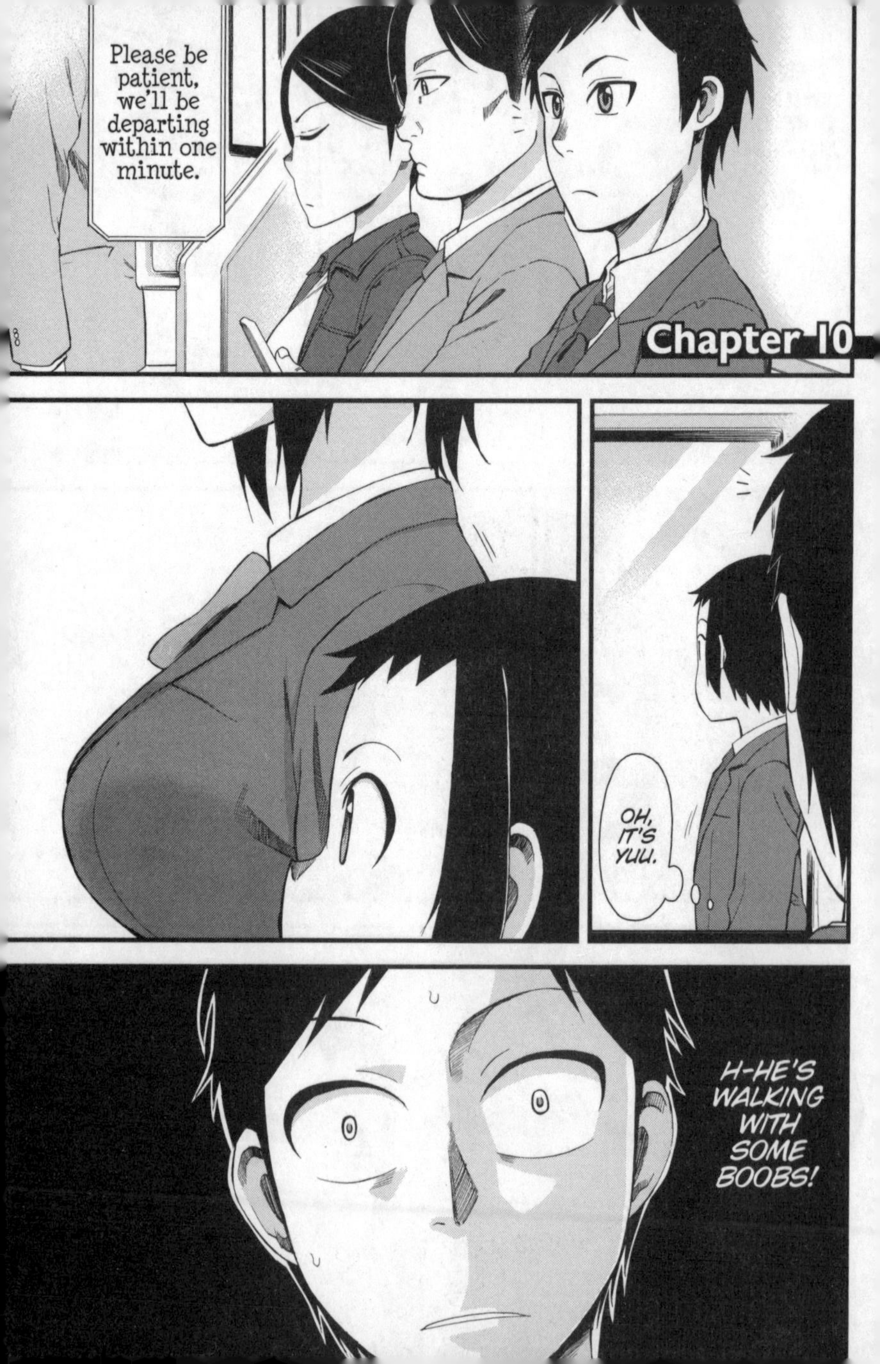
Please be patient, we'll be departing within one minute.
Chapter 10
OH, IT'S YUU.
H-HE'S WALKING WITH SOME BOOBS!

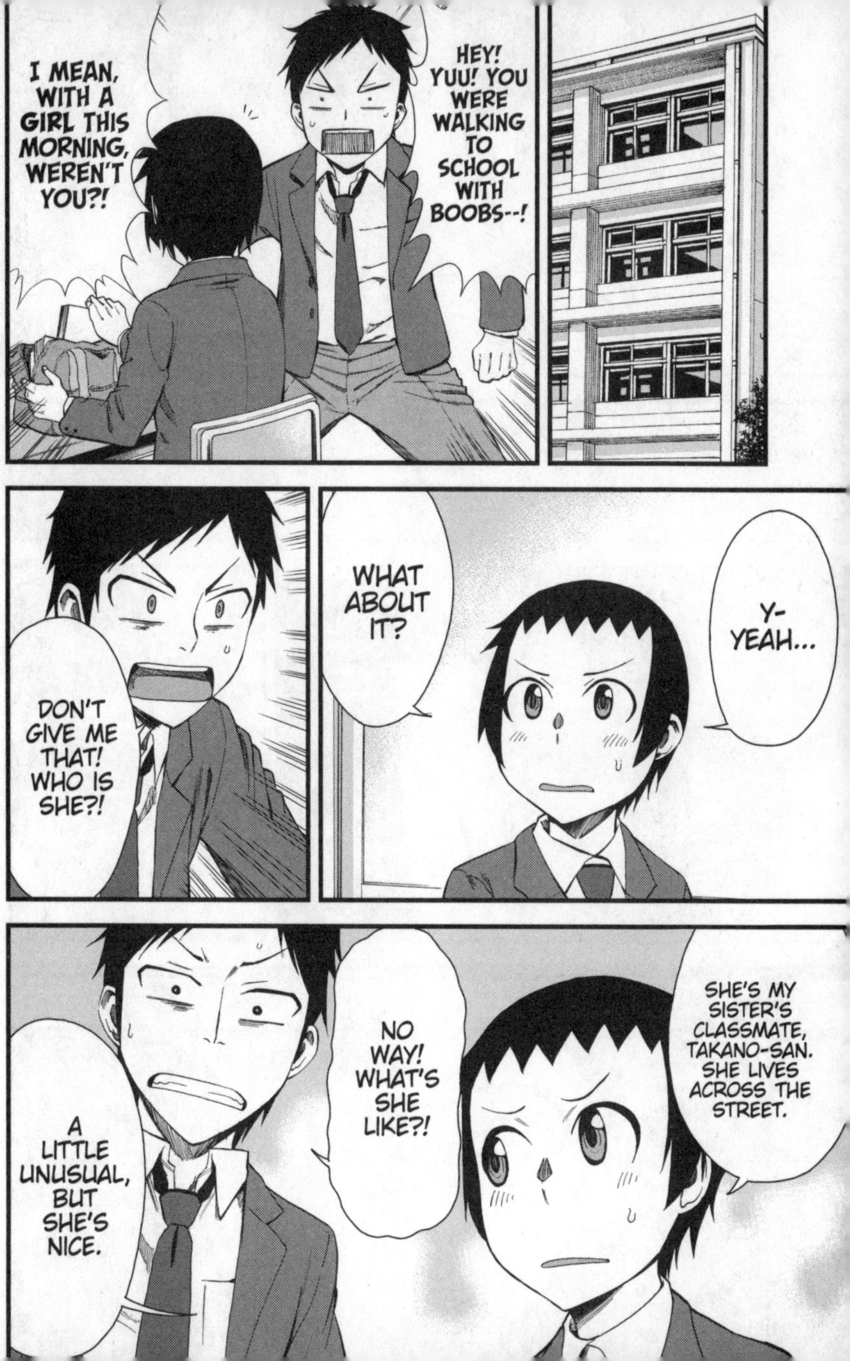
HEY! YUU! YOU WERE WALKING TO SCHOOL WITH BOOBS--!
I MEAN, WITH A GIRL THIS MORNING, WEREN'T YOU?!
Y-YEAH...
WHAT ABOUT IT?
DON'T GIVE ME THAT! WHO IS SHE?!
SHE'S MY SISTER'S CLASSMATE, TAKANO-SAN. SHE LIVES ACROSS THE STREET.
NO WAY! WHAT'S SHE LIKE?!
A LITTLE UNUSUAL, BUT SHE'S NICE.

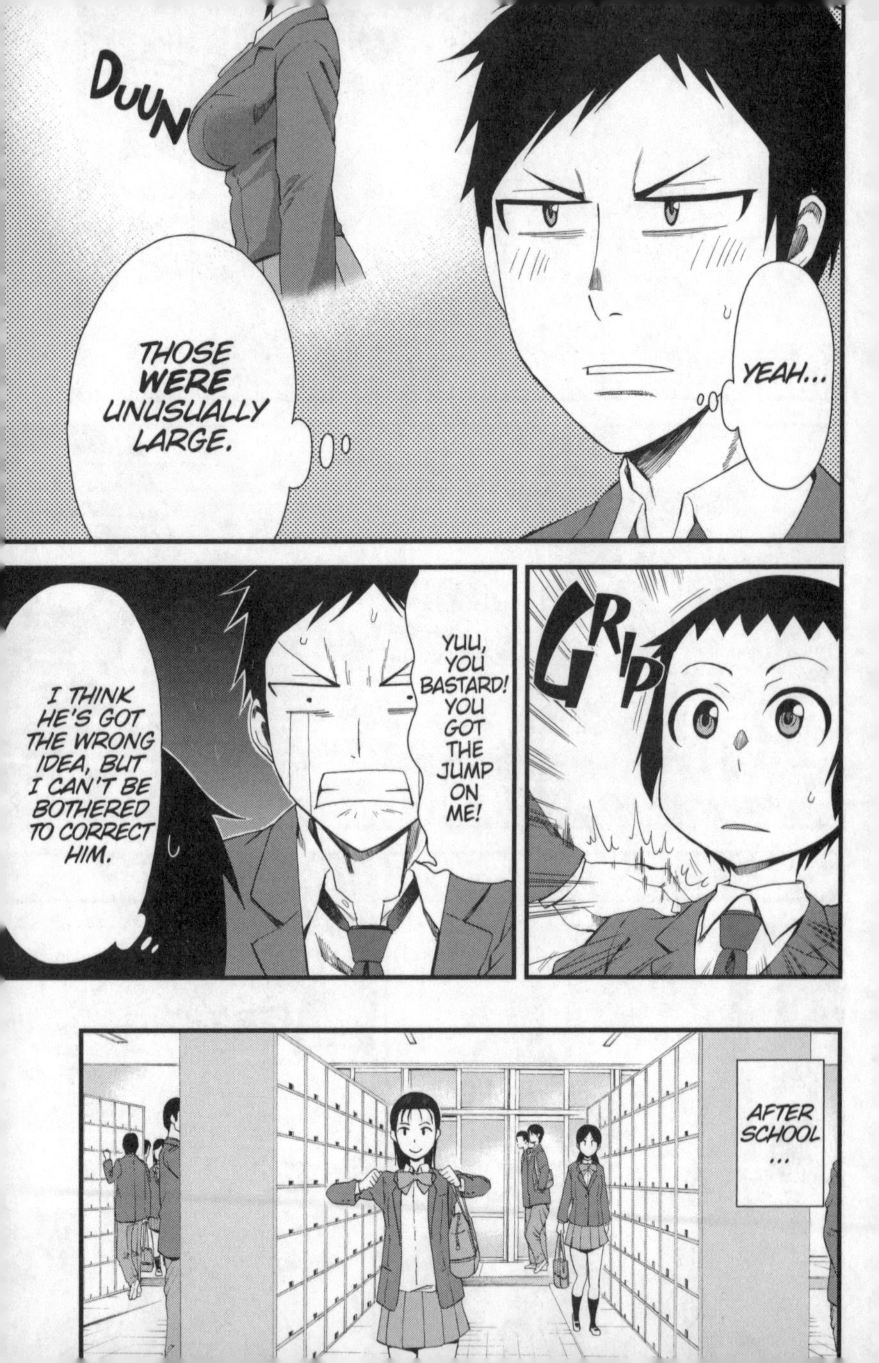
DUUN
YEAH...
THOSE WERE UNUSUALLY LARGE.
GRIP
YUU, YOU BASTARD! YOU GOT THE JUMP ON ME!
I THINK HE'S GOT THE WRONG IDEA, BUT I CAN'T BE BOTHERED TO CORRECT HIM.
AFTER SCHOOL ...

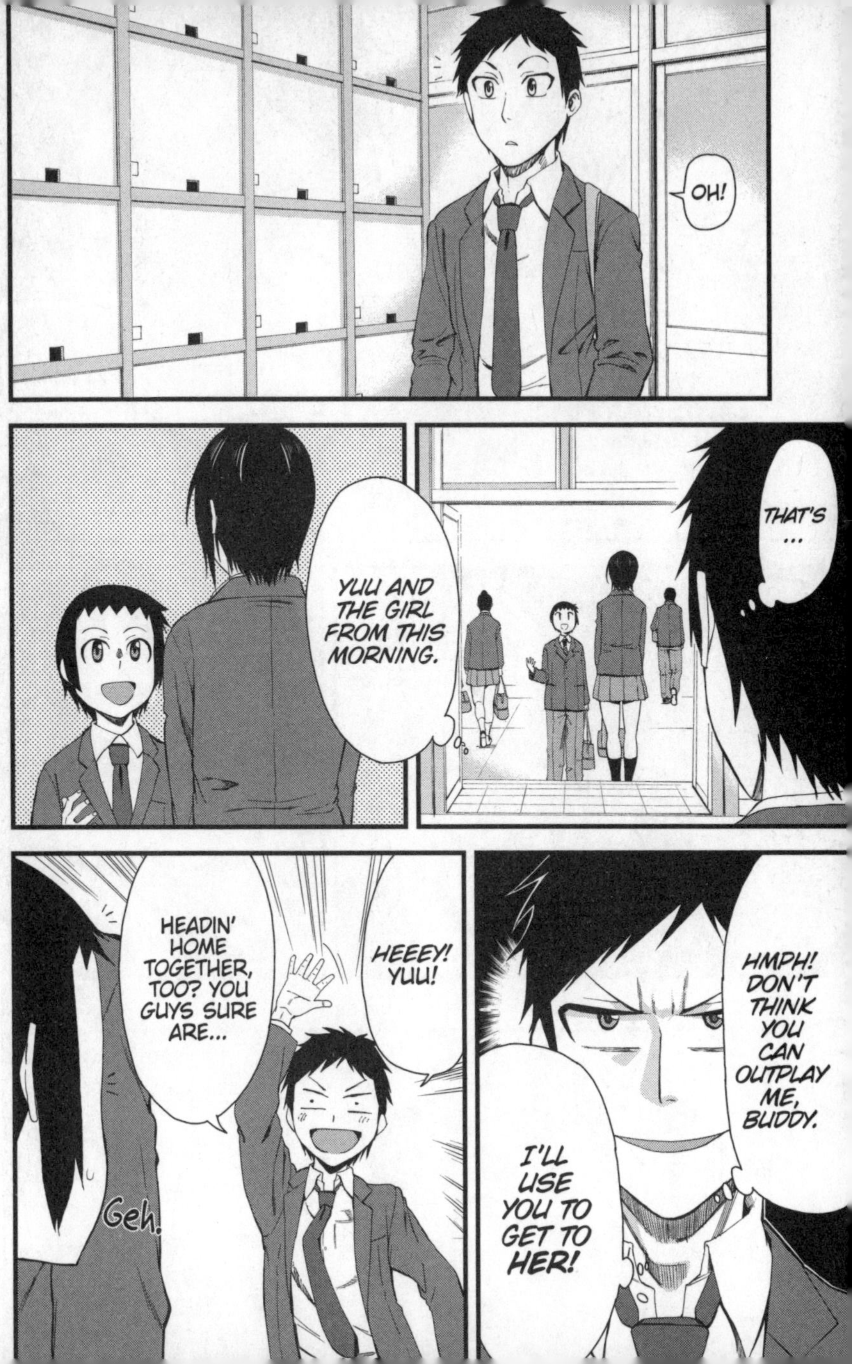
OH!
THAT'S ...
YUU AND THE GIRL FROM THIS MORNING.
HMPH! DON'T THINK YOU CAN OUTPLAY ME, BUDDY.
I'LL USE YOU TO GET TO HER!
HEEEY! YUU!
HEADIN' HOME TOGETHER, TOO? YOU GUYS SURE ARE...
Geh.

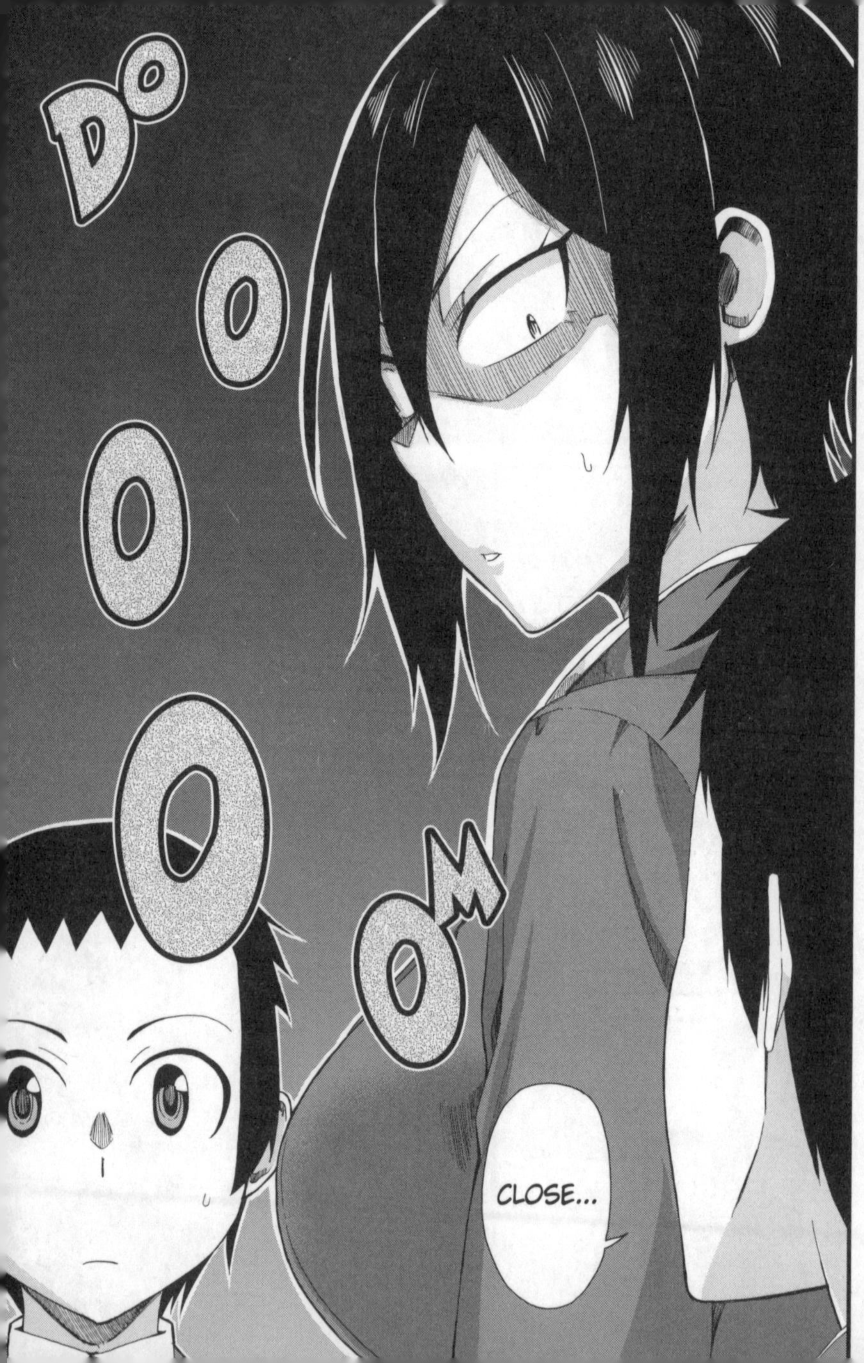
DOOOOOM
CLOSE...

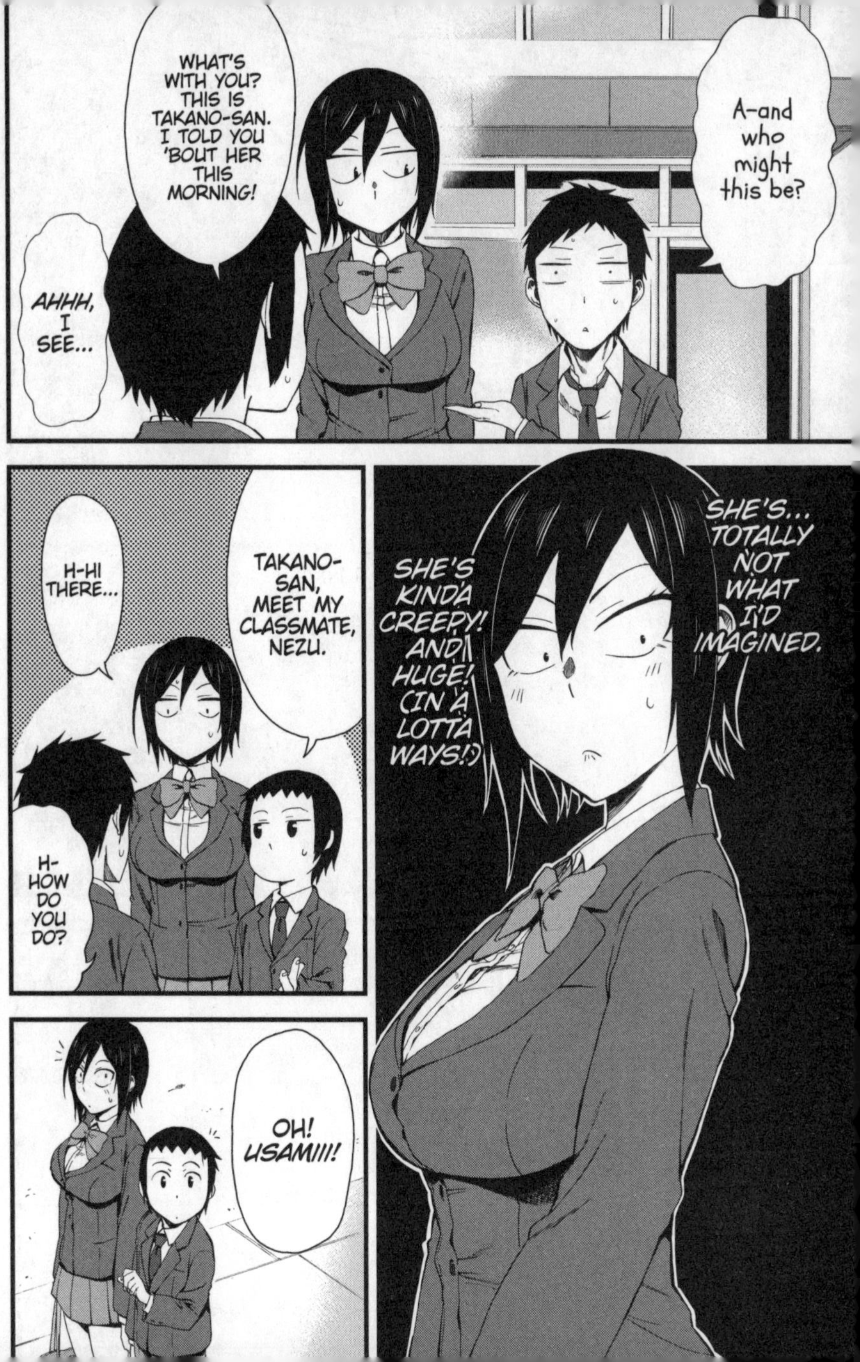
A-and who might this be?
WHAT'S WITH YOU? THIS IS TAKANO-SAN. I TOLD YOU 'BOUT HER THIS MORNING!
AHHH, I SEE...
SHE'S... TOTALLY NOT WHAT I'D IMAGINED.
SHE'S KINDA CREEPY! AND HUGE! (IN A LOTTA WAYS!)
TAKANO-SAN, MEET MY CLASSMATE, NEZU.
H-HI THERE...
H-HOW DO YOU DO?
OH! USAMIII!

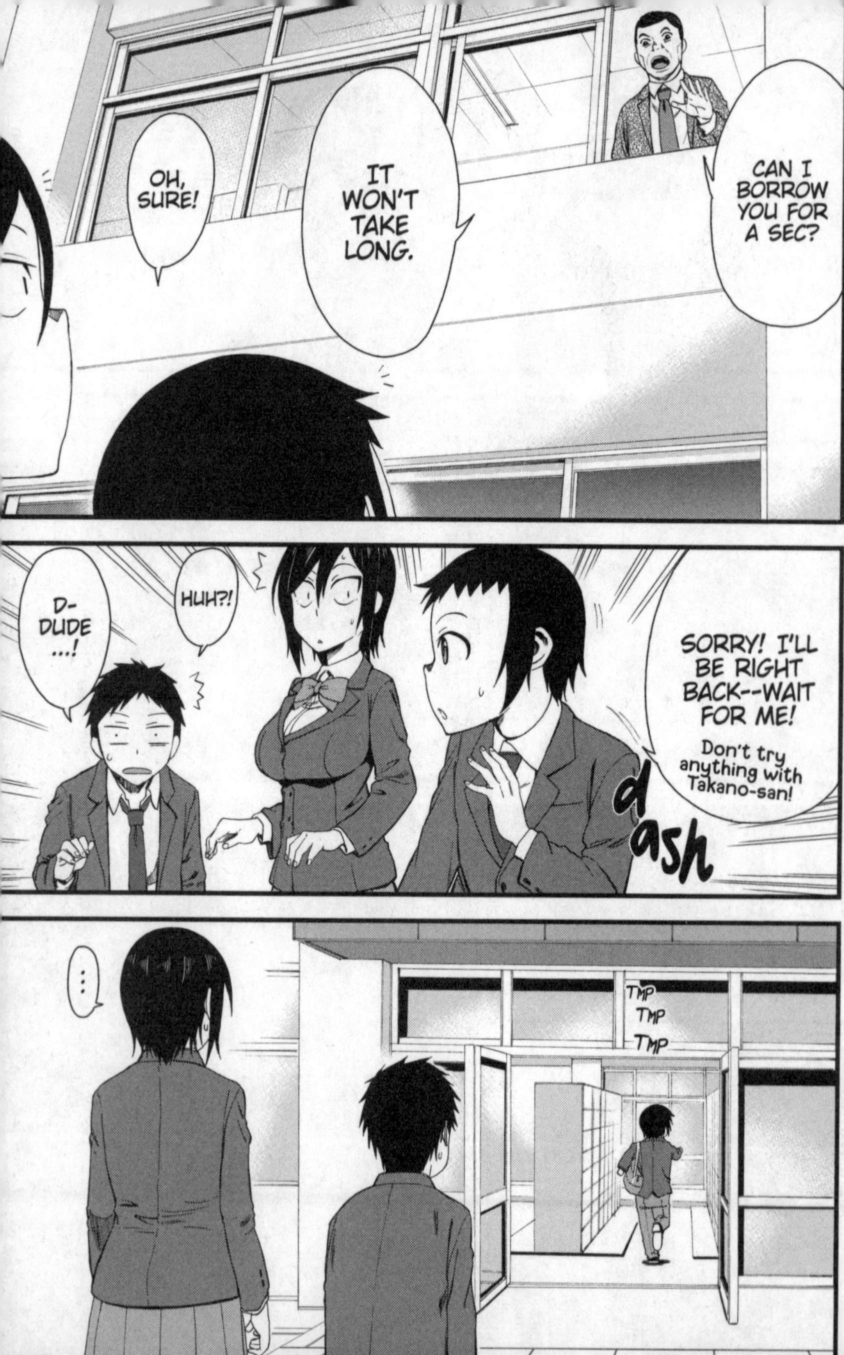
CAN I BORROW YOU FOR A SEC?
IT WON'T TAKE LONG.
OH, SURE!
SORRY! I'LL BE RIGHT BACK--WAIT FOR ME!
Don't try anything with Takano-san!
dash
HUH?!
D-DUDE ...!
TMP
TMP
TMP
...

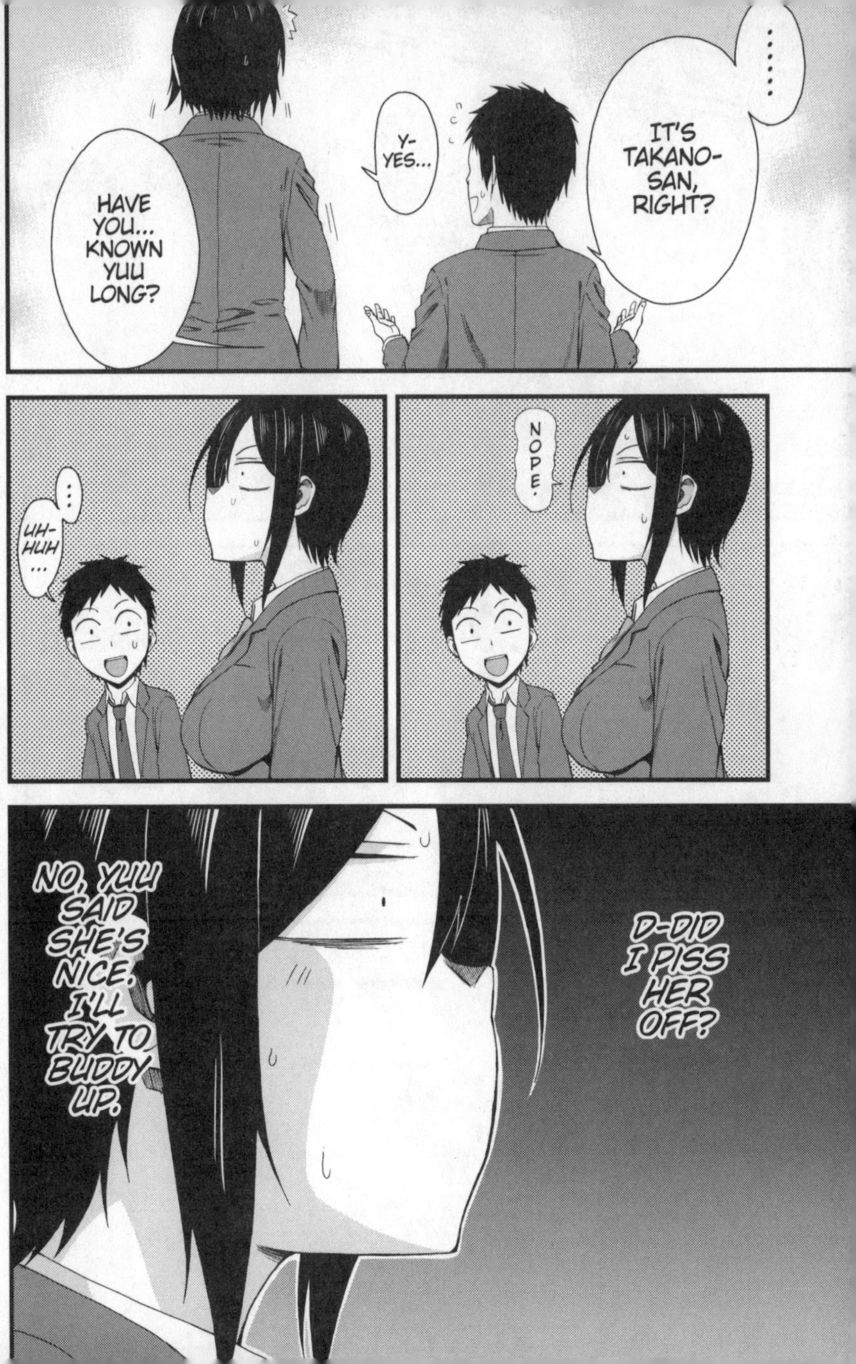
......
IT'S TAKANO-SAN, RIGHT?
Y-YES...
HAVE YOU... KNOWN YUU LONG?
NOPE.
...
UH-HUH...
D-DID I PISS HER OFF?
NO, YUU SAID SHE'S NICE. I'LL TRY TO BUDDY UP.

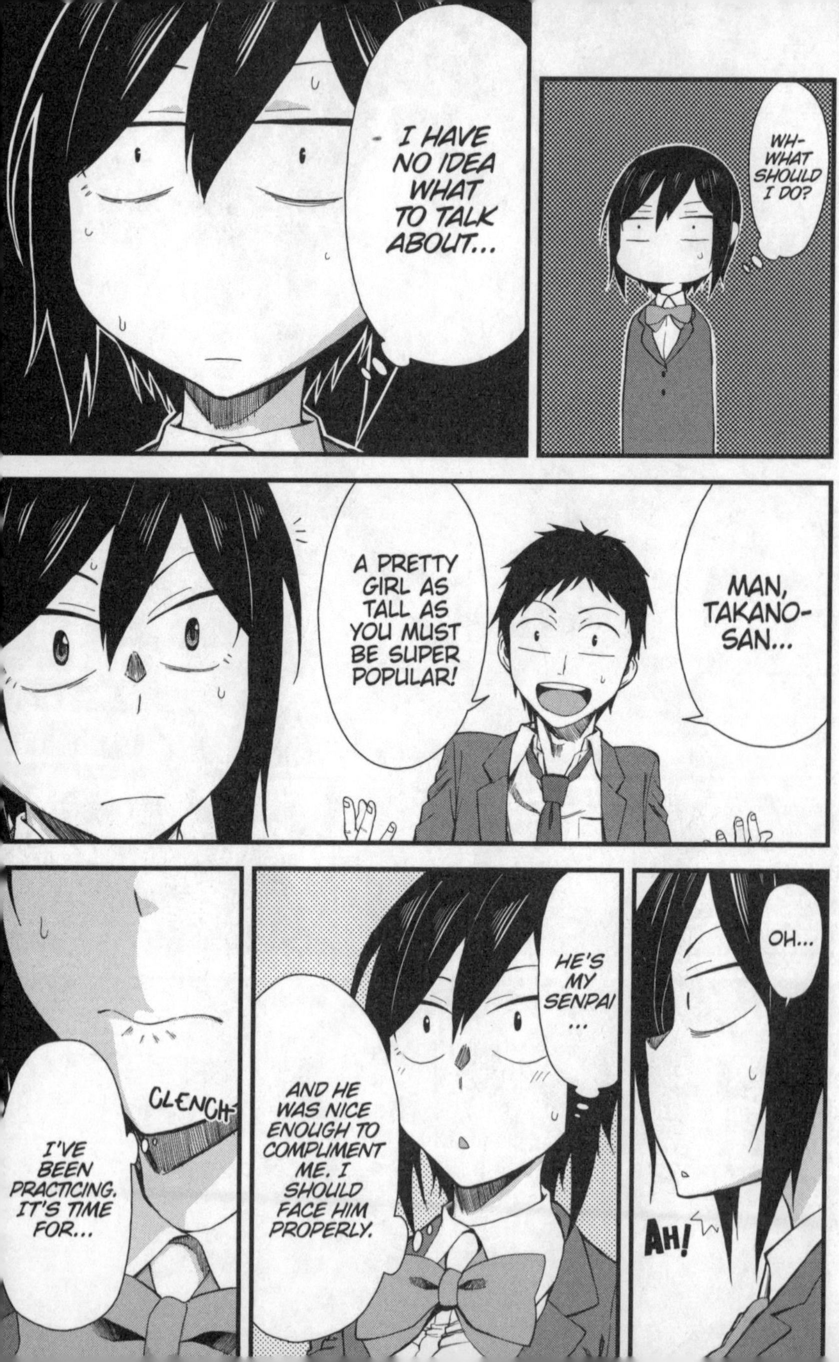
WH-WHAT SHOULD I DO?
I HAVE NO IDEA WHAT TO TALK ABOUT...
MAN, TAKANO-SAN...
A PRETTY GIRL AS TALL AS YOU MUST BE SUPER POPULAR!
OH...
AH!
HE'S MY SENPAI...
AND HE WAS NICE ENOUGH TO COMPLIMENT ME. I SHOULD FACE HIM PROPERLY.
CLENCH
I'VE BEEN PRACTICING. IT'S TIME FOR...

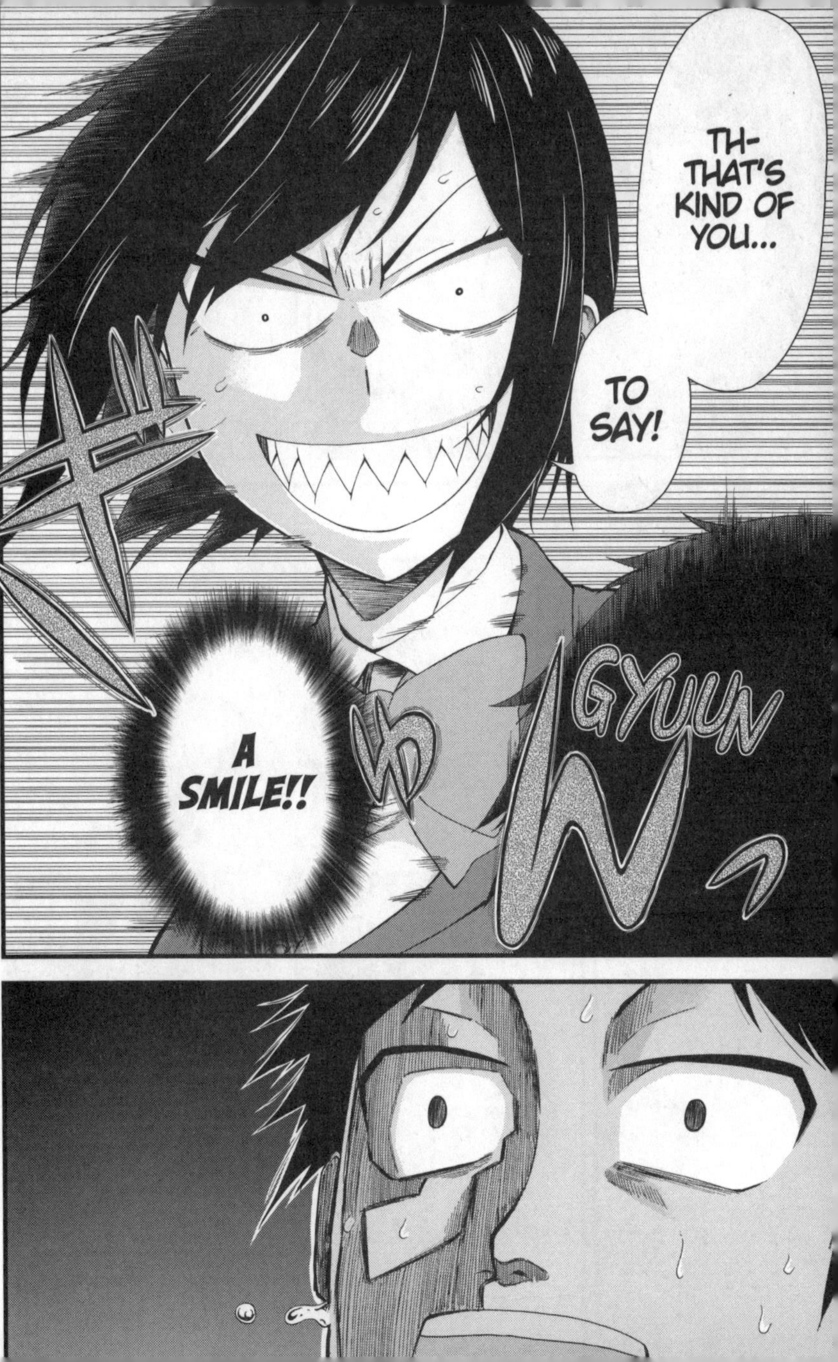
TH- THAT'S KIND OF YOU...
TO SAY!
GYUUN
A SMILE!!

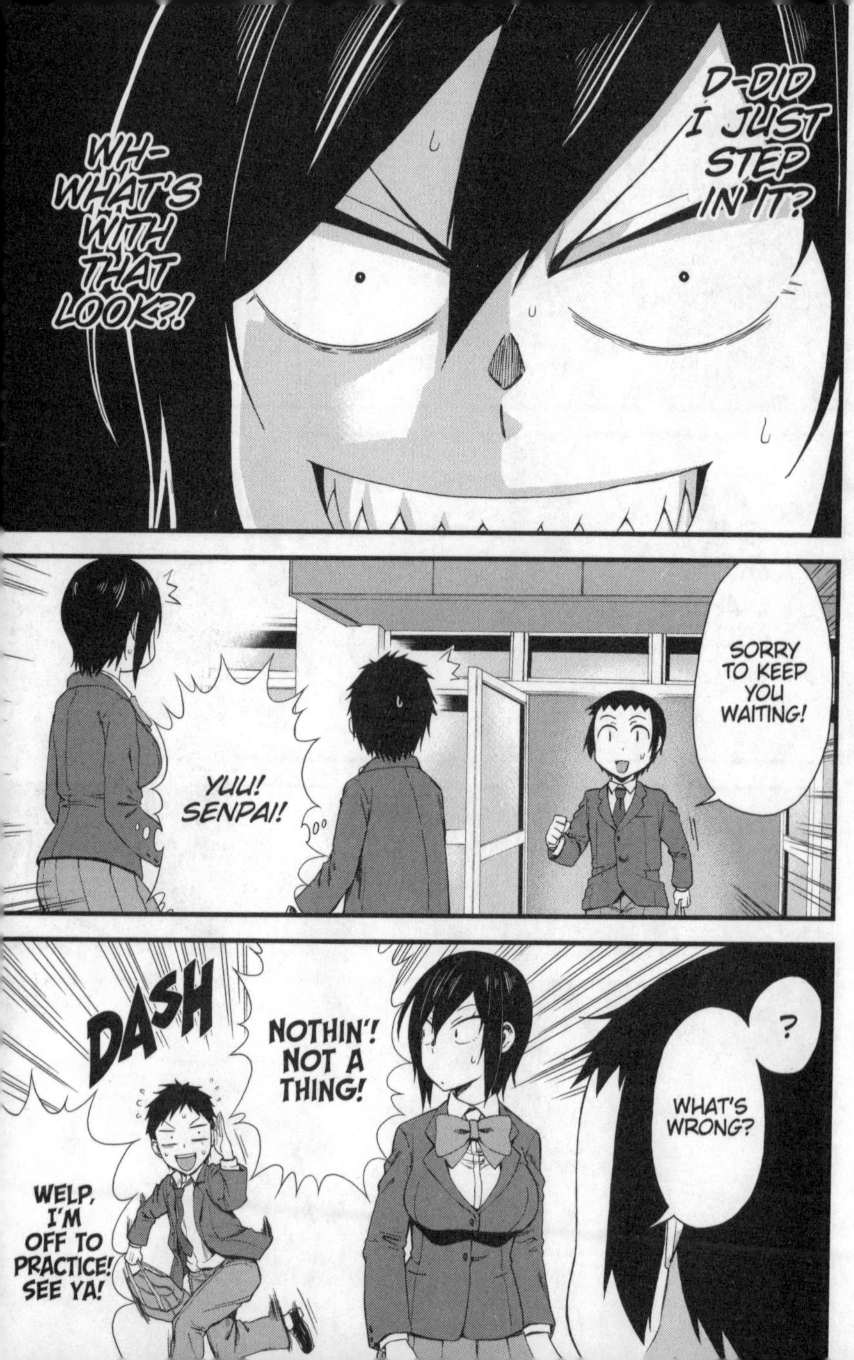
D-DID I JUST STEP IN IT?
WH-WHAT'S WITH THAT LOOK?!
SORRY TO KEEP YOU WAITING!
YUU! SENPAI!
?
WHAT'S WRONG?
NOTHIN'! NOT A THING!
DASH
WELP, I'M OFF TO PRACTICE! SEE YA!

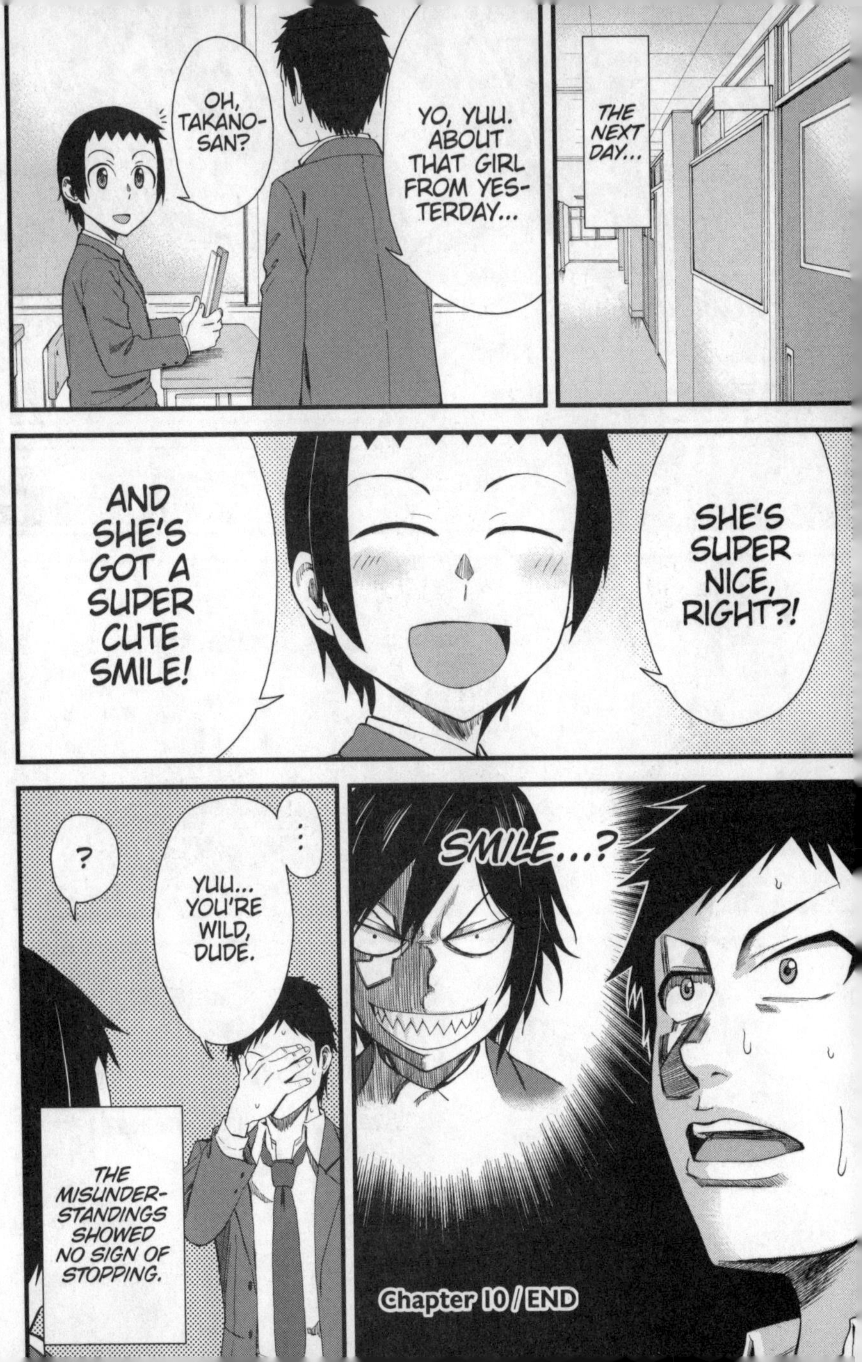

THE NEXT DAY...
YO, YUU. ABOUT THAT GIRL FROM YES-TERDAY...
OH, TAKANO-SAN?
SHE'S SUPER NICE, RIGHT?!
AND SHE'S GOT A SUPER CUTE SMILE!
SMILE...?
Chapter 10 / END
...
YUU... YOU'RE WILD, DUDE.
?
THE MISUNDER-STANDINGS SHOWED NO SIGN OF STOPPING.

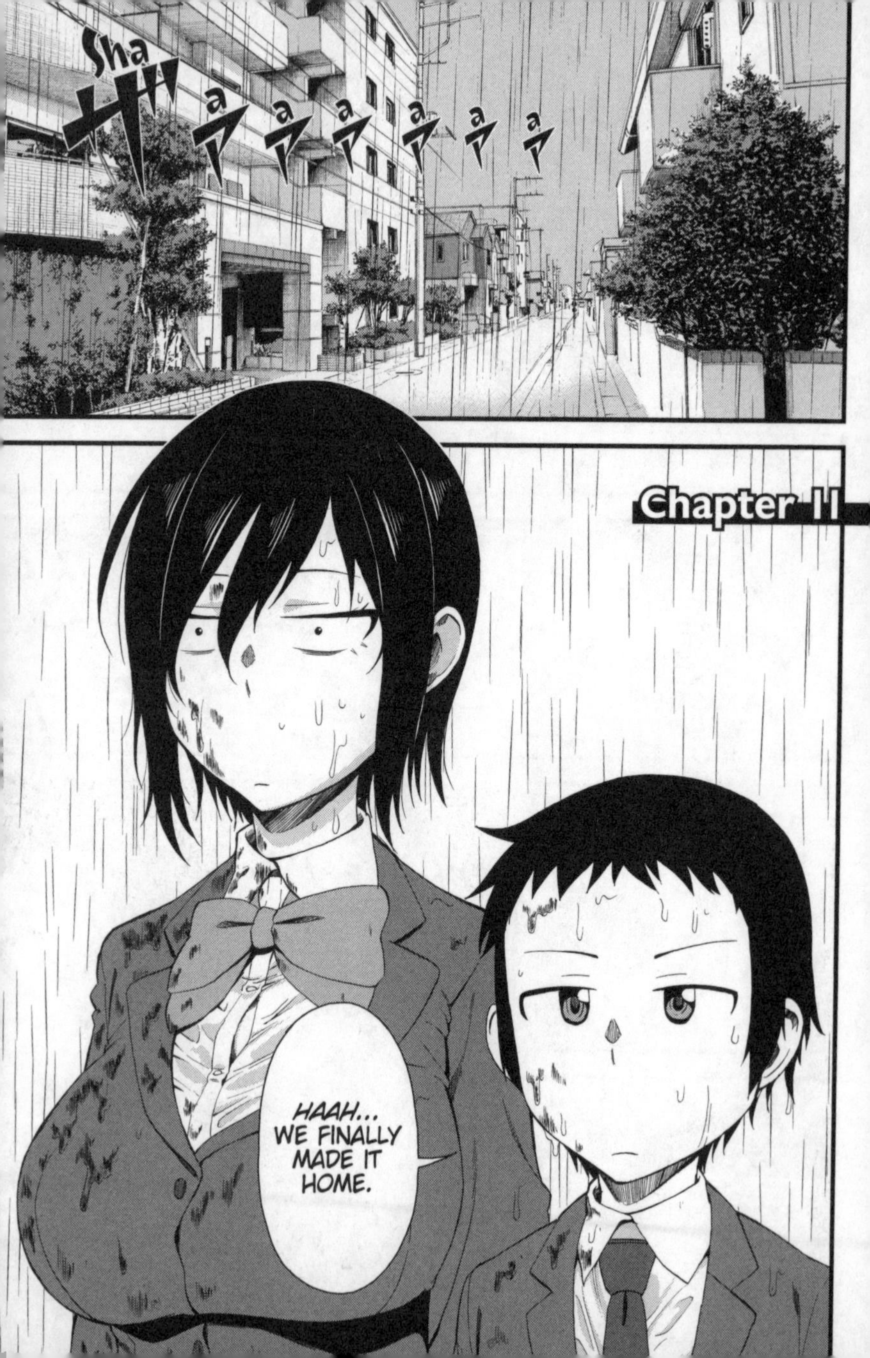
Sha a a a a a a
ザアアアアアア
Chapter 11
HAAH... WE FINALLY MADE IT HOME.

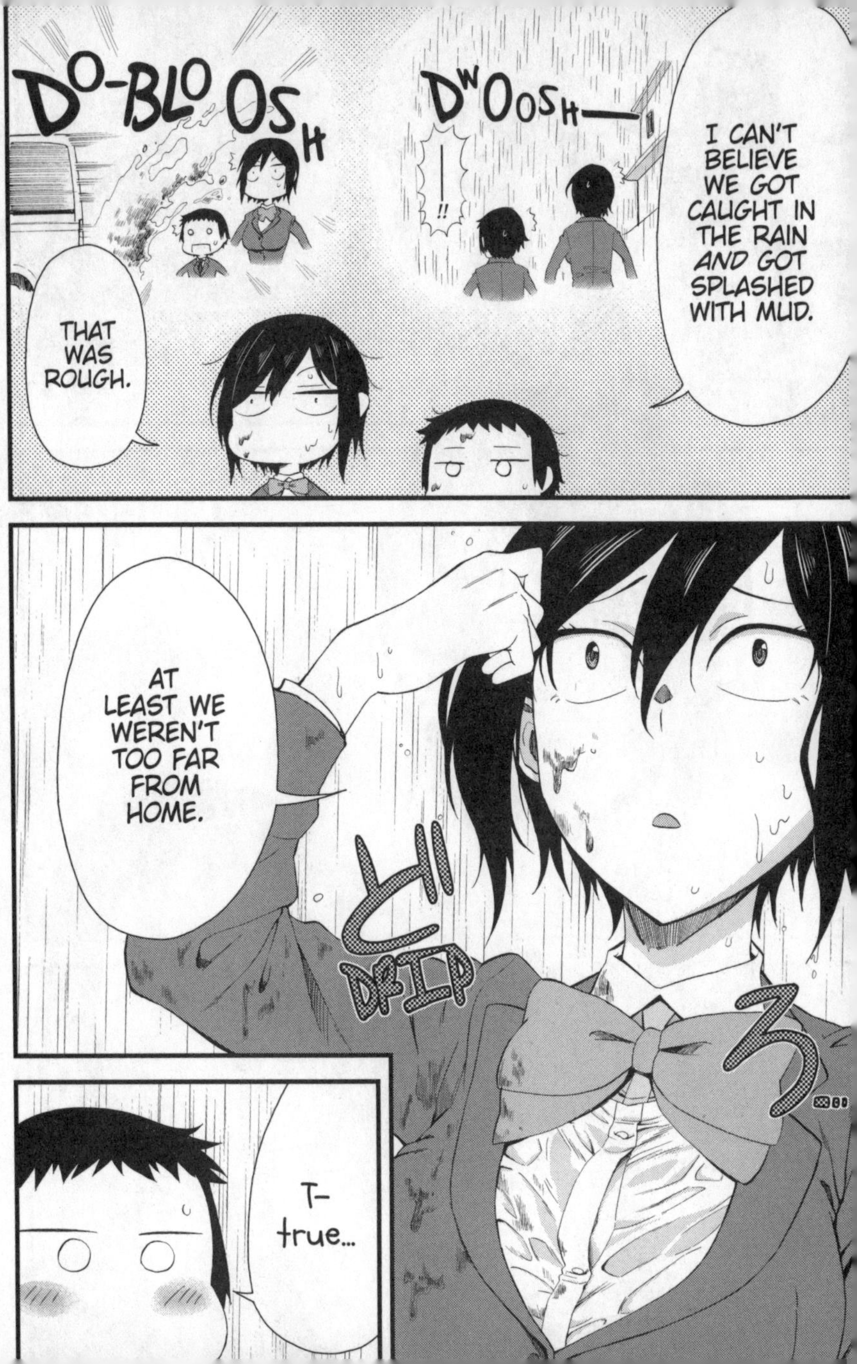
I CAN'T BELIEVE WE GOT CAUGHT IN THE RAIN AND GOT SPLASHED WITH MUD.
DWOOSH—
—!!
DO-BLOOSH
THAT WAS ROUGH.
AT LEAST WE WEREN'T TOO FAR FROM HOME.
DRIP
T-true...

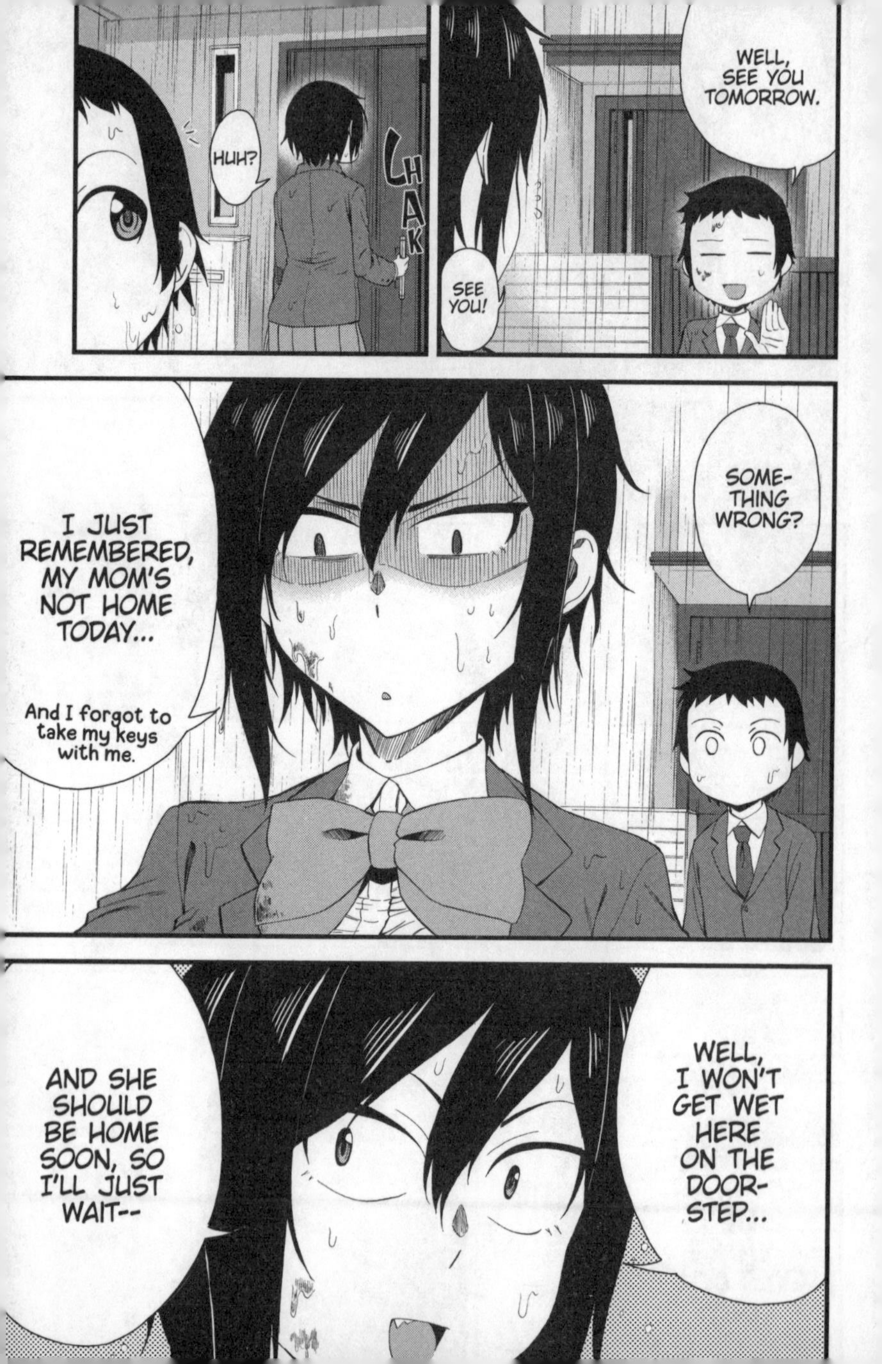
WELL, SEE YOU TOMORROW.
SEE YOU!
CHAK
HUH?
SOME-THING WRONG?
I JUST REMEMBERED, MY MOM'S NOT HOME TODAY...
And I forgot to take my keys with me.
WELL, I WON'T GET WET HERE ON THE DOOR-STEP...
AND SHE SHOULD BE HOME SOON, SO I'LL JUST WAIT--

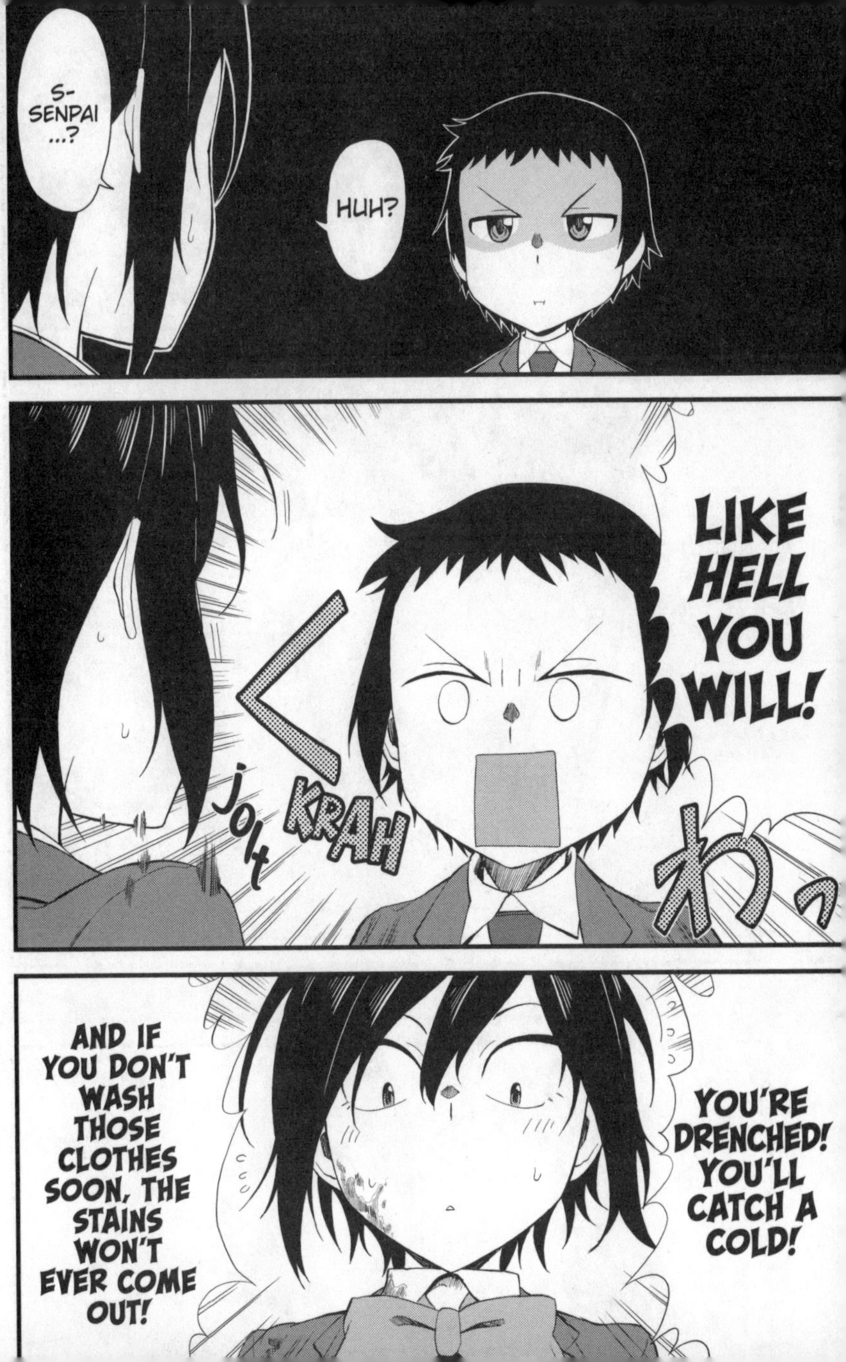
S-SENPAI ...?
HUH?
LIKE HELL YOU WILL!
わっ
KRAH
jolt
YOU'RE DRENCHED! YOU'LL CATCH A COLD!
AND IF YOU DON'T WASH THOSE CLOTHES SOON, THE STAINS WON'T EVER COME OUT!

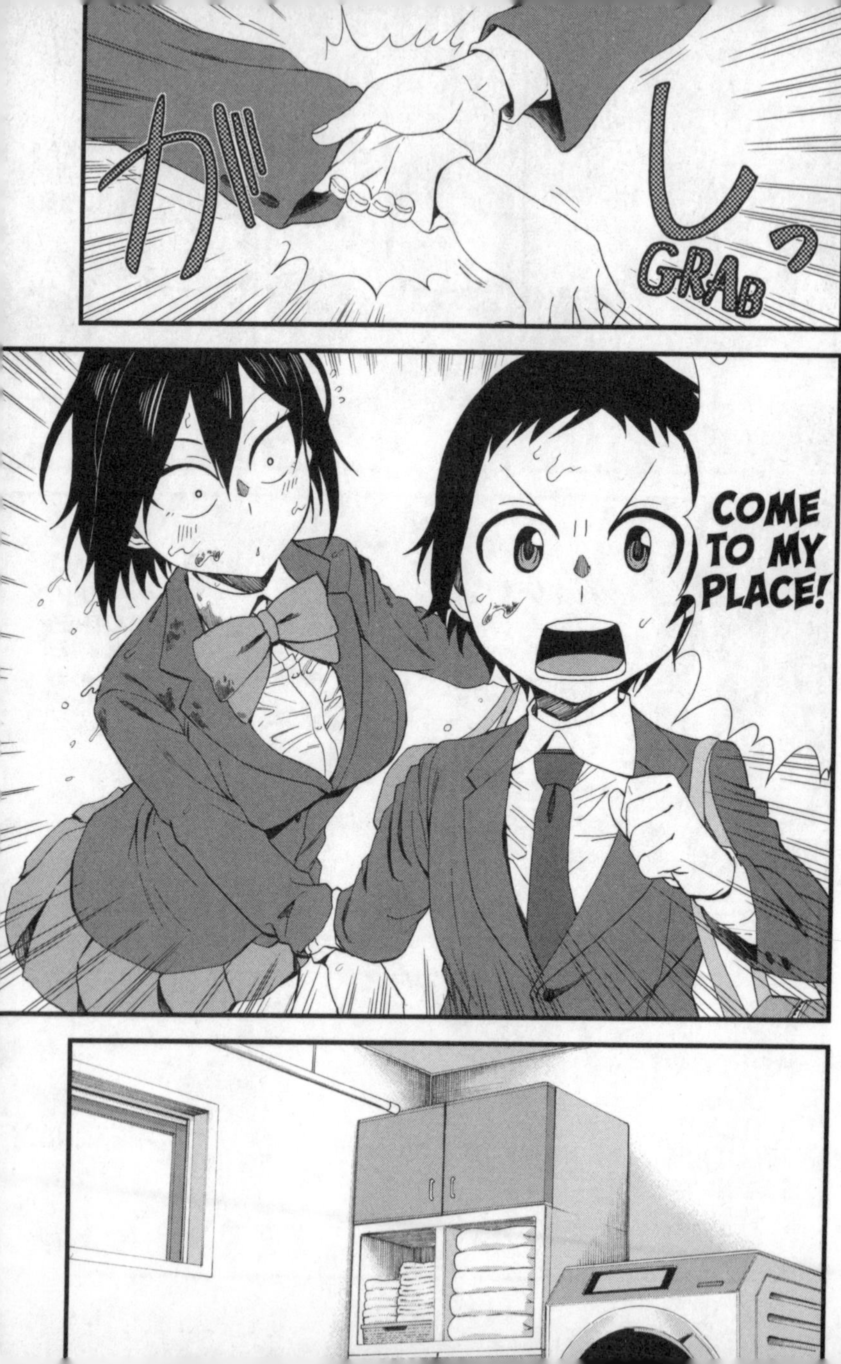

がしっ
GRAB
COME TO MY PLACE!

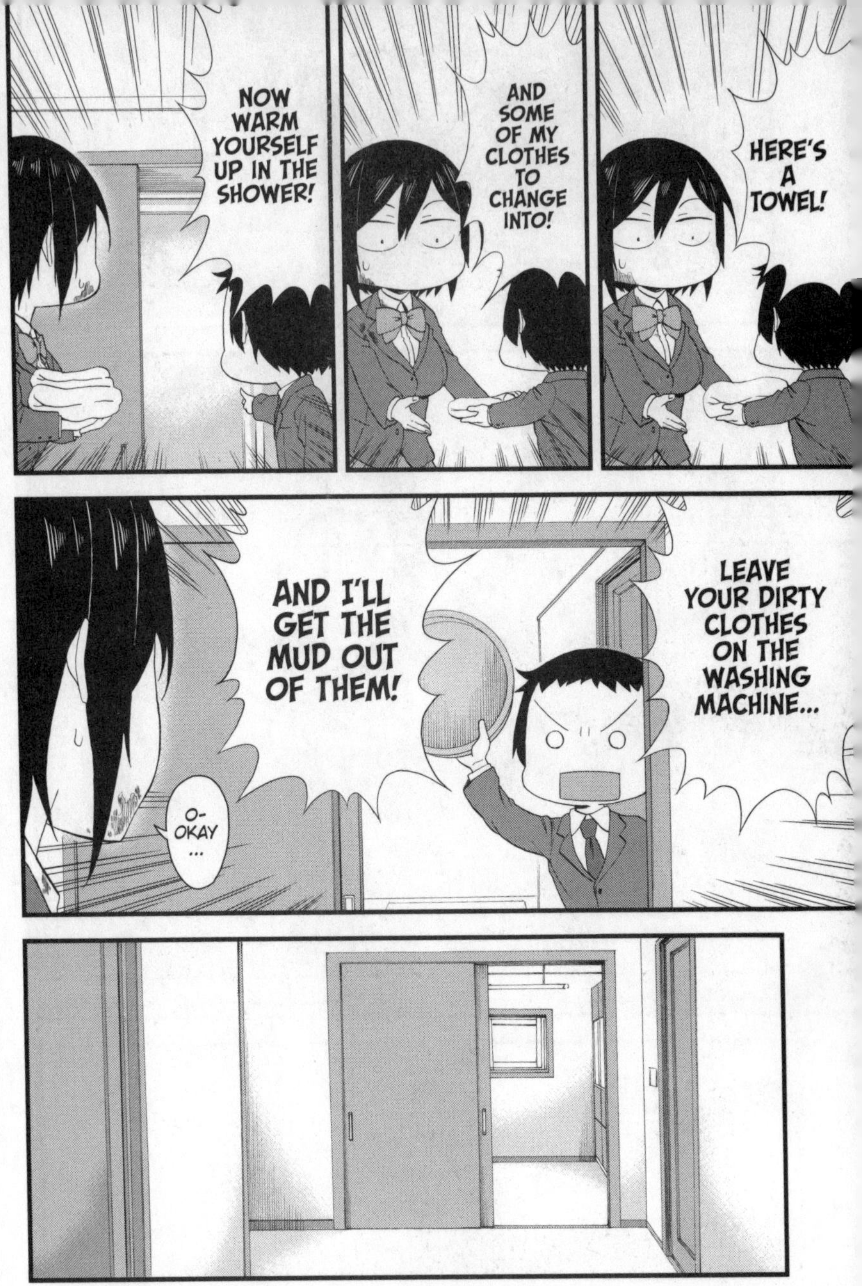
HERE'S A TOWEL!
AND SOME OF MY CLOTHES TO CHANGE INTO!
NOW WARM YOURSELF UP IN THE SHOWER!
LEAVE YOUR DIRTY CLOTHES ON THE WASHING MACHINE...
AND I'LL GET THE MUD OUT OF THEM!
O-OKAY ...

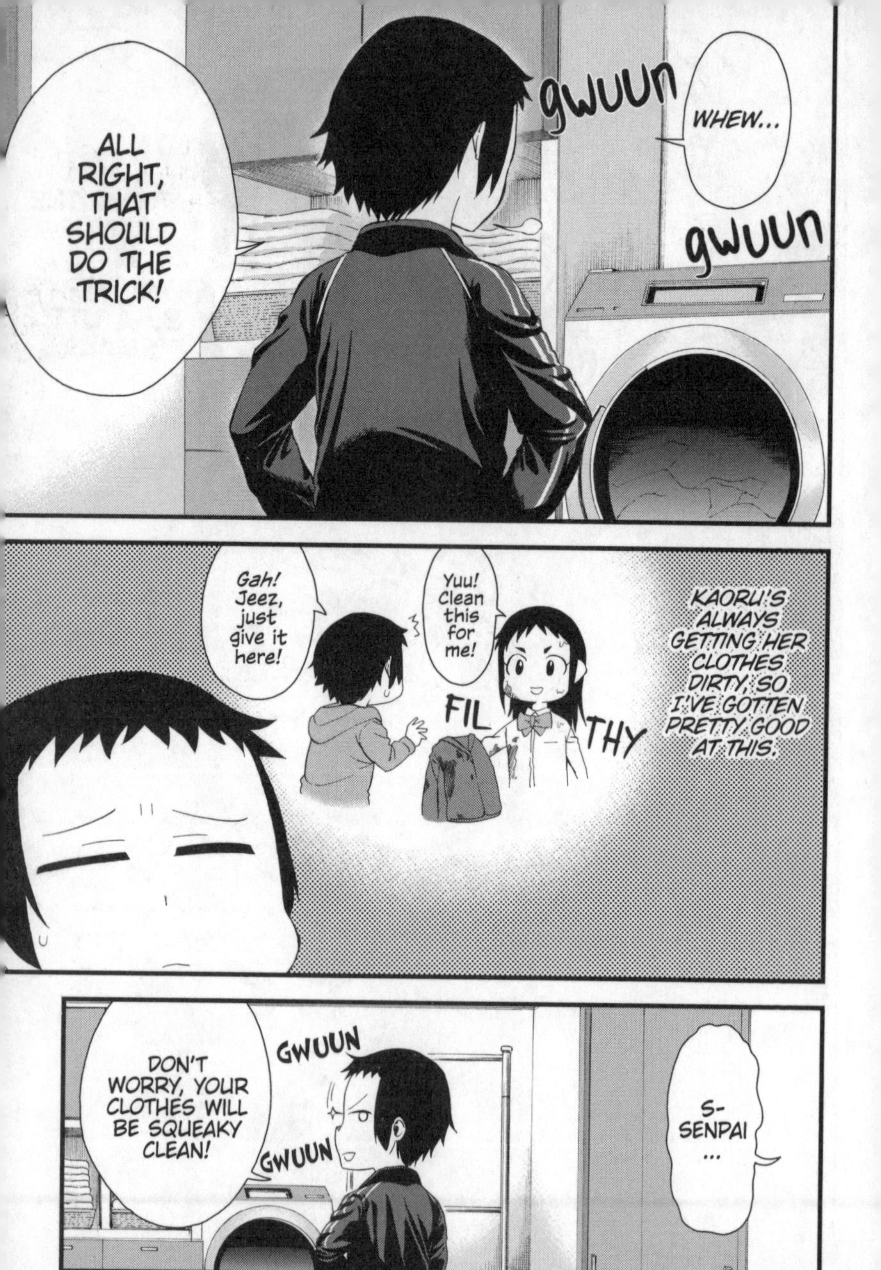
WHEW...
gwuun
gwuun
ALL RIGHT, THAT SHOULD DO THE TRICK!
KAORU'S ALWAYS GETTING HER CLOTHES DIRTY, SO I'VE GOTTEN PRETTY GOOD AT THIS.
Yuu! Clean this for me!
Gah! Jeez, just give it here!
FIL THY
S-SENPAI...
GWUUN
DON'T WORRY, YOUR CLOTHES WILL BE SQUEAKY CLEAN!
GWUUN

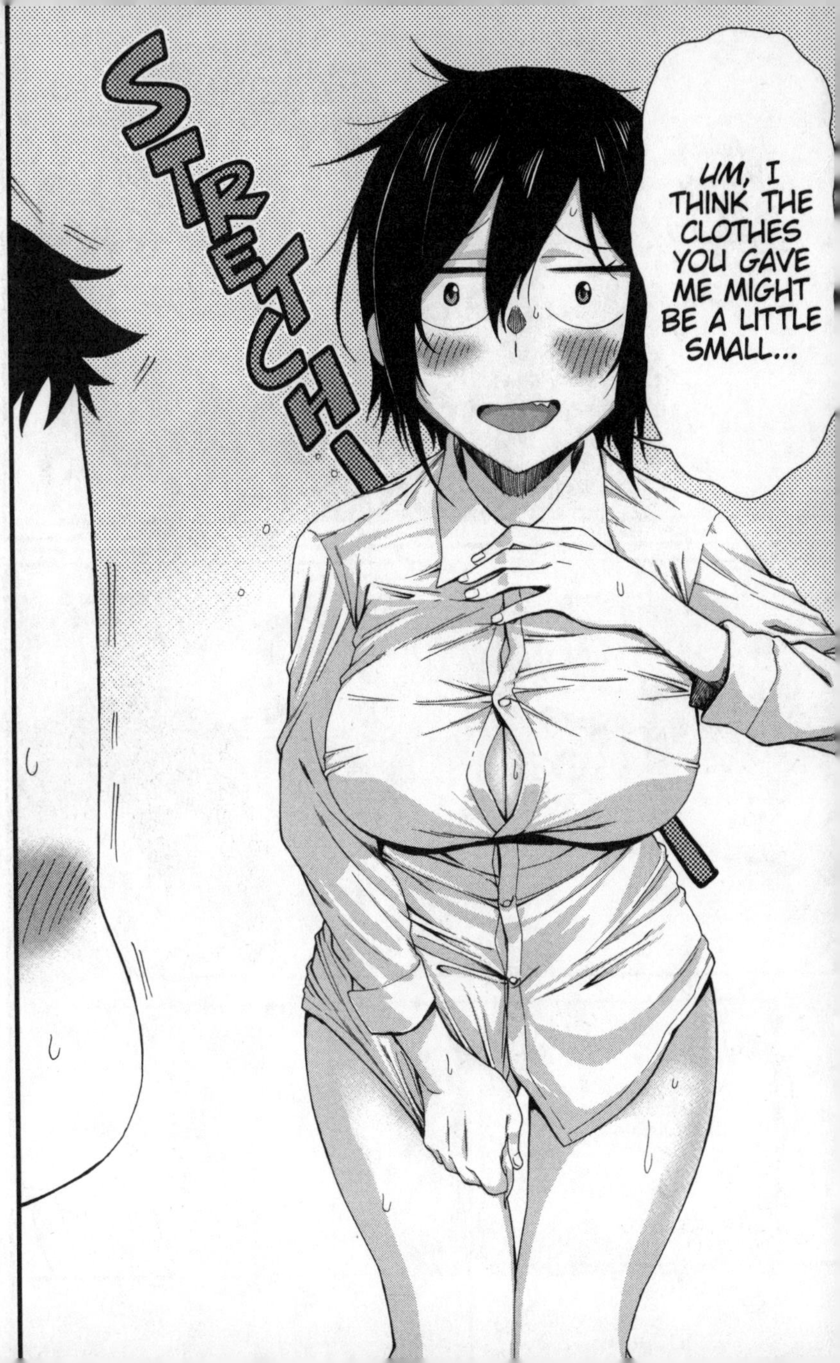
UM, I THINK THE CLOTHES YOU GAVE ME MIGHT BE A LITTLE SMALL...
STRETCH

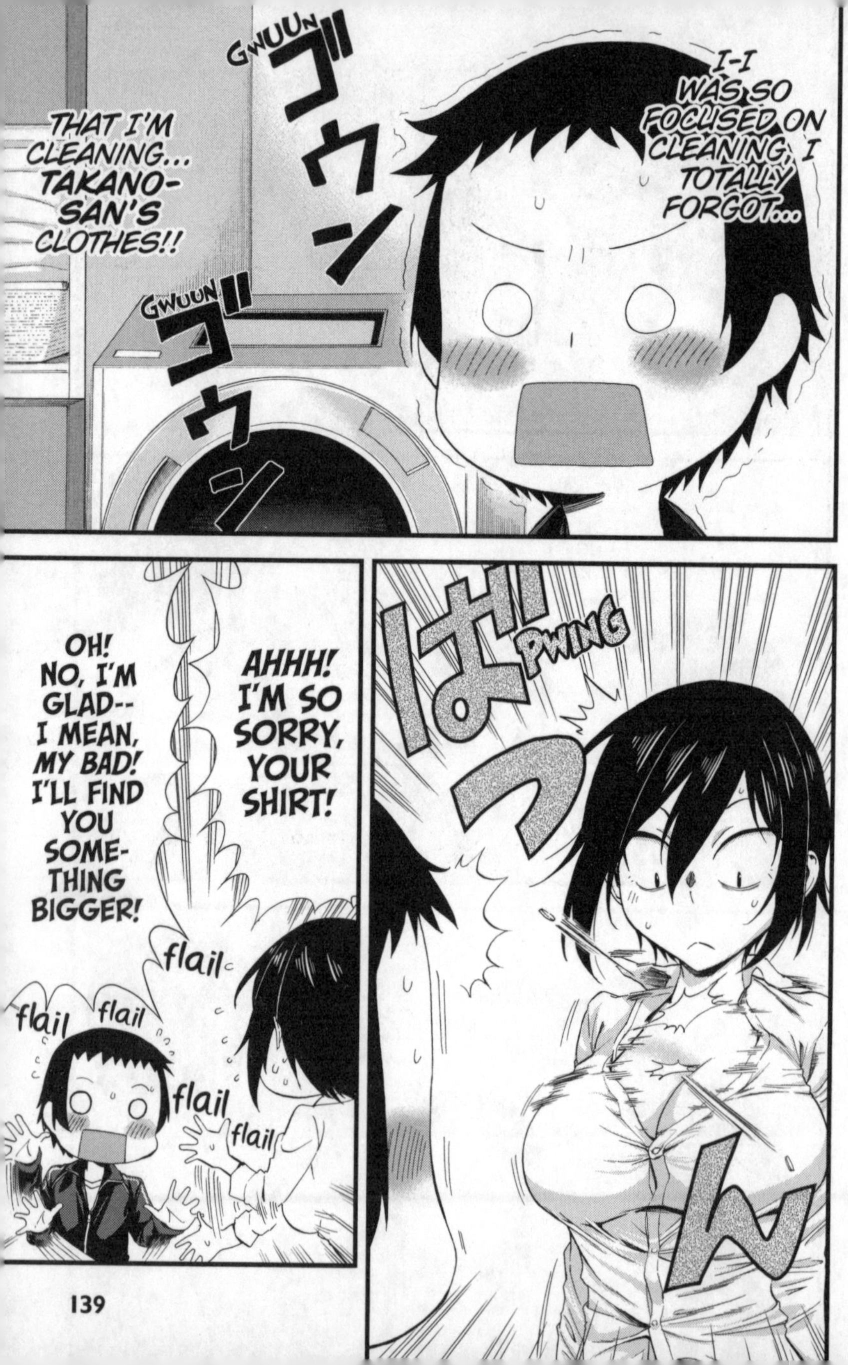
GWUUN
I-I WAS SO FOCUSED ON CLEANING, I TOTALLY FORGOT...
THAT I'M CLEANING... TAKANO-SAN'S CLOTHES!!
GWUUN
PWING
AHHH! I'M SO SORRY, YOUR SHIRT!
OH! NO, I'M GLAD-- I MEAN, MY BAD! I'LL FIND YOU SOME-THING BIGGER!
flail
flail
flail
flail
flail

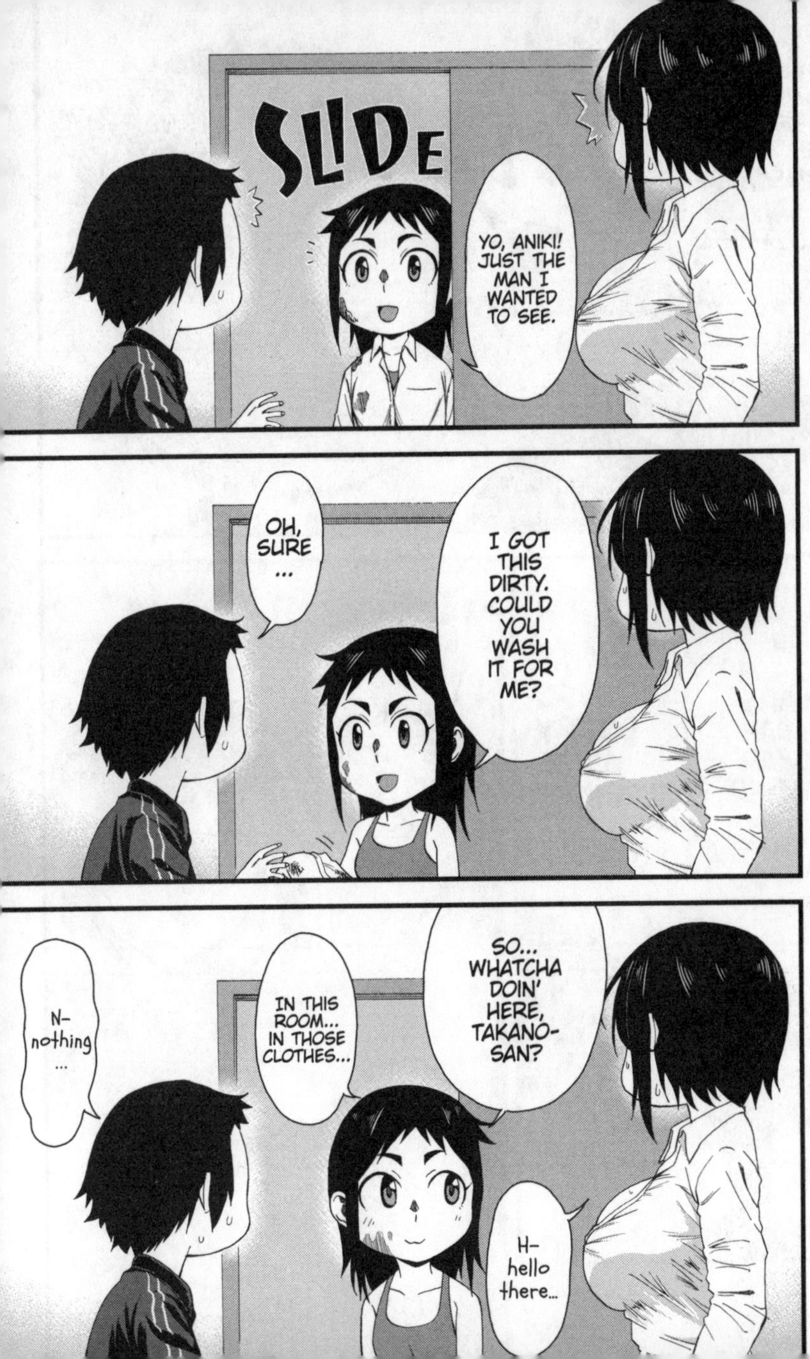
SLIDE
YO, ANIKI! JUST THE MAN I WANTED TO SEE.
I GOT THIS DIRTY. COULD YOU WASH IT FOR ME?
OH, SURE ...
SO... WHATCHA DOIN' HERE, TAKANO-SAN?
IN THIS ROOM... IN THOSE CLOTHES...
H- hello there...
N- nothing ...

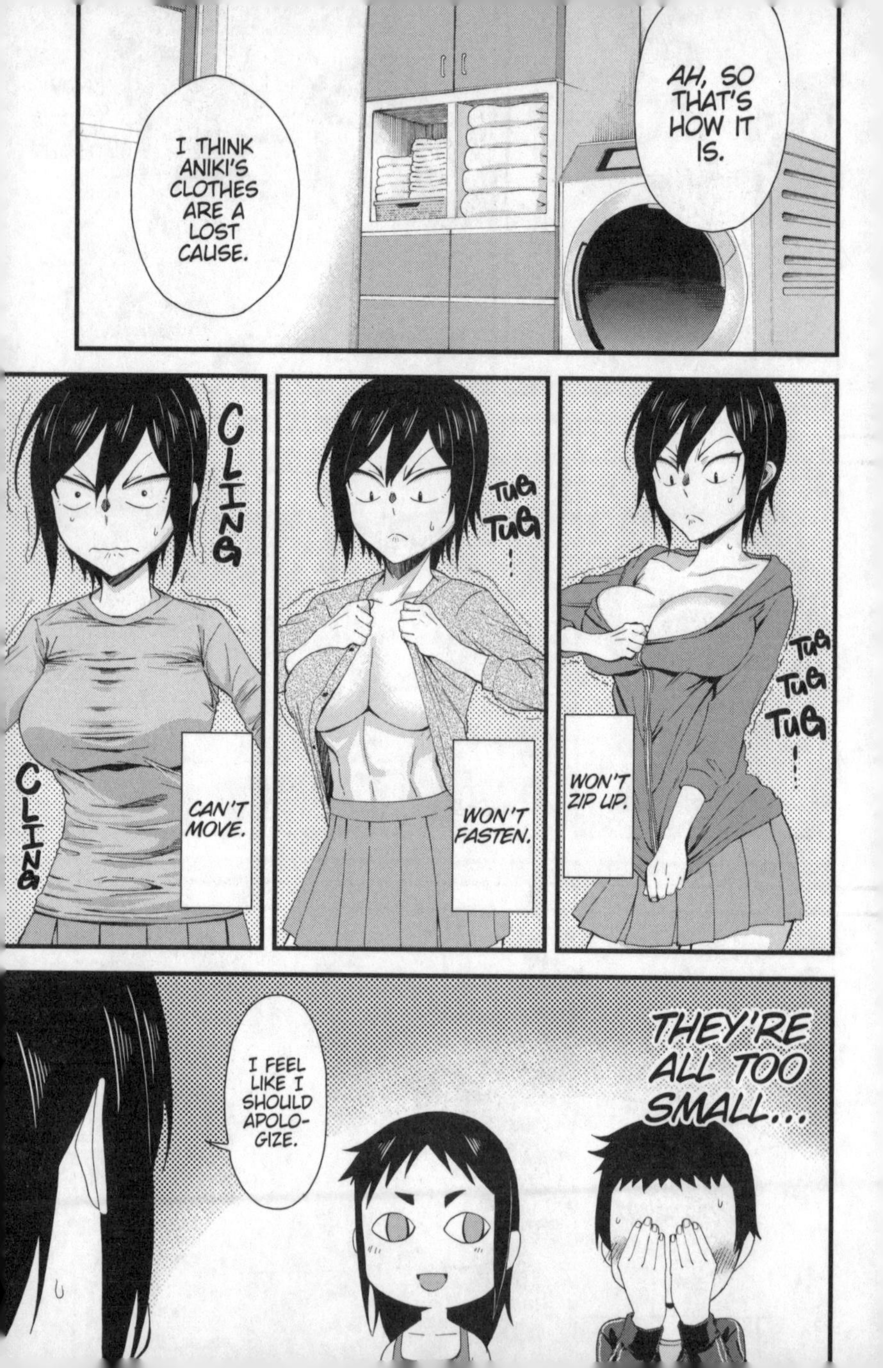
AH, SO THAT'S HOW IT IS.
I THINK ANIKI'S CLOTHES ARE A LOST CAUSE.
TUG TUG TUG...
WON'T ZIP UP.
TUG TUG...
WON'T FASTEN.
CLING CLING
CAN'T MOVE.
THEY'RE ALL TOO SMALL...
I FEEL LIKE I SHOULD APOLO-GIZE.

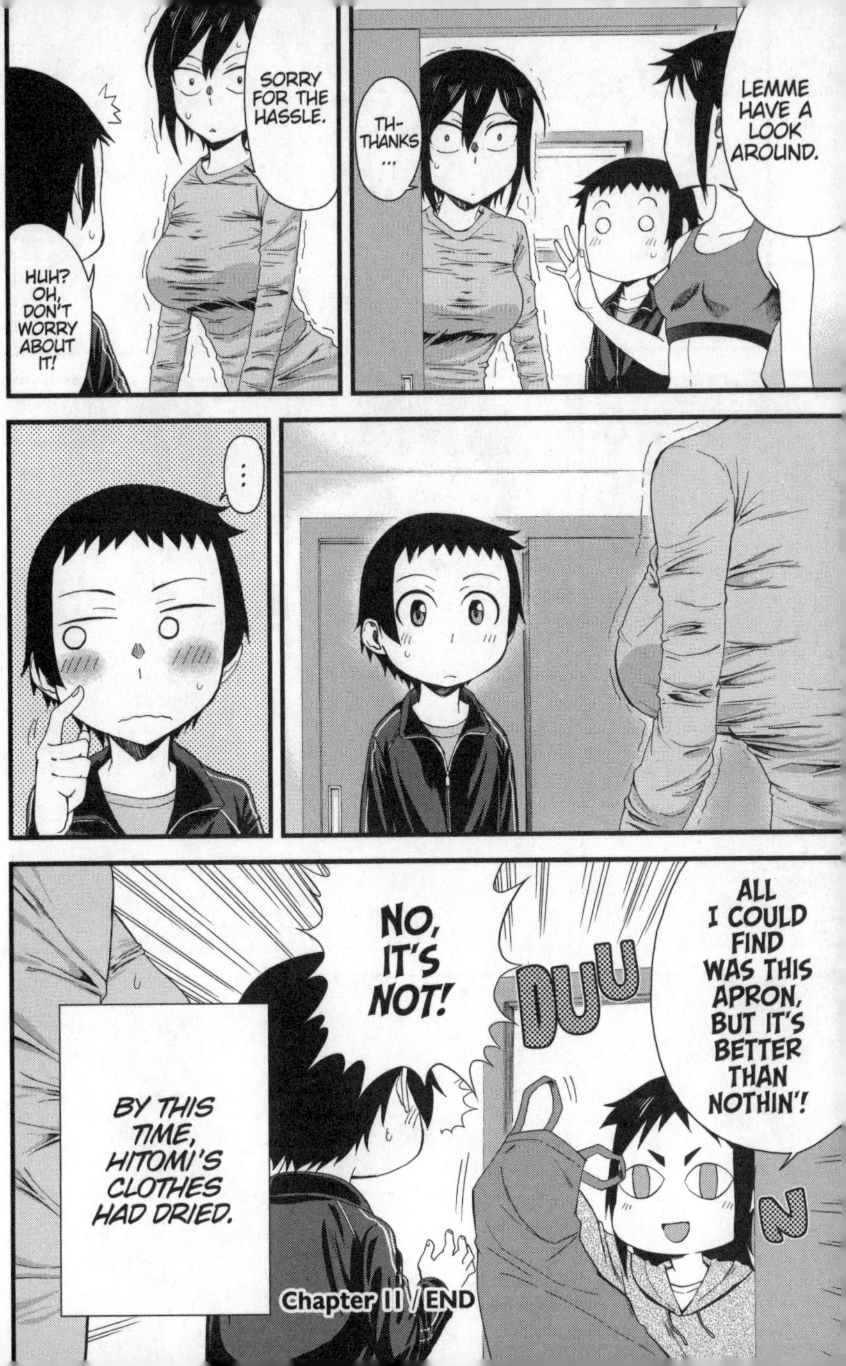
LEMME HAVE A LOOK AROUND.
TH-THANKS...
SORRY FOR THE HASSLE.
HUH? OH, DON'T WORRY ABOUT IT!
...
ALL I COULD FIND WAS THIS APRON, BUT IT'S BETTER THAN NOTHIN'!
DUUN
NO, IT'S NOT!
BY THIS TIME, HITOMI'S CLOTHES HAD DRIED.
Chapter 11 / END

Chapter 12

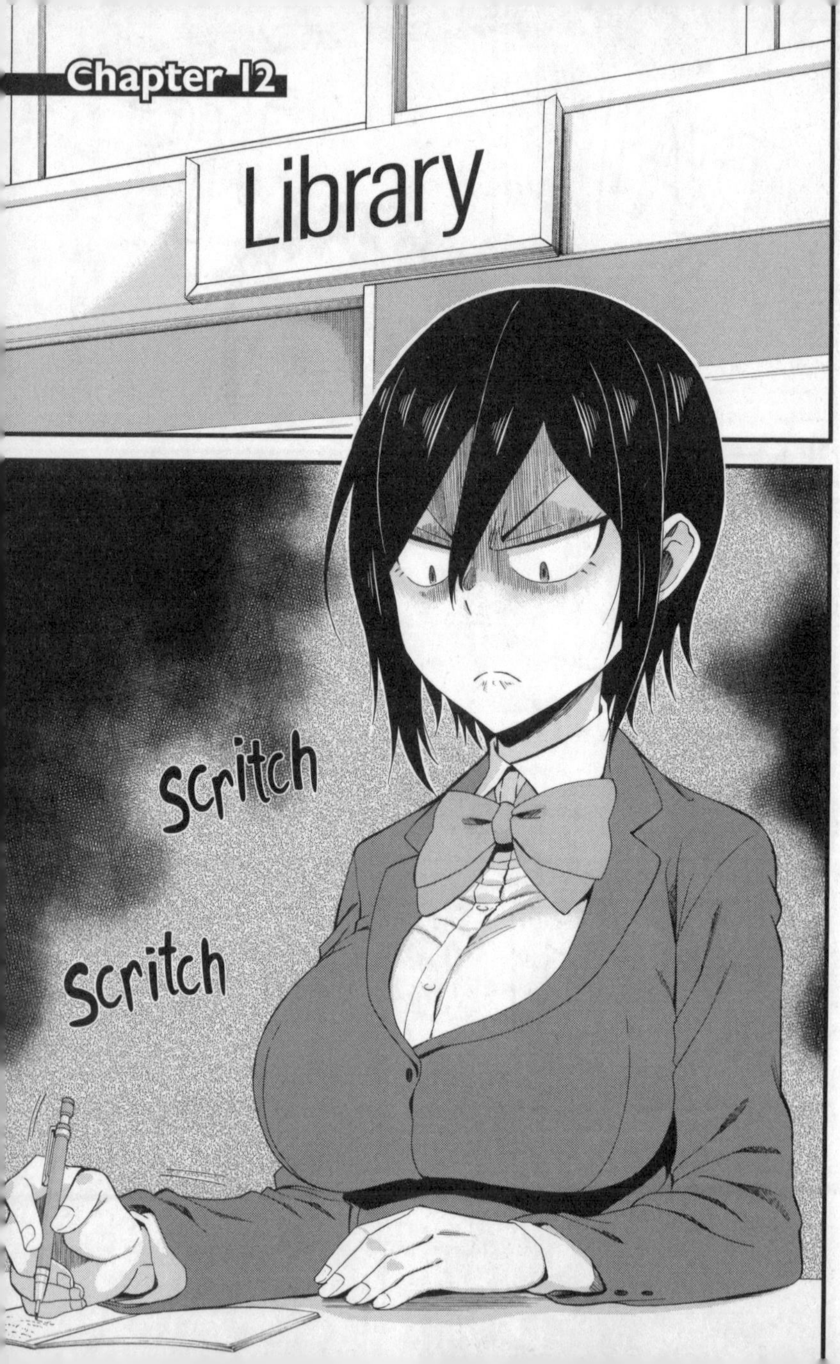
Library
scritch
scritch

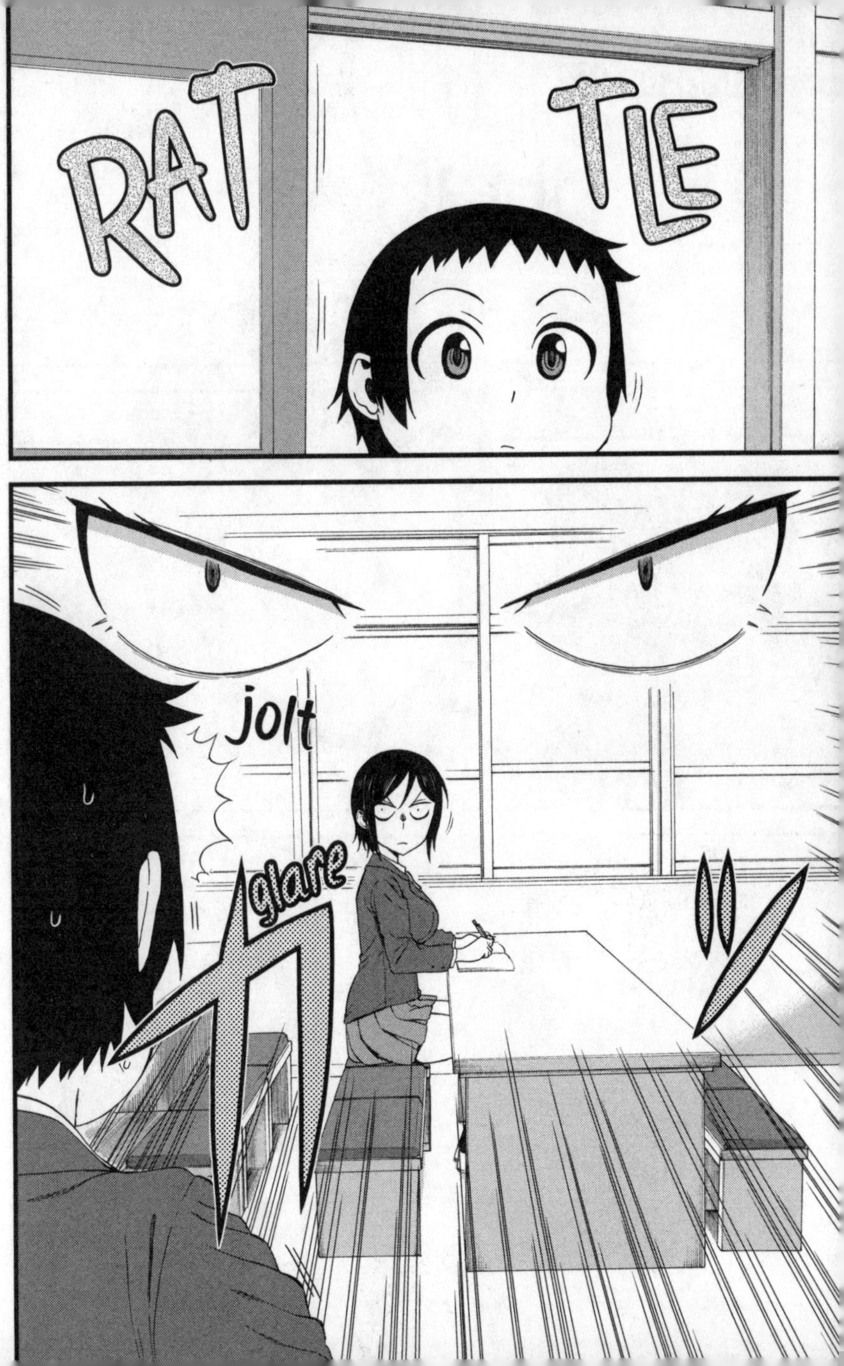
RAT
TLE
jolt
glare

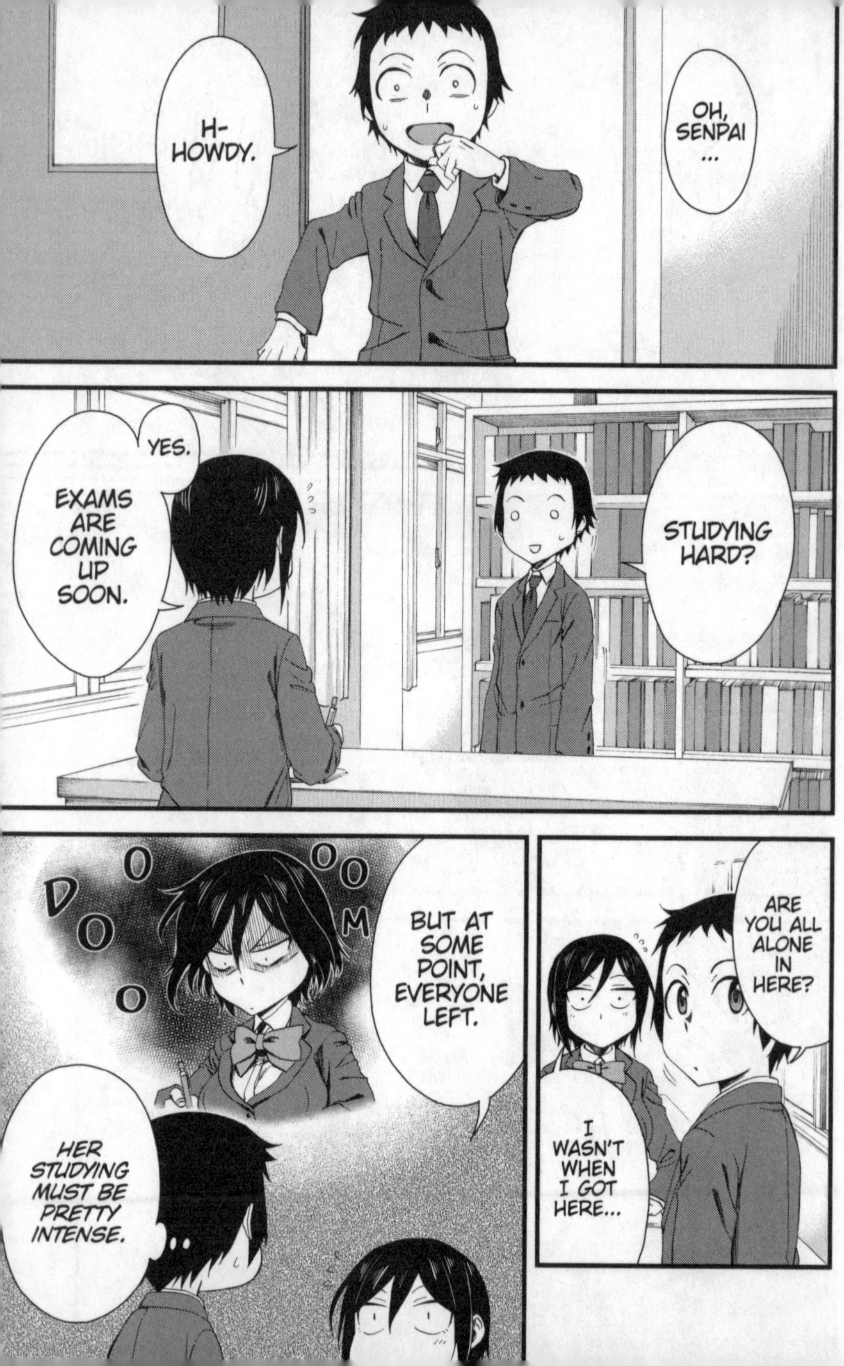
OH, SENPAI...
H-HOWDY.
STUDYING HARD?
YES.
EXAMS ARE COMING UP SOON.
ARE YOU ALL ALONE IN HERE?
I WASN'T WHEN I GOT HERE...
BUT AT SOME POINT, EVERYONE LEFT.
DOOOOOM
HER STUDYING MUST BE PRETTY INTENSE.

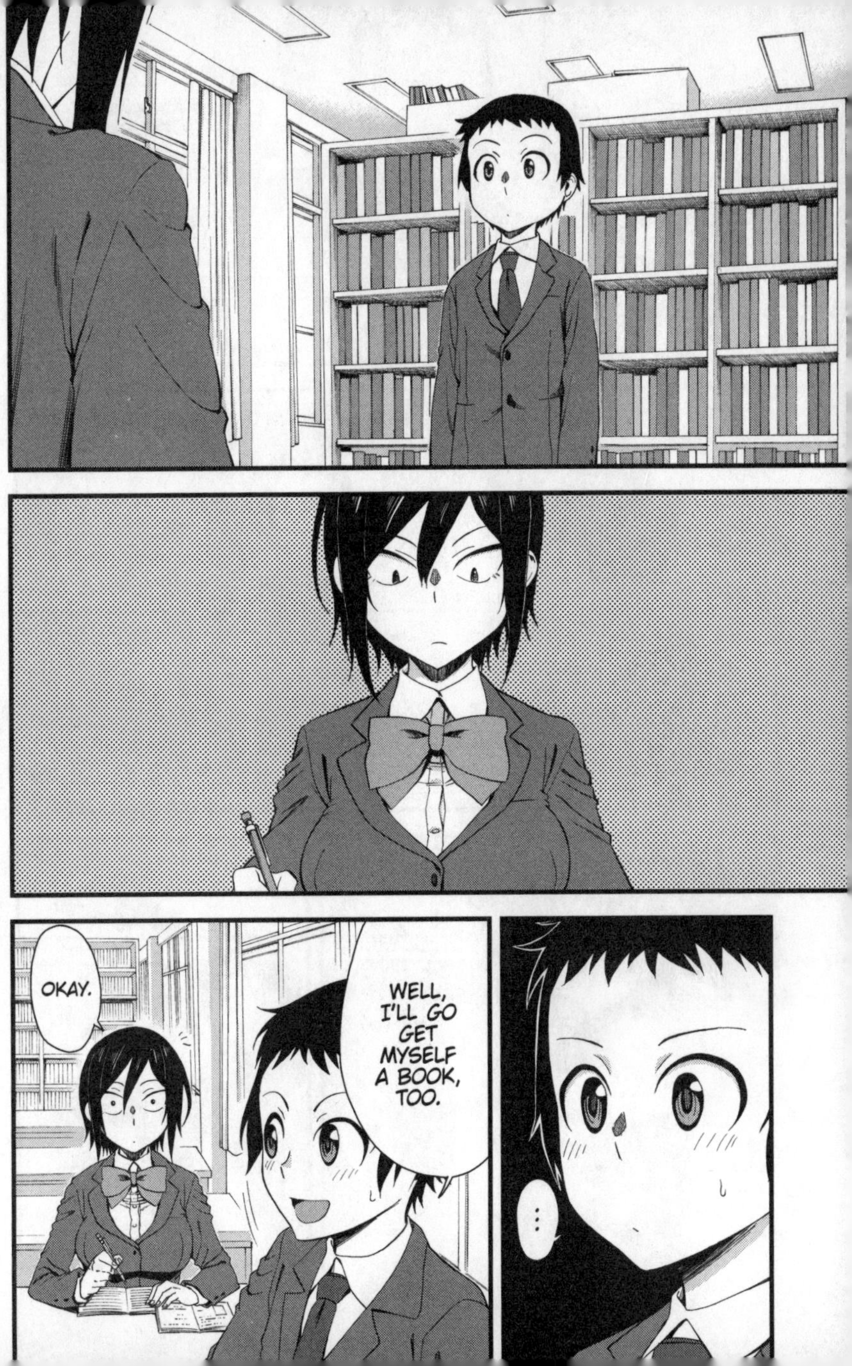
...
WELL, I'LL GO GET MYSELF A BOOK, TOO.
OKAY.

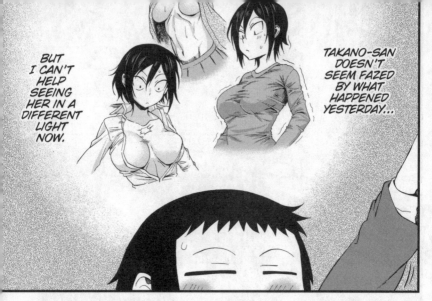

BUT I CAN'T HELP SEEING HER IN A DIFFERENT LIGHT NOW.

TAKANO-SAN DOESN'T SEEM FAZED BY WHAT HAPPENED YESTERDAY...

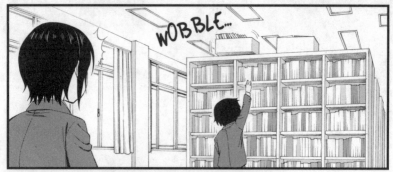

WOBBLE...

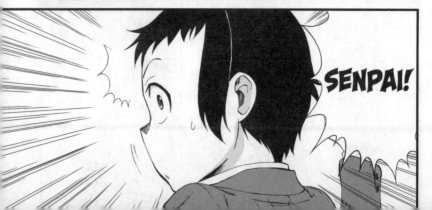

SENPAI!

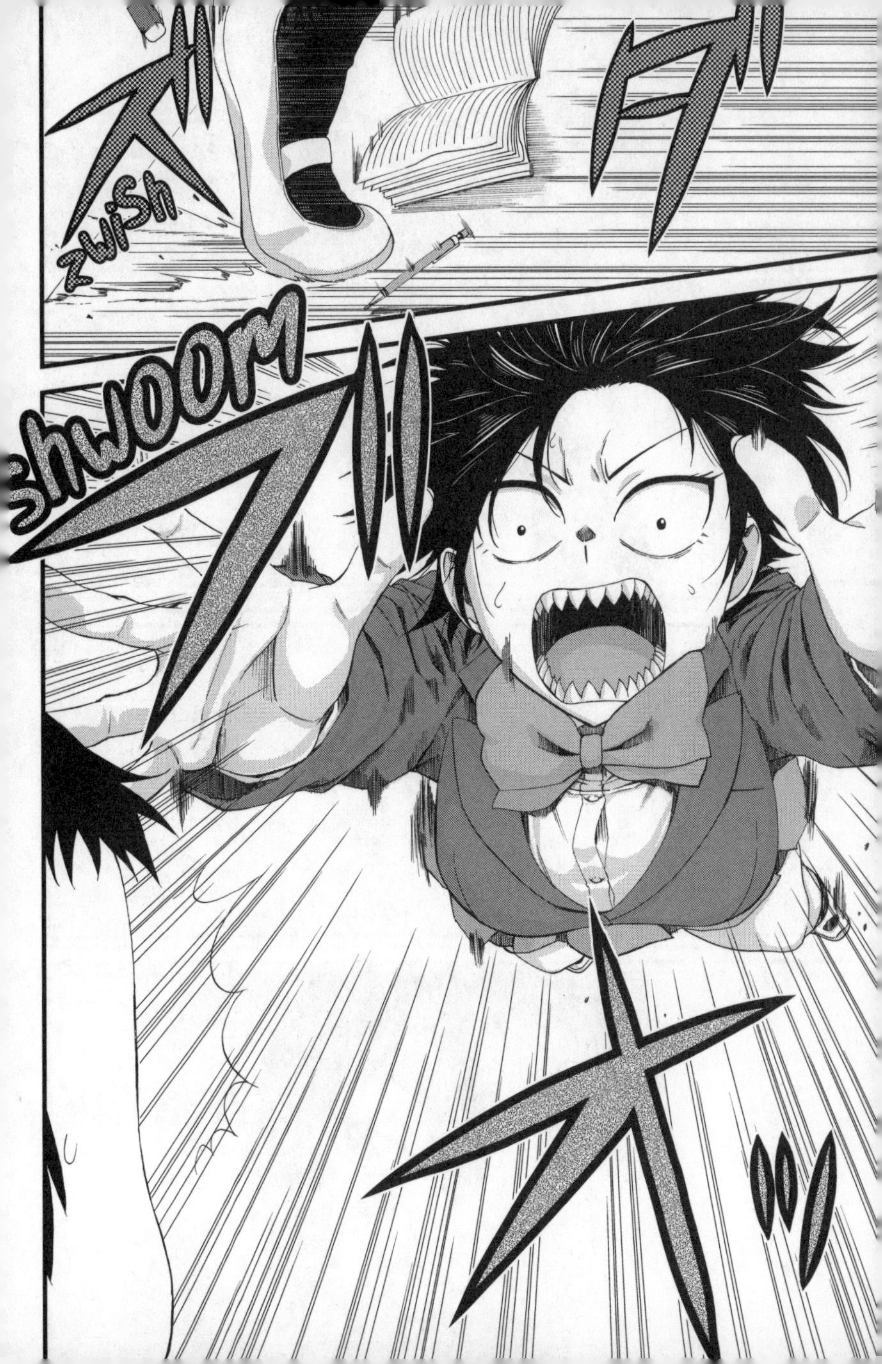
zwish
shwoom

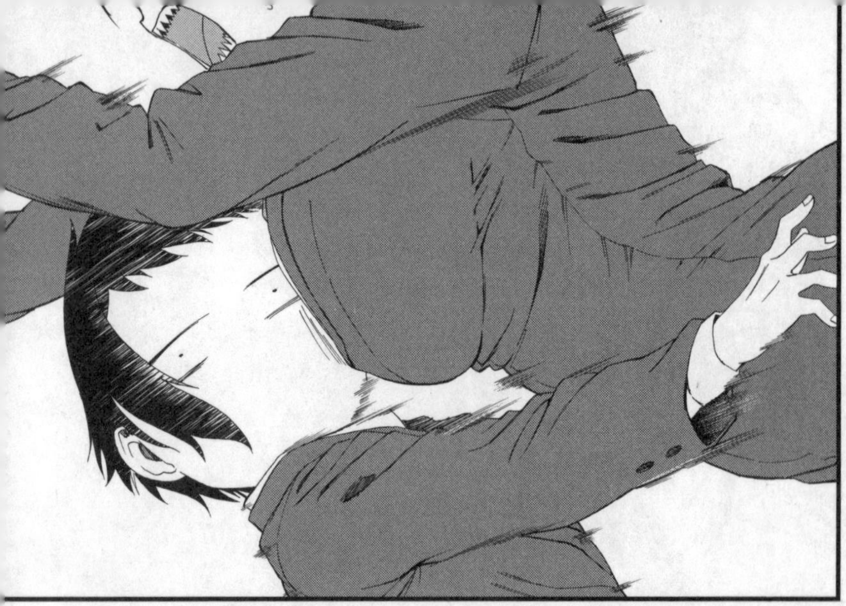

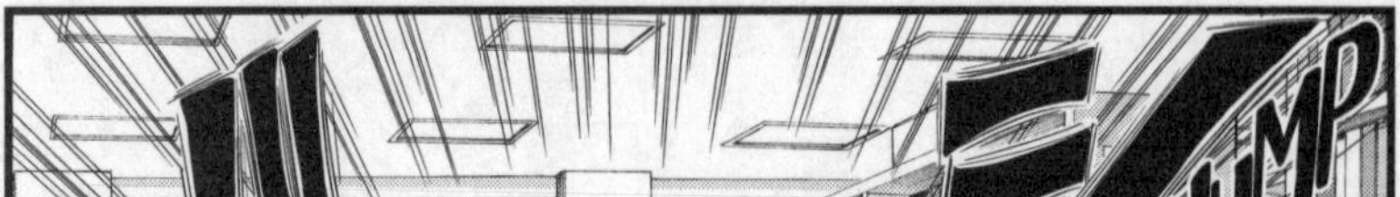
WHUMP

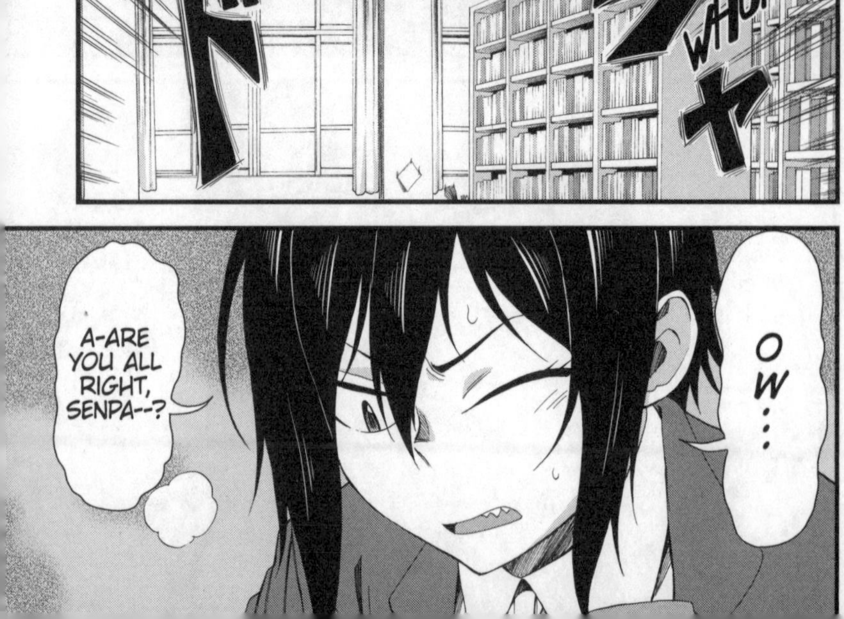
OW...
A-ARE YOU ALL RIGHT, SENPA--?

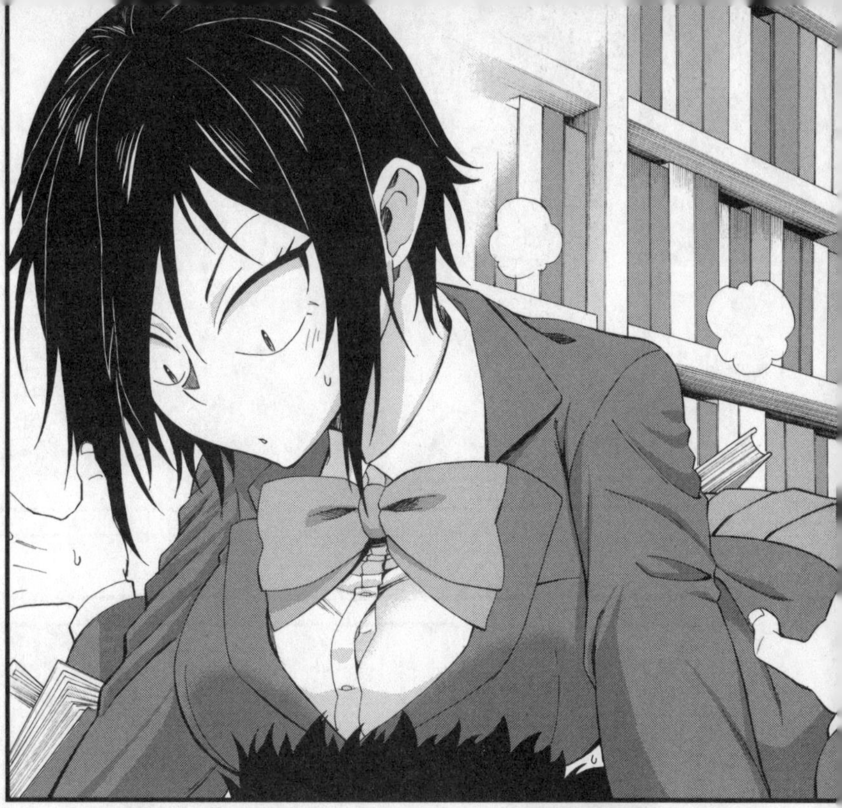

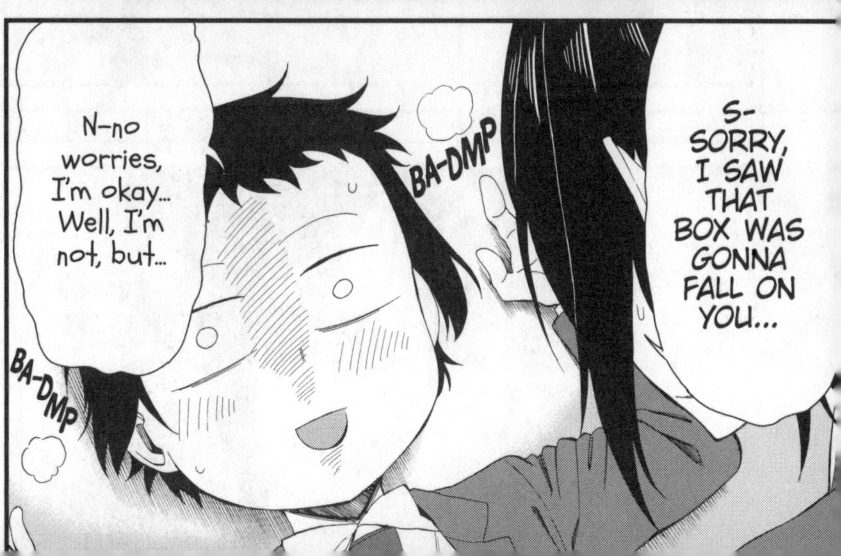
S-SORRY, I SAW THAT BOX WAS GONNA FALL ON YOU...
BA-DMP
N-no worries, I'm okay... Well, I'm not, but...
BA-DMP

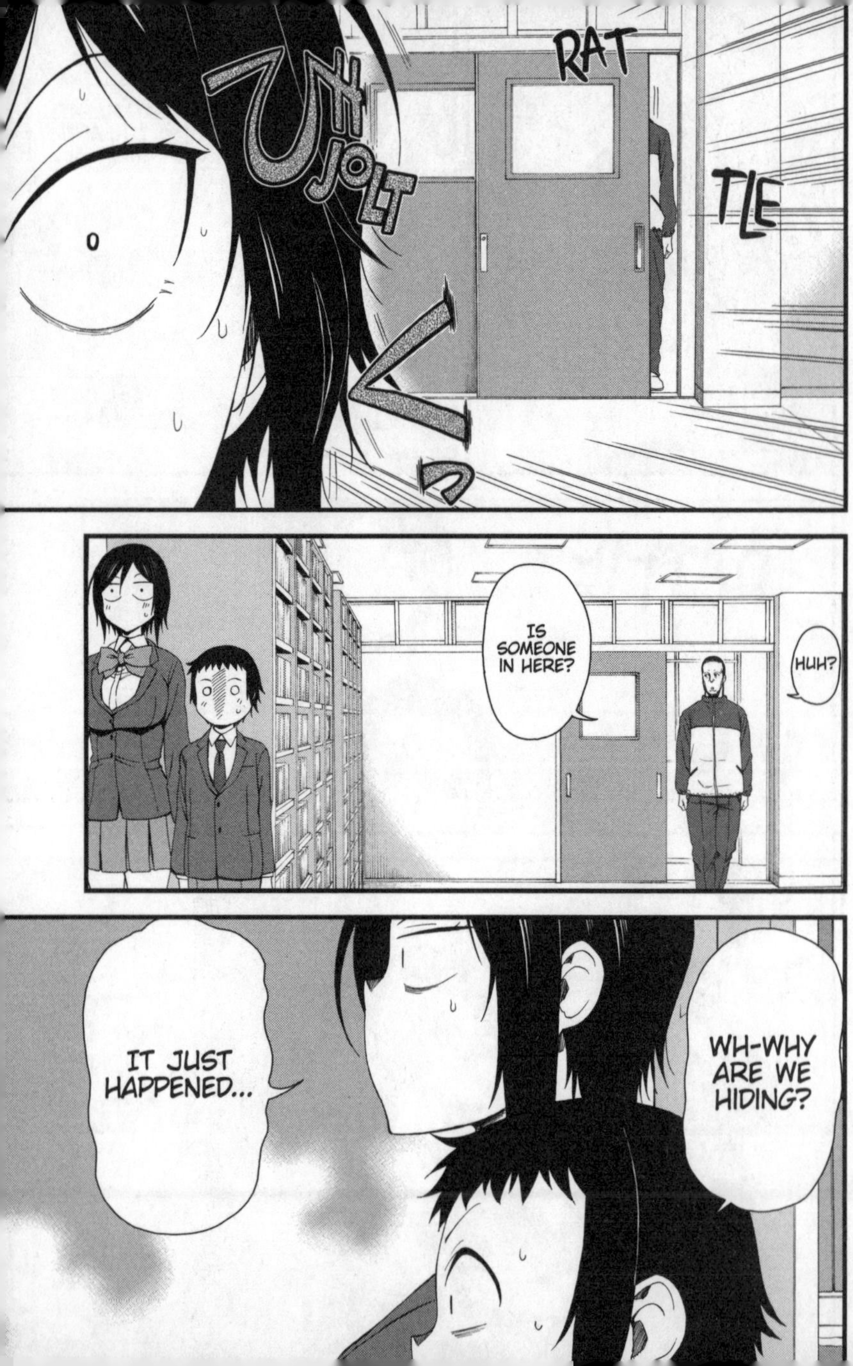
RAT
TLE
UH
JOLT
HUH?
IS SOMEONE IN HERE?
WH-WHY ARE WE HIDING?
IT JUST HAPPENED...

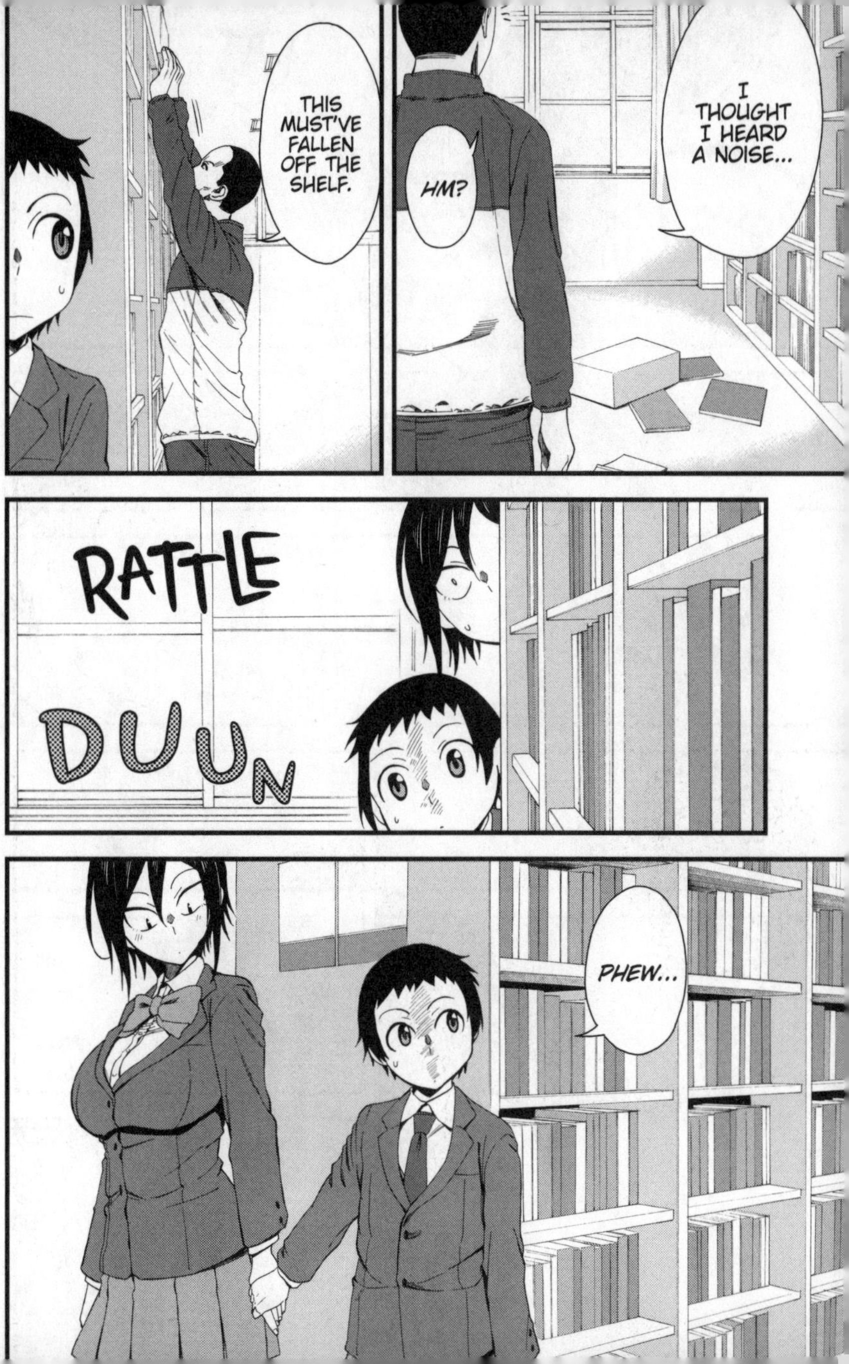
I THOUGHT I HEARD A NOISE...
HM?
THIS MUST'VE FALLEN OFF THE SHELF.
RATTLE
DUUN
PHEW...

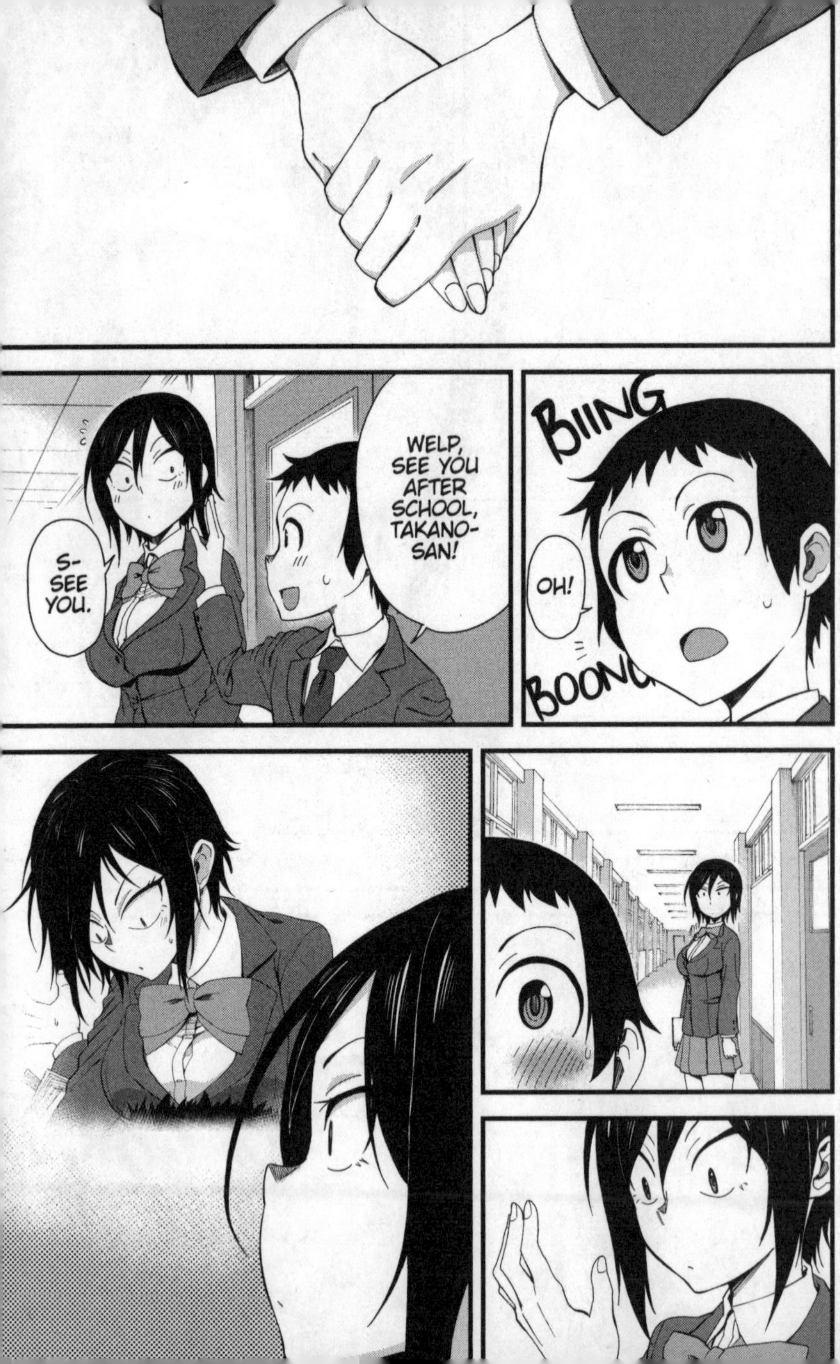
BIING
OH!
BOONG
WELP, SEE YOU AFTER SCHOOL, TAKANO-SAN!
S-SEE YOU.

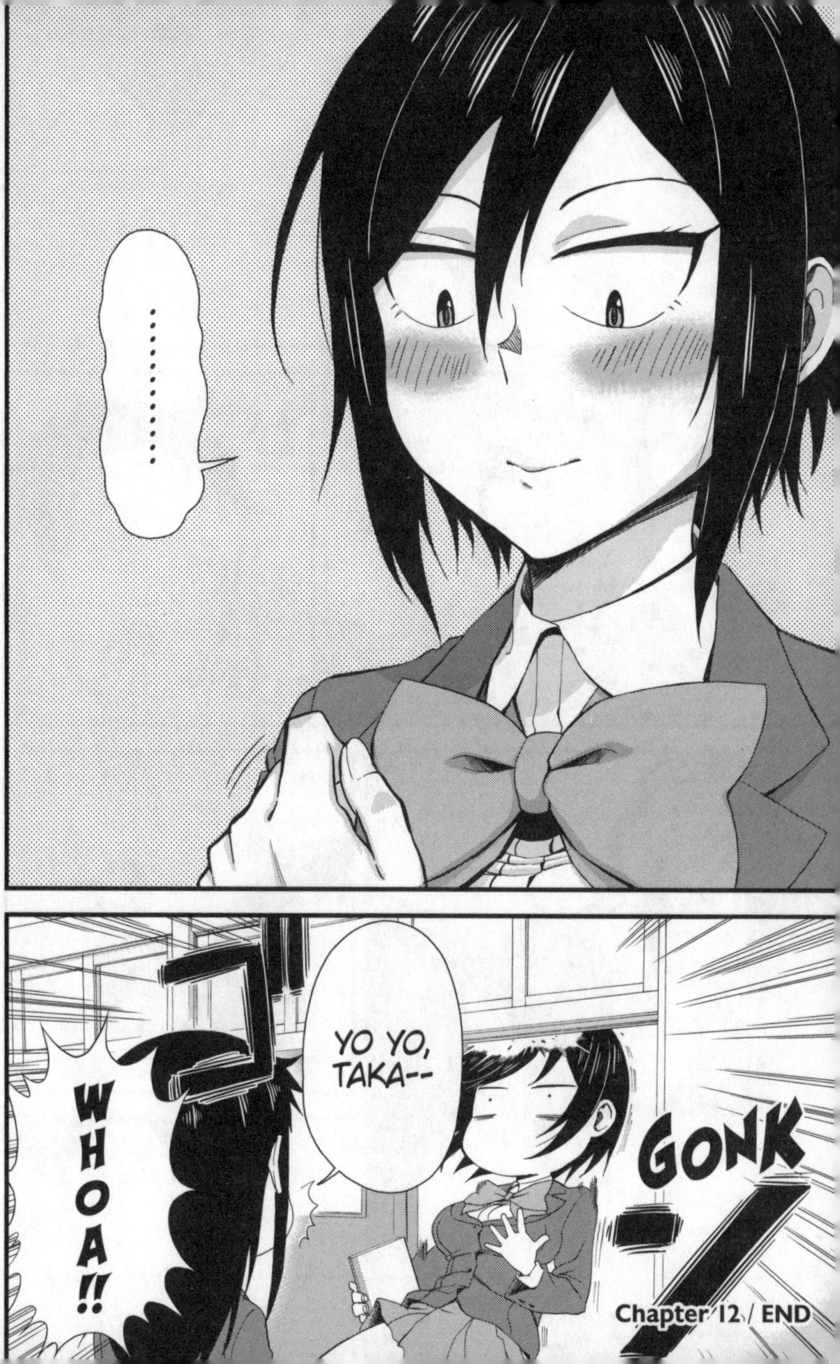

......
GONK
YO YO, TAKA--
WHOA!!
Chapter 12 / END

Hitomi-chan is Shy With Strangers

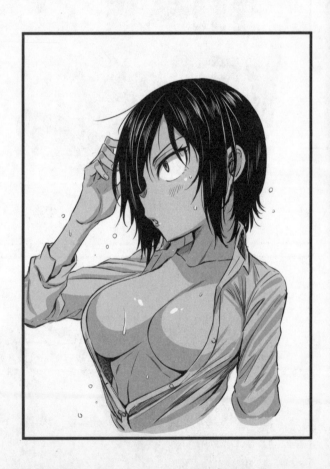

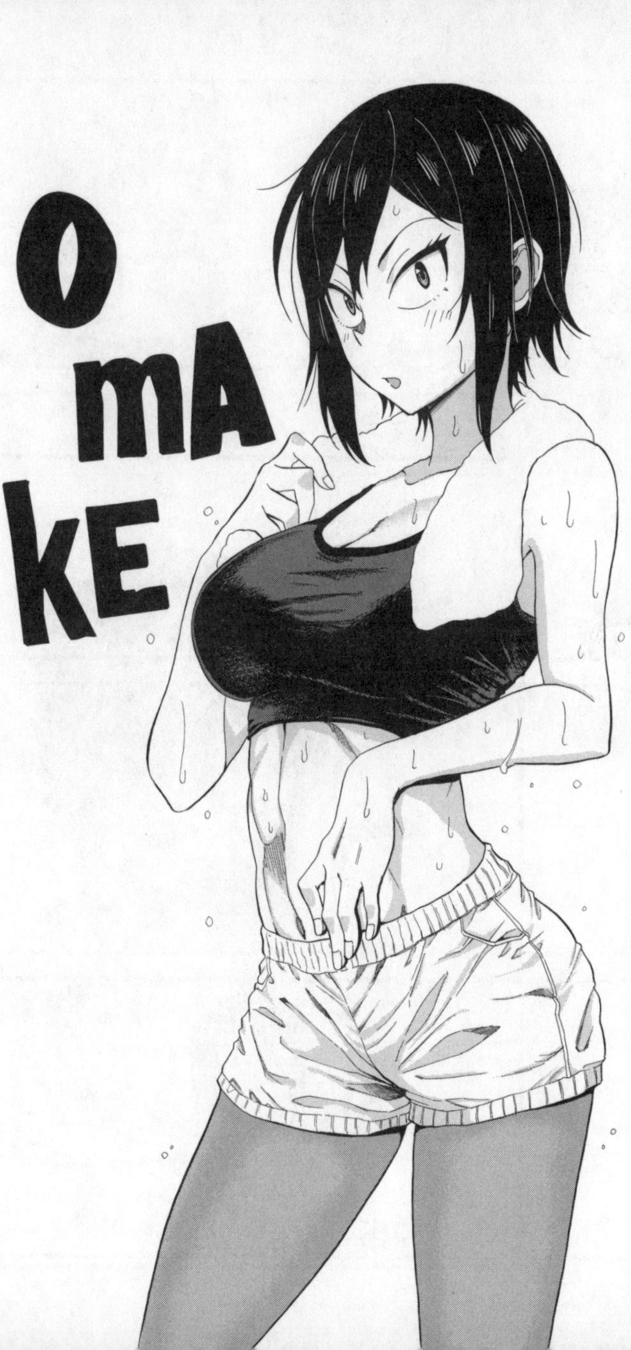
OMAKE

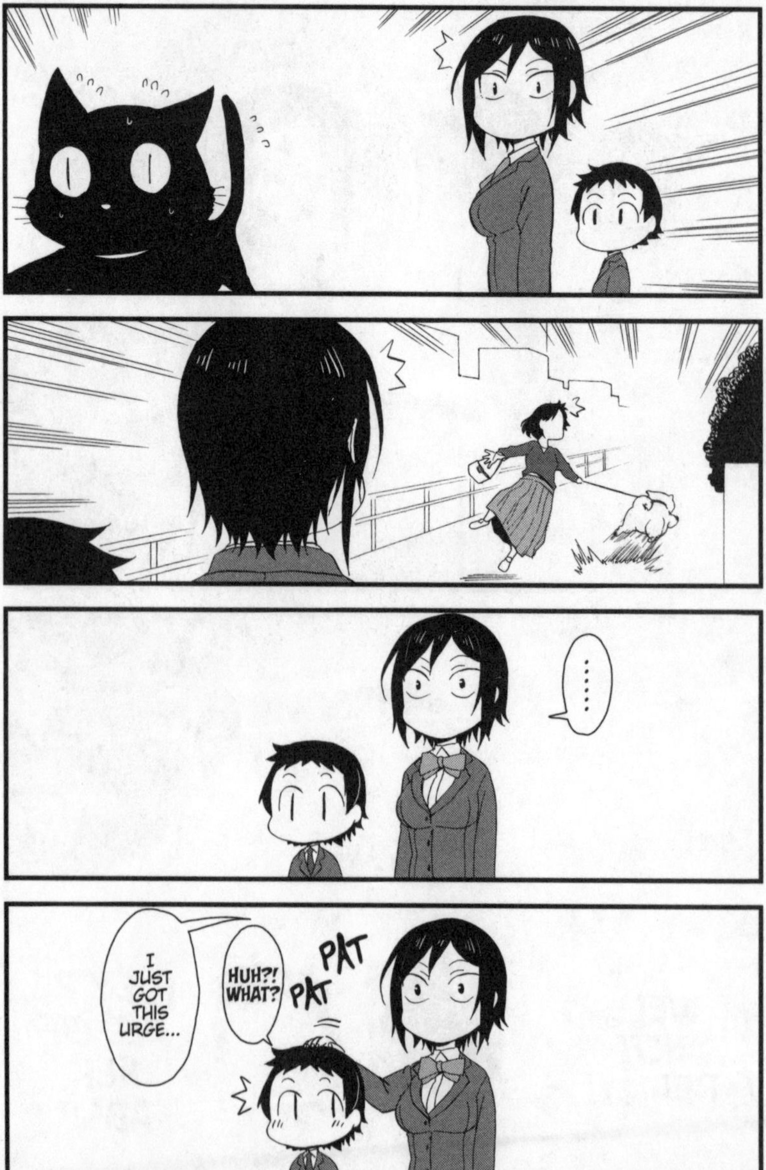
......
PAT PAT
HUH?! WHAT?
I JUST GOT THIS URGE...

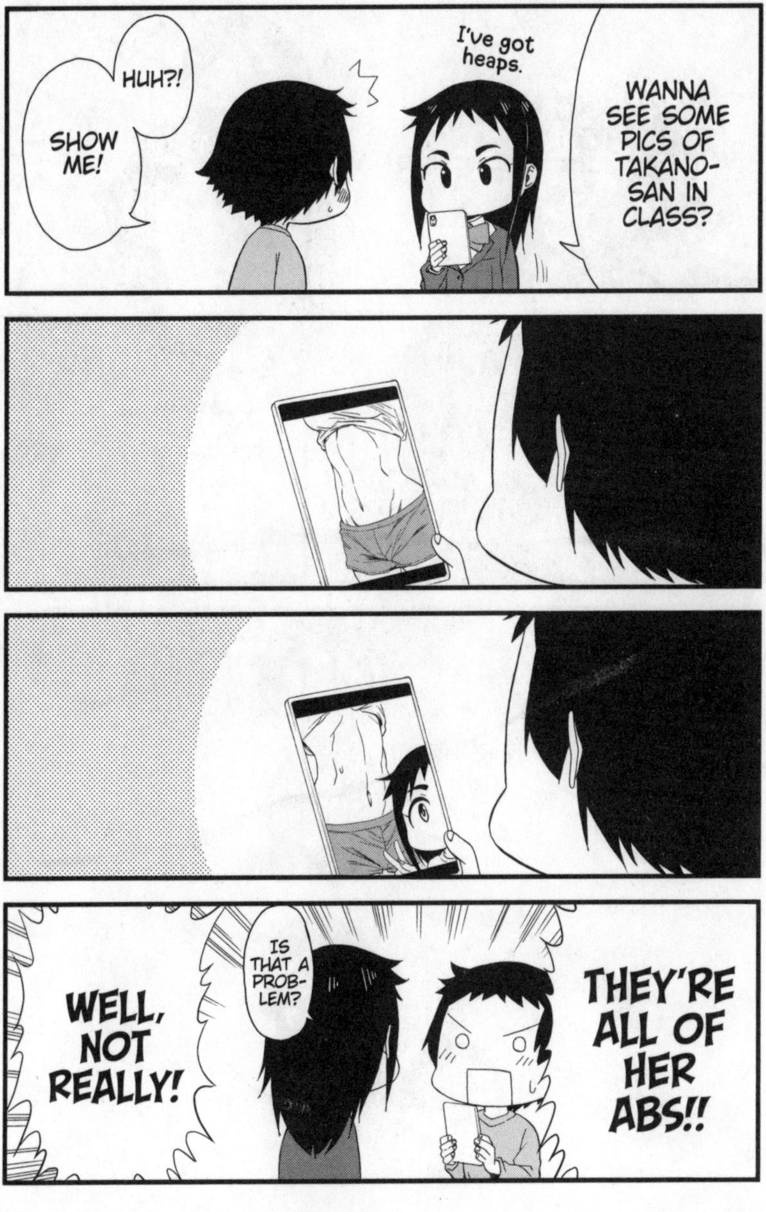
WANNA SEE SOME PICS OF TAKANO-SAN IN CLASS?
I've got heaps.
HUH?!
SHOW ME!
THEY'RE ALL OF HER ABS!!
IS THAT A PROB-LEM?
WELL, NOT REALLY!

Afterword

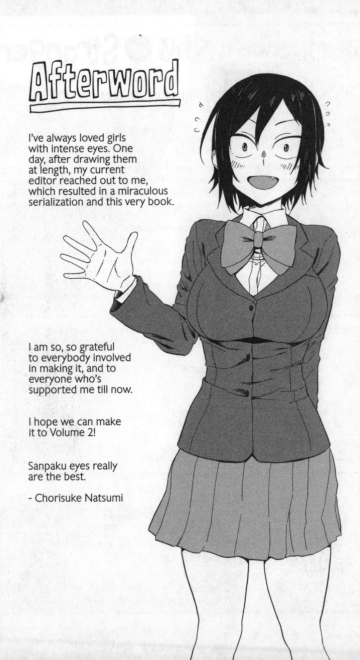

I've always loved girls with intense eyes. One day, after drawing them at length, my current editor reached out to me, which resulted in a miraculous serialization and this very book.

I am so, so grateful to everybody involved in making it, and to everyone who's supported me till now.

I hope we can make it to Volume 2!

Sanpaku eyes really are the best.

- Chorisuke Natsumi

SEVEN SEAS ENTERTAINMENT PRESENTS

Hitomi-chan is S...

story and art by CHORISUKE NATSUMI

Vol. 1

TRANSLATION
Avery Hutley

ADAPTATION
Patrick King

LETTERING
Carolina Hernández Mendoza

COVER & LOGO DESIGN
Hanase Qi

PROOFREADER
B. Lana Guggenheim

COPY EDITOR
Dawn Davis

EDITOR
Jenn Grunigen

PREPRESS TECHNICIAN
Rhiannon Rasmussen-Silverstein

PRODUCTION ASSOCIATE
Christa Miesner

PRODUCTION MANAGER
Lissa Pattillo

MANAGING EDITOR
Julie Davis

ASSOCIATE PUBLISHER
Adam Arnold

PUBLISHER
Jason DeAngelis

Hitomichan ha hitomishiri Vol. 1
© Chorisuke Natsumi 2019
Originally published in Japan in 2019 by Akita Publishing Co., Ltd.
English translation rights arranged with Akita Publishing Co., Ltd.
through TOHAN CORPORATION, Tokyo.

Seven Seas press and purchase enquiries can be sent to Marketing Manager Lianne Sentar at press@gomanga.com. Information regarding the distribution and purchase of digital editions is available from Digital Manager CK Russell at digital@gomanga.com.

Seven Seas and the Seven Seas logo are trademarks of Seven Seas Entertainment. All rights reserved.

ISBN: 978-1-64827-663-7
Printed in Canada
First Printing: October 2021
10 9 8 7 6 5 4 3 2 1

READING DIRECTIONS

This book reads from *right to left*, Japanese style. If this is your first time reading manga, you start reading from the top right panel on each page and take it from there. If you get lost, just follow the numbered diagram here. It may seem backwards at first, but you'll get the hang of it! Have fun!!

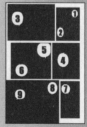

Follow us online: www.SevenSeasEntertainment.com